FLAWED CAPITALISM

Also by David Coates and published by Agenda Publishing

Reflections on the Future of the Left (editor)

FLAWED CAPITALISM

*The Anglo-American Condition
and its Resolution*

DAVID COATES

agenda
publishing

First published in 2018 by Agenda Publishing

Agenda Publishing Limited
The Core
Science Central
Bath Lane
Newcastle upon Tyne
NE4 5TF

www.agendapub.com

ISBN 978-1-911116-33-2

British Library Cataloguing-in-Publication Data
A catalogue record for this book is available from the British Library

Typeset in Nocturne by Patty Rennie

Printed and bound in the UK by TJ International

For Eileen and Jonathan,
Emma, Ben and Anna, Tom and Ed
With love and thanks!

Contents

Acknowledgements

As even a cursory glance at the many footnotes to each chapter must make abundantly clear, volumes of this kind depend entirely on the fine work of others. In this instance, I owe an enormous debt of gratitude to a vast list of research academics in both the US and the UK, to the members of research teams at a myriad of progressive think tanks on both sides of the Atlantic, and to a seemingly endless supply of fine investigatory journalists based in each national capital – an enormous debt owed, that is, to a large set of people without whose skills, dedication and courage a volume of the kind that follows here could simply never have been written. Those debts are particularly huge to the research teams at the Economic Policy Institute, the Center for American Progress, and the Brookings Institution in the United States, and to their equivalents at the Resolution Foundation, the Sheffield Political Economy Research Institute, and the Centre for Economic Performance in the UK – plus, of course, to the gifted journalists working at *The Washington Post* and *The New York Times* in the US and at *The Guardian* and *Financial Times* in London. Then in addition, I owe a set of more personal debts: primarily to Alison Howson, Matthew Watson, and Agenda Publishing for supporting this venture, to Tony Payne at SPERI for his guidance throughout, to colleagues at Wake Forest University who read and commented on parts of what now follows, and to my magnificent children – both in the UK and in America – who did the same. The book is dedicated to them, and to Eileen, my wonderful partner in all of this: partly in gratitude – certainly in love – and partly in the hope that by acting together, we can still yet make a better world than that foreshadowed by the arrival in office of Donald J. Trump and Theresa May.

DAVID COATES
Wake Forest University, November 2017

Abbreviations

AIG	American International Group
ARRA	American Recovery and Reinvestment Act
CAP	Center for American Progress
CBI	Confederation of British Industry
CBO	Congressional Budget Office
CFPB	Consumer Financial Protection Bureau
CIA	Central Intelligence Agency
CME	Coordinated Market Economy
EPI	Economic Policy Institute
FDI	Foreign Direct Investment
GSE	Government Sponsored Enterprise
G7	Canada, France, Germany, Italy, Japan, the UK and the US
G20	Forum for governments and central banks of top 20 economies
IFS	Institute for Fiscal Studies
ILP	Independent Labour Party
IMF	International Monetary Fund
JAM	"Just about Managing" family
LME	Liberal Market Economy
NAFTA	North American Free Trade Agreement
NATO	North Atlantic Treaty Organization
NBER	National Bureau of Economic Research
NEDC	National Economic Development Council
NEF	New Economic Foundation
NIER	National Institute of Economic Research
NPI	New Policy Institute
OBR	Office for Budget Responsibility

OECD	Organization for Economic Cooperation and Development
ONS	Office of National Statistics
PISA	Programme for International Student Assessment (OECD)
SOCOM	Special Operations Command
SNAP	Supplemental Nutrition Assistance Program
SPERI	Sheffield Political Economy Research Institute
SPM	Supplementary Poverty Measure
SSA	Social Structure of Accumulation
STEM	Science, Technology, Engineering & Math
TANF	Temporary Assistance for Needy Families
TARP	Troubled Assets Relief Program
TUC	Trades Union Congress
UKIP	United Kingdom Independence Party
UNFAO	United Nations Food and Agriculture Organization
VA	Veterans Administration

Introduction

Every book has its moment of conception and its period of drafting. This book has been a long time in the making, but its drafting began only very recently and at a particularly awesome moment. Drafting began in the interregnum between two US Administrations, just as Donald Trump was poised to become the forty-fifth president of the United States; and on the day in which, in the United Kingdom, the new Conservative Government led by Theresa May lost its first by-election in a strong Tory seat, as buyer's remorse about the Brexit vote began belatedly to surface. Because of developments of this kind, early 2017 seemed to be both a good and a bad time to begin to write. Given all that was happening around us, it seemed a particularly appropriate moment to put together a systematic reflection on the future of both societies, and on the likely strength of the economies on which those societies rest. But it was also a moment at which such a reflection was bound to be difficult to deliver, because there was suddenly so much political novelty and uncertainty in both London and Washington, DC. Any reflection written to illuminate the times would, therefore, need to explain that novelty and uncertainty, as well as throw light on the continuities that make the novelty so disturbing.

For just twelve months earlier, when Barack Obama gave his last State of the Union Address and David Cameron returned from Brussels with his renegotiated settlement with the European Union, neither Donald J. Trump's occupancy of the White House, nor Theresa May's of No. 10, was visible on the political radar of any serious public commentator. But here we were, facing 2017 with both newly in charge: the one poised to substantially reconfigure America's already inadequate welfare net (and to do an additional set of entirely unclear things to "make America great again"); the other poised to

1

somehow negotiate the UK's route out of the European Union without damaging still further the already vulnerable UK economy. Of course, neither of these political figures will necessarily be with us for long – May, if her weakened condition after her unsuccessful general election continues, Trump if he is eventually impeached – but even if either/both fall from power as sharply as they rose, the political volatility from which they both benefited will undoubtedly persist.

So, as we explore now the future of two economies under new and uncertain political leadership, it is initially worth noting the extent to which, for all their recently achieved solid rates of GDP-growth and job-creation – both the US and UK are running at near full employment as this volume goes to press – serious indicators are readily available to demonstrate just how *fundamentally flawed* both economies continue to be. Take the US economy for example, where:

- Total household debt is on the rise again – up by 70 per cent from its post-crash trough of 2010 – peaking in the first three months of 2017 at $12.7 trillion (a peak higher even than that realized in 2008). This, in the wake of over four decades of stagnant real wage growth for most Americans, and of steadily increasing inequality in the distribution of income and wealth.

- Post-recession manufacturing employment growth in the US economy that is still sluggish and low. The US manufacturing sector, which in 2000 absorbed 17.3 million American workers and by 2010 absorbed just 11.5 million, still only accounted for 12.3 million jobs by mid-2015, a 37 per cent drop from the June 1979 manufacturing employment peak of over 19 million.[1] This at a time when the US trade deficit with what is now the world's leading producer and exporter of manufactured goods – China – is running at a record level: $365.7 billion in 2015, and still $347 billion in 2016.

- Labour market participation rates for working-age men in America are down and falling, at the very time when death rates among those men are creeping up. In the US, some 11.5 million men aged 24–55 are currently neither employed nor looking for a job; but the white non-Hispanic members of that same demographic are reportedly consuming pain-killers at twice the rate of employed Americans,[2] and – as Figure I.1 indicates – are now dying at a faster rate and at a younger age than did their equivalents in the generation before, and younger and at a faster rate than their equivalents abroad. It used to be only the black working class who died young in America, but apparently not any more.

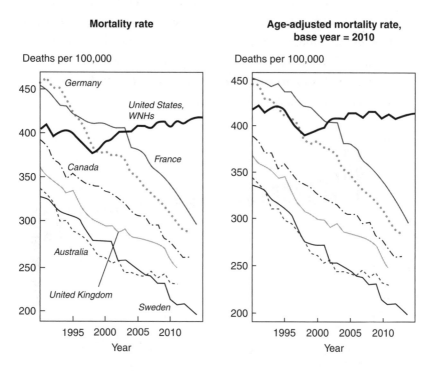

Mortality rate

Age-adjusted mortality rate, base year = 2010

Figure I.1 Rising morbidity and mortality in midlife among white non-hispanic Americans in the twenty-first century
(Source: Anne Case & Angus Deacon, "Mortality and Morbidity in the 21st Century", Brookings Papers on Economic Activity, Spring 2017, p. 406).

But the United States is not alone in supposedly facing a difficult and demanding economic and social future, one characterized by dire statistics on such things as income and debt, job security, and health. There are powerful signs of adverse headwinds in the United Kingdom too, if you know where to look for them. Among these are at least the following:

- Wage stagnation: just a month after the Brexit vote in June 2016, the Trades Union Congress (using OECD data) reported that average real wages in the UK had fallen by nearly 10 per cent since the onset of the financial crisis in 2008, a fall exceeded in the entire OECD – as Figure I.2 indicates – only by Greece, Hungary and the Czech Republic.[3] If true, that means that the British are currently in the middle of their worst decade for wage growth since the end of the Second World War, and on average will not earn more in real terms in 2021 than they did in 2008.[4] On the Government's own figures, indeed, and because of Brexit, "real average earnings are now forecast to be £830 lower in the UK than expected in 2020 – thanks to a double whammy of weak pay rises and higher inflation".[5]

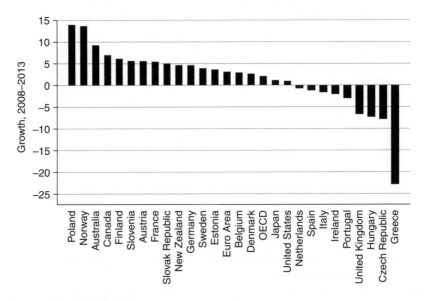

Figure I.2 International real hourly earnings growth, 2008–13 (Source: OECD Employment Outlook, 2014).

- Productivity shortfall: the productivity of UK workers – measured by output per hour – fell in the last two quarters of 2015 faster than at any time since the fourth quarter of 2008, when the UK economy was officially in recession. That shortfall left the UK with the largest productivity gap with the G7 average since records began, with UK output per hour now a full 36 percentage points less than the figure for Germany, 31 per cent less than that for France, and 30 per cent down on the figure for the United States.[6] This is no small matter, given the critical role that labour productivity plays in sustaining and increasing overall living standards. It means that currently the British "are no richer relative to the EU-15 average than they were 15 years ago, and [that] the average Briton has to work more hours than the EU-15 average to achieve that income".[7]

- Rising personal debt: what is even more troubling are the signs, emerging again, that in the UK those incomes are being inflated only by the acquisition of larger and larger quantities of personal and household debt. In the twelve months to July 2017, if the Bank of England's figures are correct, "household incomes had grown by just 1.5 per cent but outstanding car loans, credit card balances and personal loans had risen by 10 per cent" as "terms and conditions on credit cards and personal loans had become easier".[8] So, it is not just in America that the ghosts of 2007–8 are beginning once more to stir.

* * * *

With all this in mind, one important recent political experience shared by the US and the UK might now begin to make more sense than perhaps it initially did: their shared experience of two major elections/referenda in which the outcome came as a surprise, not just to those who lost them but to their winners as well. In both countries, new political leaders and agendas now hold centre-stage because of a widespread and largely unexpected rejection in 2016 of more mainstream candidates and programmes by first the British and then the American electorate. It is true that the margin of victory for the Leave Campaign was very tiny in the British case, and that Donald Trump's winning margin was restricted to the electoral college (Hillary Clinton's popular vote exceeding his by more than 3 million): but victories, however problematically earned, count in elections – because to the victors go the spoils.

The Brexit vote was quickly understood at the time, and is still largely seen now, as a protest vote against their persistent neglect (from many governments and over many decades) by communities situated far from

5

London – communities that are currently full of non-college educated, pre-dominantly white, working-class voters.[9] The unexpected election of Donald Trump was equally grounded in a protest vote against economic neglect by their US equivalents.[10] In neither case was white working-class anger the only factor in play: but in both countries it was in play, and being in play, it made the electoral difference. For the first time since at least 1945, the old political order in both Washington, DC and London was rattled to its core by the protest votes of those who found their present circumstances unsatisfac-tory – rattled by voters, moreover, who were prepared on this occasion to blame existing political parties for the things they found unsatisfactory. In each country, that is, elections held in 2016 demonstrated more clearly than in recent elections past that a significant section of each electorate found their circumstances to be intolerably *flawed*.

Which takes us to the title of this comparative text: *Flawed Capitalism: The Anglo-American Condition and its Resolution.* Long before Donald Trump and Theresa May came to dominate the political headlines, it was increasingly obvious to many progressive commentators on both sides of the Atlantic that there were flaws in both countries that needed to be recognized and understood, addressed and rectified.[11] As we shall see, those flaws were (and remain) partly nationally-anchored and country-specific, and need to be dealt with as such. But they were, and are, also partly common to the eco-nomic model underpinning both societies; and to the degree that they are, are equally and similarly remediable. That much at least was clear before the 2016 political tsunamis.[12] But what those unexpected developments have now added to this ongoing reform effort is both a new urgency and a new question. The new urgency comes from the new uncertainty, and the new question becomes this. Will the new centre-right solutions now on offer in Washington, DC and in London bring those much-needed remedies closer, or push them further away? As you will see as you read on, the answer on offer here is that the new politics of the centre-right will only make things worse on both sides of the Atlantic – that by shifting to the right in so unexpected a fashion, both countries have just scored spectacular own-goals – and that these are own-goals which are likely to undo much, and perhaps even all, of the limited progressive gains that had been put in place in both the US and the UK on either side of the financial crisis of 2008.

Donald Trump's proposed retreat from globalization in the United States, and the Brexit retreat from the European Union in the United Kingdom, both suffer from what Ben Clift recently and properly characterized as "the dangerous illusion of 'taking back control'".[13] Why that control will not come back the centre-right way, but can be recaptured by the development and implementation of more progressive politics, will be the focus of the second half of *Flawed Capitalism*. The book's first task is more modest but equally vital. It is to take stock of where we are, of how and why we got here, and of the adequacy of our current condition.

1

The Anglo-American Condition: Similarities and Differences

"We have always been kin: kin in blood, kin in religion, kin in representative government, kin in ideals, kin in just and lofty purposes; and now we are kin in sin, the harmony is complete, the blend is perfect, like Mr. Churchill himself, whom I now have the honor to present to you."

> Mark Twain, introducing Winston Churchill at a meeting on the Boer War at the Waldorf Astoria in New York in December 1900: showing his own distaste for British and American imperialism[1]

"Anglo-American households are broke. Too many households have endured years of declining real incomes, bouts of unemployment, rising indebtedness and without sufficient savings: they are bearing the brunt of the economic downturn and are disproportionately paying for the costs of fiscal austerity without any evidence of a lasting recovery."

> Johnna Montgomerie[2]

There is nothing particularly forced or arbitrary about putting the words "Anglo" and "American" together in a single and hyphenated adjective. On the contrary, if only by dint of common usage, it is any opening moment of conceptual separation and doubt that requires some effort: a moment at which the apparent "naturalness" of the coupling between the two terms needs to be explored. But that exploration is necessary: because, as is immediately obvious whenever we stop to reflect upon it, the United Kingdom and the United States are very different places, and there is nothing preordained in the existence of any similarities between them. So, if we are going to study them together, as we are now – and particularly if we are going to make statements

9

that encompass them both, as we definitely will – it behoves us first to justify the underlying design of the exercise upon which we are poised to embark.

Putting the two countries together and setting them apart

So why put the two countries together, separate them off from the rest, and seek out statements that encompass them both? Two different reasons initially spring to mind. The first is that we can undertake that exercise with some confidence because we are not moving into new territory – because there have been many occasions in the past on which governments in both countries have done something similar. They have acted together. They have separated themselves off from significant others; and they have made general statements about their shared conditions and interests. Putting "Anglo" and "American" together in a single hyphenated adjective captures verbally, therefore, the existence of something that is actually real, and something that on occasion has been extremely important in world history: namely a "special relationship" between the two countries, one firmly grounded in overlapping histories, similar institutions and shared languages and culture.

The second reason is this: that we can also put the two countries together because many other scholars have done so before us. In treating the two countries as a single and interconnected subject of analysis, we necessarily join an already existing large and rich literature on those interlinked histories, institutions and cultures.[3] We also become a new player in a particular body of scholarship – in comparative political economy – within which it is now common to postulate the existence of an Anglo-American "model" of how to run a modern economy and society. This volume will contribute to that last body of work in particular: and in relation to it at least, the obligation of these opening pages will be less to justify talking about the two economies as similar than to justify characterizing them as being, because similar, equally flawed.

The United Kingdom and the United States go back together a long way in time. The 13 colonies that initially created the United States did so – as America annually celebrates – in rebellion against the British crown. What the fourth of July fireworks tend to illuminate less than the brave separation, however, is the extent to which the breakaway colonies, as just half of the

26 American and Caribbean colonies of the first British Empire, like the other 13 had been constructed internally under British direction. Each shared a language with the "mother country". Each shared similar legal codes and judicial practices. Each shared similar commercial activities and constitutive social classes. And many of their leading citizens even shared – right to the very end of the colonial period – a common desire to be British: Benjamin Franklin in particular came to his own revolutionary break very reluctantly and very late in the day. For what linked the newly-independent United States most to the British Isles from which the former colonists or their fore-bears had once come, were the people who first populated particularly the northern-most set of the 13 breakaway states. After 1620, significant parts of the most progressive sections of the emerging British middle class ended up precisely there, freer in the new world than in the old to pursue their own religious predilections, and freer too to create a modern capitalist economy untrammelled by feudal legacies. They came for freedom, and most of them came as, and wanting to remain, British.

Yet in spite of all that, the relationship between the new nation and the old was understandably initially rather fraught – the two countries fought a brief second war, after all, between 1814 and 1816 – a war from which the United States then drew the imagery for the national anthem which it uses to this day. But thereafter, the linkage between the two grew. They grew in volume; they grew in regularity; and they grew in ease: as people continued to migrate from key parts of the United Kingdom to the United States (especially from Ireland); as UK technology and capital crossed the Atlantic in ever greater quantities to develop the post-Civil War American economy; and as the sharing of a common language between the British and the North Americans left each society particularly open to the exchange of intellectual products and to the creation of a shared cultural universe. As Jim Cronin rightly put it, "intercourse and ex-change between Britain and the United States have been ... constant and criti-cal, and they have occurred at the very highest levels; and the two countries have chosen to be each other's best ally in all the geopolitical conflicts that have dominated international relations in the [twentieth] century".[4]

Throughout the nineteenth century, the United Kingdom was the senior partner in the emerging relationship between the two. Economically and militarily, the United States was the junior actor then – playing catch-up economically, and normally restricting itself globally only to interventions in its own self-appointed sphere, namely the Americas. That changed, of course, quickly after 1941. For by then, the US economy was already larger and more dynamic than the British – the economic imperative to "catch up" had already shifted across to the European side of the Atlantic long before the attack on Pearl Harbor – and by the end of the Second World War, the equivalent military shift had also followed. For by 1945, the decline of the British Empire was as visible to much of the rest of the world, if not always to key figures in the British political elite, as was the rise of its less formal but no less real American equivalent.

This resetting of leadership within the military and economic interplay between two great imperial powers was also reflected in a more subtle and nuanced shift in the interplay between the two socially and culturally: the thinning of the social and ideational relationship between them over time, with the emergence – especially in the United States – of social categories and localized histories that set the US and the UK apart. The two societies had never been totally similar, of course. The nineteenth century British one was heavily scarred (and the twentieth century one was still vestigially so) by a feudal past that America lacked, a feudal legacy that left a British aristocracy in place, if not a peasantry. From its inception, the United States was totally free of such feudal shadows, but it remains scarred to this day (and scarred even more severely than were the British by feudalism) by the legacies of the slavery it once consolidated in its southern states, and of the genocide it practiced on the native Americans who resisted the encroachment of European settlement on the lands they had occupied for millennia. The nineteenth-century British had their immigrants too – Irish immigrants fleeing famine in the 1840s just like the United States, and Eastern European Jews fleeing pogroms in the 1890s, again with American parallels – but the biggest difference between the two by then was the predominant composition of the labour forces filling the factories of the industrial economies that both societies were developing apace in the second half of the nineteenth century.

The nineteenth-century British drew their factory labour force, in the main, from their own urban and rural areas – at the end of a two-century period of conversion of an English and Scottish feudal peasantry into a wage-based agrarian (and then industrial) working class. The United States, by contrast, had neither a similar length of time within which to operate, nor the same internal sources of labour on which to draw. So instead, and on either side of the Civil War, its entrepreneurial class recruited to American factories the geographically-mobile sections of other countries' displaced peasantries: taking labour first from Ireland, then from northern and eastern Europe, then from the Mediterranean basin, and always – on its west coast – from China as well. The eventual result was the emergence in North America of a society made up almost entirely of immigrants (both voluntary and involuntary in nature) and their descendants: a mosaic of peoples in the United States with their own non-British histories and cultures. It was a mosaic that pulled the two societies – the American and the British – increasingly apart over time: united for years in spite of the mosaic by the residual white, Anglo-Saxon and Protestant character of America's ruling groups, but increasingly pulled apart after 1945, as America's ruling groups slowly lost much of their waspishness.

The cumulative result, politically, of this different pattern of nineteenth-century working-class formation was the emergence in the twentieth century of two societies divided by a common language. In the United States, the term "liberal", for example, means someone who is willing to use the state for purposes of social justice, whereas in the United Kingdom, the term "liberal" often means just the reverse. It can mean progressive in an American sense, but it more normally carries the connotation of "neoliberalism" – more Adam Smith than John Maynard Keynes. From a British perspective, both Margaret Thatcher and Ronald Reagan were liberals, the very thing that Americans know they were not! It can all be very confusing:* until we note the way in which the legacy of feudalism, and the weight of "class identity" in the UK case, has left the political centre of gravity in London further to the left – and in that sense, in a more commonly Western European position – than

---

* There is also, of course, the colour-coding confusion. Across the entire world (and that included, it should be said, in the United States), for most of the twentieth century the colour "red" signified "leftness" in politics – the "red menace" of the Cold War era, "Red Square" in Moscow, the "red flag" celebrated in song at every Labour Party conference, and so on. In the UK at least, "blue" was the equivalent colour of the right: Margaret Thatcher dressed regularly in that colour. But somewhere along the line, around the year 2000 and in the United States alone, the colour-coding shifted. "Red" became Republican. "Blue" became Democrat. Readers following both political systems simultaneously need to remember that. It is all very confusing!

its American equivalent in Washington, DC. For the twentieth-century UK labour movement eventually shaped the way that British people still understand politics – and left a social democratic culture in place – to a degree not matched by the US labour movement, except in its brief New Deal moment of dominance. In consequence, current economic policy-choices are played out in the United States within a political framework heavily molded by libertarian ideas, and by mobilized religious conservatives, that have no easy UK equivalents; just as in the United Kingdom, those same economic policy-choices are now being settled by a minority Conservative Government, many of whose leading figures subscribe to an "one nation" Tory tradition that is simply not there in the modern American Republican Party. Barack Obama may have seemed far too progressive for many American conservatives, but ironically it is likely that he would have been politically comfortable in a UK context to have been simply a progressive Conservative.

These emerging differences between the two component elements of the Anglo-American world, that are so vital to the day-to-day story of politics in both, are not just "political and ideological". They are also "political and institutional". The United States is, after all, a very big country: whereas the United Kingdom, though smaller, is a European nation; and both size and geography matter here. The US political system is a federal one, with a written constitution and a well-established set of checks and balances. The UK political system has neither. Policy change at the national level is, in consequence, much more difficult to effect in Washington, DC than is policy change in the London-focused UK parliamentary system. But equally, the federal nature of the US political structure leaves a significant space for "state-led" initiatives that are far more difficult to orchestrate at the "local level" in the heavily-centralized UK equivalent. Political activists – both conservatives and progressives – if blocked at the national level, often turn *down* to exploit state-level opportunities in the United States, when their UK counterparts (pre-Brexit at least) would more likely turn *out*, to seek support in EU-based social legislation and development funding.* As we now watch these two

---

* The two biggest examples in the contemporary US being the use of state-level power by social conservatives to limit the availability of abortion, and by progressives in a state like California to slowdown the Trump Administration's policies on climate change and immigration control.

14

economies struggle with a shared agenda of competitive difficulties, these variations of size and geography will ghost everything that follows. The United States is dealing with a globalized capitalism, from which it is separated by two great oceans. The United Kingdom is doing the same, separated from the rest of Western Europe only by the width of the English Channel.

The emergence of a similar economic model

The United States was, from its inception, a commercially-oriented society; and by the time it was created, so too was the Britain from which it broke. In fact, initially at least, Britain was the more commercially-developed of the two. The British aristocracy had long made their peace with an emerging capitalist class, converting the land it owned into commercial units worked by tenant farmers and wage-paid day labourers, while sustaining its own non-commercial style of life by increasing the rental income it drew from that farming. Aristocratic money sustained mercantile capitalism extensively in the years after the English Civil War, so that by the time of the American Revolution, British trade was a global force, British factory production was already on the rise, and British interest in the application of science to new forms of production was already evident. Indeed, in the mid/late eighteenth century Scottish Enlightenment that gave us Adam Smith and David Hume among others, Benjamin Franklin was also a major player: as commercially-minded and scientifically-curious middle classes emerged in both societies, divided by the Atlantic but linked by regular intellectual intercourse and intimate social networks.

The result in both cases was essentially the same: the emergence – first in the newly-named United Kingdom after 1801* and in the United States either

---

* Countries that call themselves "United' rarely are. If they were genuinely united, they would hardly need the adjective. The north-south divide left behind by the American Civil War is still very much alive and well in contemporary America; and the various labels used to describe the UK continue to confuse many. Prior to 1707, the London state was an English one, also ruling Wales and maintaining a less than total hold on Ireland through a parliament in Dublin. In 1707, England (and Wales) and Scotland voluntarily merged. The new political entity was called Britain – and as its first empire grew, eventually Great Britain. In 1797, aping the Americans, the Irish Protestants rebelled against English rule, basing their

side of its civil war – of an increasingly industrially-based capitalist economy led and owned by a new class of private entrepreneurs. This was not state-led industrial development. It was privately-initiated and middle-class owned economic change in industries as diverse as coal and textiles, iron ore and railways. Indeed, in both countries industrial development began primarily in textile factories relying on coal-driven steam power, only to be surpassed quickly by more broadly-based factory production driven by investments in iron and steel, railways and shipbuilding. In consequence, both societies had created a recognizably modern factory-based working class by the 1880s. Both by then had shed labour from agriculture, moved production from the countryside to the town, and sustained urban life by the development of commercial farming linked to its markets by railways and financed in its development by banks. And in all of this early industrial change, the state had played only a limited though essential role: disciplining labour, protecting property rights, and encouraging private investment and entrepreneurial activity without developing the strong capacity for leadership played by governments in economies that industrialized later such as Germany, Japan and eventually (in a different way) Russia.

The global economic leadership enjoyed by the British economy in the nineteenth century allowed its political class to develop an imperial role, and its leading financial institutions to act as a conduit between the British economy and the more developed parts of the global system it led. Aspiring industrial nations and companies came to London in the nineteenth century to borrow English money, to use that money to buy English-made goods, and to return home with those goods to develop industrial capacity of their own. The global leadership of the American economy after 1945 enabled its political class and its leading financial institutions to play a similar set of roles. In

---

rebellion in Belfast in the north of the island. That rebellion was crushed, the Dublin parliament was closed, Irish MPs were redirected to the London parliament, and the whole system was relabelled as "the *United* Kingdom" – just in case any remaining Irish rebels were in any doubt. They were, of course, and more than a century later – between 1916 and 1922 – they forced the London Imperial Parliament to allow southern Ireland to break away from the British Empire, to become eventually the state we now know as (the Republic of) Ireland. To date, the remainder of the United Kingdom – England, Wales, Scotland, and Northern Ireland – remain part of the UK, even though lately the Scots have been having serious doubts about the wisdom of remaining so, and may now soon leave.

each case, that economic dominance lasted, at most, for one or two generations before the economies that had initially done the borrowing caught up with the technologies of the globally-dominant British or American firms, and then undercut that dominance with technological developments of their own.

But while the dominance lasted, similar patterns of institutional change bedded themselves in. Governments – first the British, later the American – opened overseas markets for their domestic producers by the force of their diplomacy, and where necessary by the force of their arms. To maintain that capacity to use force, each globally-dominant economy then developed its own military-industrial complex, and the preoccupations of government incrementally shifted from protecting the interests of all its producing sectors into one of protecting primarily those producing military equipment and financial advantage. For as foreign borrowers came first to London and then to New York, the size, importance and political weight of financial institutions grew within each globally-dominant economy in turn, and the major industrial companies in each looked increasingly outside the domestic economy for their resources, their markets and eventually even their production sites. The result in each case was the slow emergence of an economy – first in the United Kingdom and then in the United States – dominated by large financial institutions and globally-oriented transnational corporations, an economy in possession of a large and state-supervised engineering sector geared to military production, and a domestically-focused civilian economy that was increasingly vulnerable to foreign competition in both its overseas and its domestic markets.

When the Cold War was at its height, the relevant academic literature on types of modern economies tended to treat all capitalist ones as basically similar, and as necessarily superior to their state-socialist alternative. But when that superiority was underscored by the unexpected collapse of the Soviet Union at the end of the 1980s, and with it the disappearance of the Cold War, a new body of academic literature emerged – one focused on the relative strengths of different *types* of capitalist economy. In that new literature on comparative political economy, it has become conventional to treat the US and UK economies that we have just described here as broadly similar in kind, and to label them as "liberal market economies" (as "LMEs", with the term "liberal" being used here in its European rather than its contemporary American sense) to be compared to the more "coordinated market economies" ("CMEs") of the continental European and East Asian sort.[5] In this literature, such liberal market economies are understood to be ones in which investment and production decisions are anchored overwhelmingly in the hands of the senior management of private companies, who are then:

> left free to pursue their own short-term profit motives and to raise their capital in open financial markets. In such capitalisms, workers enjoy only limited statutory industrial and social rights, and earn only what they can extract from their employers in largely unregulated labour markets. State involvement in economic management is limited largely to the creation and protection of markets; and the dominant understandings of politics and morality in the society as a whole tend to be individualistic and classically-liberal in form.[6]

Such a view of a "liberal market capitalist model" is normally presented as simply that – a model, an ideal type, a framework to allow comparative analysis of economic performance over time. No economy – not even the two that concern us here – are ever presented in the comparative political economy literature as pure liberal market economies against that definition. But since the definition does capture key core elements of how the US and UK economies do indeed now operate, the label of "LME" is normally applied to them. Of course, the US economy was not always a liberal market one. It certainly was not during the New Deal; and some of its key sectors now – not least those linked to the Pentagon – do not fit the model to this day. And as we shall see, the UK was certainly not a liberal market economy in the heyday of state planning and incomes policy development when first Harold Macmillan led the Conservatives in Government and then Harold Wilson led Old Labour. But both economies do now exhibit many of the features of a liberal market economy as normally defined: and because they do, it is worth treating them together for comparative purposes, and worth understanding both their strengths and their weaknesses through the lens of this LME–CME distinction. That is certainly what we shall do here, in the chapters that follow.

But we shall also do one other thing that much of the literature on comparative political economy often does not do. We shall avoid treating liberal market economies as necessarily superior as a form of economic organization and practice. On the contrary, both the US and UK economies will be understood here as model types of liberal market economy, and for that reason, economies that are necessarily fundamentally flawed.

Flawed capitalisms in the making

To attach the label of "flawed capitalism" to a systematic examination of the Anglo-American condition is to take a particular position in an ongoing and often bitterly contested academic and political debate. It is to make a serious challenge to the claims about American exceptionalism and superiority that are currently such a feature of conservative political discourse in the United States; and it is to call into question the validity of the view, more generally held in America, that there is something different and special about the United States, a view that persists even in the minds of those who feel that currently things in America are not going in quite the direction that they should. It is also to challenge a parallel sense of difference, and even superiority, in contemporary British political culture – to call into question that often-expressed sense of the unique and important nature of Britain's past and present global role, position, character and contribution. It is to challenge a view of British exceptionalism that remains particularly prevalent in much of the UK's political class – a view that particularly afflicts British prime ministers of the Blair and Thatcher mould – and also a view (of what it means to be British) that in a more moderate form informs the worldview of broad swathes of the UK electorate.

In both countries, that is, something that we might term a "defensive nationalism" is widespread in the popular culture – one that was very evident in both the Brexit vote and the Trump victory in 2016. It is a defensive nationalism that does not take kindly to criticism from outside, and it is one that is linked in complicated ways in both cases to the past/present imperialism of their respective states. For as we have already seen, and as we shall discuss in much more detail later, both the United Kingdom and the United States possess a substantial and well-documented imperial past: and arguably the United States possesses an equally substantial and well-documented imperial present,[7] even though the prevailing self-image projected by current US political elites regularly denies that central fact. By contrast, the self-image presented by past UK elites was never so coy about Britain's capacity and willingness to strut its stuff on the world stage. On the contrary, the size of the British Empire was invariably presented by them as something to be universally celebrated and welcomed – and there is even now some residual nostalgia in ruling circles for what are still thought of there as Britain's greatest days.

Denial of the existence and importance of imperial power goes only so far, however, even in a contemporary America that tells itself endlessly that it was (and remains) the first "new nation" – the first one born out of an anti-imperial struggle – so that paradoxically, popular culture in the United States is currently more imperial at the very moment when popular culture in the United Kingdom is becoming ever more visibly less so. You only have to note the greater willingness of contemporary Americans than of their British equivalents to sing their national anthem with gusto, and to honour both their soldiers and the flag at every public opportunity, to see that faith in the country's imperial mission – with all its underlying notions of exceptionalism and superiority – is still widespread in the United States in ways it was once in the United Kingdom but is no more. The ruling orthodoxy remains in much of America that the United States is a country like no other, that its uniqueness gives it a moral superiority over the rest of the system of nation-states, and that because it does, America always conducts itself in the world as *the* model to which all others legitimately aspire. In the ruling orthodoxies of the day – in conservative America at least – the world has much to learn of a positive kind from the United States; but the United States, by contrast, has little to learn from those who live beyond its shores.

Indeed, in both countries – the one imperial, the other post-imperial – popular culture is still more self-congratulatory than it is self-critical; which is why anyone arguing that there are deep flaws in the economies and societies of both contemporary America and modern-day Britain will find themselves, as we shall do here, running against the dominant tide of popular sentiment and in tension with broadly-held understandings of conventional common sense. But run against that tide we must. For there are weaknesses in each economy and society that need to be addressed, and addressed fully – weaknesses which link back in important ways to the imperial practices that the British once celebrated and which many Americans still do. It is to the character and origin of those weaknesses that the opening chapters of this volume will be directly addressed.

Building a progressive alternative

There is a sense, of course, in which the term "flawed capitalism" is the ultimate oxymoron; because capitalism, no matter how it is organized, is inherently and inescapably flawed by the central contradiction around which it is fundamentally organized – that between capital and labour. The existence of that contradiction was, after all, why Marx and Engels both argued for the system's entire replacement, and why later generations of Marxists remain dissatisfied with the politics of social democracy.[8] But given capitalism's apparent permanence in our modern condition, it is surely worth noting that some capitalisms are, in a less basic sense than that, *more* flawed than others: depending on the degree to which the private ownership of investment resources at their core escapes regulation by the democratic state, or subverts that democratic control by resetting those regulations to advance the interests of capital rather than those of labour. The argument to be developed here is that contemporary Anglo-American capitalism is flawed in precisely this undemocratic way; and that in consequence the job of the democratic left in both political systems is to call into existence a more inclusive form of capitalism – fundamentally resetting relationships between capital and labour, the better to leave their economies and societies significantly *less* flawed. Capitalisms that are managed only in the interests of the privileged few are damaged in ways that capitalisms managed in the interests of the majority are not; and the job of the Left now is to move us away from a capitalism flawed by privilege into one made less privileged by the assertion of popular control.

If your interests are simply in the detail of this less flawed and more civic form of capitalism, then please turn directly to the last chapter, where those details are explored. But if, as I hope, you are also interested is how exactly the Anglo-American model is flawed, the better to know precisely what those details should be, then please take the longer route to the conclusion by reading on.

PART I

Flawed Economies

2

The Rise and Fall of American Economic Leadership

"Financiers live in a world of illusion. They count on something which they call the capital of the country which has no existence. Every five dollars they count as a hundred dollars; and that means that every financier, every banker, every stockbroker is 95 per cent a lunatic. And it is in the hands of these lunatics that you leave the fate of your country!"

George Bernard Shaw[1]

"The service and sacrifice of our men and women in uniform has promoted peace and prosperity from Germany to Korea, and enabled democracy to take hold in places like the Balkans."

Barack Obama[2]

It is not too great an exaggeration to say that there was a time, in the decades immediately following the Second World War, when across the advanced capitalist world as a whole the vast majority of people looked to the United States as a model economy and society – one to whose affluence, freedoms and stability so many of them then aspired. It is also not too much to say that, in the decades since, America has continued to enjoy that status in the eyes of at least the more conservative sections of the electorate in each major industrial economy with which the United States now competes. But even in those circles, America's reputation abroad is now no longer what it once was. There are flaws in the contemporary character and performance of the US economy – and in the society which that economy sustains – which are now too visible to be easily ignored. And because they are, if we are ever fully to grasp the contemporary Anglo-American condition and its resolution, it is

25

essential that we begin with a careful examination of exactly why the American economy was once so untarnished a model, and why it is untarnished no longer.

The rise and fall of the initial postwar settlement

As we have just noted, the American economy in the immediate post-Civil War period was a catch-up one, industrializing behind a substantial tariff-wall as it borrowed technology and capital from the United Kingdom and a labour force drawn from primarily Europe. The late-nineteenth century "Age of the Robber Barons" in US economic history was one of extraordinarily rapid economic growth built on fierce internal competition and brutal working conditions, the interplay of which moved the economy as a whole from a position of global backwardness to that of global leadership within a generation. For as the size of the domestic American market grew, and as the leading firms servicing it grew with it, American corporate capital exploited the technology of the second industrial revolution (the 1890s revolution built on electricity and modern science) and the competitive advantages of the emerging managerial revolution to build an industrial base that was more advanced, and more productive, than the British one it had once sought to emulate. So productive and dynamic was this new American economy that by 1929 it fell into a decade-long depression that was ultimately rooted in the lack of levels of consumer demand capable of keeping American industrial companies operating at full capacity. It was only the political changes triggered by the New Deal – particularly those strengthening the bargaining rights of organized labour – and the mobilization of productive capacity required by global warfare that eventually lifted the entire American economy out of depression: moving it away from the mass unemployment and stagnant living standards of the 1930s, and placing it instead onto a postwar trajectory of sustained growth and rising wages for at least the unionized sections of the American economy's by then fully-employed labour force.

Pessimists on the right and the left of the American political spectrum – drawing largely on the experience of continental Europe immediately after the First World War – had anticipated during the Second World War that the end of global hostilities would return the United States to the depression conditions of the 1930s. But their pessimism proved misplaced, as the surrender of the Axis powers in 1945 opened an era of American global economic leadership that both lifted living standards at home for a generation and eventually triggered an equivalent trajectory of economic growth and rising prosperity in a select and chosen number of leading economies abroad.

THE RISE

The international foundations for a sustained period of US global economic leadership were laid well before the war ended, in a series of negotiations between the allied forces that brought into existence a new set of international institutions that included the World Bank and the International Monetary Fund. Key to the way in which each of those would initially operate were negotiations held at Bretton Woods in New Hampshire in the spring of 1944. Determined not to see a return to the competitive devaluations and closed trade blocs of the 1930s – so essential to the prolongation of the interwar depression – US-led policy-makers created the framework for a postwar system of fixed but adjustable exchange rates and open trading relationships based on the dollar. Cold War politics then unexpectedly divided the wartime allies into hostile camps, leaving the non-communist bloc fully dependent on US military protection and economic support.

In consequence, there was no return to isolationism for the United States in the late 1940s, in the manner of US foreign economic and military policy at the end of the First World War. Instead, the capitalist side of the Cold War divide was organized militarily in a NATO alliance that kept large American armies in position at each end of the communist bloc – in Germany at one end, in Japan (and later South Korea) at the other – and placed the dollar at the centre of a developing set of trade flows between non-communist economies struggling to rebuild after the ravages of war. To lubricate that rebuilding, and thereby keep Western Europe and East Asia free from communism, the United States settled into a new global economic role: as the emerging system's "consumer of last resort" – one that initially ran a surplus on its balance of trade (American exports exceeding imports throughout the 1950s) but a deficit on its balance of payments (as US dollars flowed abroad to maintain

US armies, and to fuel the demand for American products in economies still too battered by war from easily producing their own).

The willingness of the United States to play this expanded global role was largely a product of Cold War politics; but its capacity to do so was rooted in something entirely other. It was rooted in the superior productive capacity of the internal US economy. The semi-automation of wartime production systems in the United States had been key to the Allied victory, first in Europe and then in Asia, as the United States had transformed itself into the "arsenal of democracy" that FDR had advocated even before the dark days of Pearl Harbor. The Allies won ultimately because of that economic (and associated military) superiority; and in the moment of victory, the United States stood alone as the one economy totally mobilized for war that had not also been entirely decimated by it. In 1945, the economic infrastructure of both Germany and Japan had been bombed into temporary total collapse, and even the British economy (though less damaged) bore the scars of pre-war under-investment and heavy wartime damage. Only the US economy was full of undamaged factories and unexhausted resources: and because it was, its problems were qualitatively different from those of both its allies and its wartime enemies. What the United States faced was not wartime dislocation because of bombing, but rather the danger of postwar recession for want of adequate consumer/military demand.

It was a danger that the United States ultimately avoided by the unexpected fusion of a remarkable triad of developments. It was a danger that was avoided partly by the US decision to maintain a large and permanent military presence abroad. In that sense, the United States avoided an economic downturn at the end of hostilities by ensuring that hostilities did not entirely end! It was a danger – of domestic factory closures – that the US economy then also partly avoided by the federal government giving dollars to consumers abroad as Marshall Aid, so ensuring that those dollars would return to the United States in the form of demand for the output of American factories that might otherwise have closed. And it was a danger – of a downturn in domestic demand triggered by the scaling down of military spending and by the extensive demobilization of military personnel – that the US economy initially avoided by cashing in on the accumulated unspent wages of its wartime soldiers, and later by the development of a limited but distinct internal

28

compact between its two basic contending classes. And in that very important sense, the United States economy flourished after 1945 in spite of the wishes (and indeed best efforts) of those who owned and directed it. It flourished because so many of the soldiers returning from war were sufficiently determined not to go back to the bad old days of the 1930s that they forced – through the trade union militancy they displayed – agreements on reluctant major employers that for the very first time in American history linked wages, productivity and profits together in a mutually supporting trajectory of growth.* American capital may have fuelled the continuing prosperity of the US economy after 1945 but it was American labour that made that prosperity happen.

In other words, the first postwar period of US global economic dominance rested on what later radical scholars categorized as a particular "social structure of accumulation"[3] – an SSA – a particularly delicate balance between demand and supply in the US economy as a whole: one with both an internal and an external face.

Internally the prosperity enjoyed by more-and-more Americans in the 1950s and 1960s ultimately rested on the significant increase in the productivity of labour, within the American economy, created by the generalized application of semi-automated production systems into one manufacturing sector after another (the spread, that is, across much of the supply side of the American economy of what the relevant academic literature calls *Fordism*†). Generalized rises in living standards are only ever attainable if labour productivity itself rises. What stopped this particular rise from collapsing into

---

* Trade union membership peaked early in the United States: at 37.5 per cent in 1953. But as David Kotz observed much later, the impact of their collective bargaining was much wider than that: "... for two reasons. First, the number of employees covered by collective bargaining contracts exceeds the number of union members. Second, when a substantial percentage of companies are unionized, non-unionized companies are under pressure to offer wages and working conditions that approximate those won through collective bargaining in order to discourage their employees from unionizing." (David Kotz, *The Rise and Fall of Neoliberal Capitalism*, Cambridge, MA: Harvard University Press, 2015, p. 27).
† The term developed by French Marxist sociologists from the 1970s to capture the complex character of modern economies: where production is based on semi-automated production systems of the kind first developed by Henry Ford, and where the viability of the firms requires both high productivity and output on the supply side and reliable and growing numbers of consumers on the demand side. On this, see David Coates, *Capitalism: The Basics* (London: Routledge, 2016), pp. 15–17.

another generalized recession was the maintenance of an appropriate level of aggregate demand via the limited capital–labour accord with which the spread of Fordism was accompanied. The demand side of the delicate balance between social classes in immediate postwar America was sustained, that is, by an accord between capital and labour that was both novel and limited. It was novel, as an accord linking rising productivity to rising wages through a series of collective agreements negotiated at the heart of the US manufacturing sector – particularly in the automotive industry – between large US corporations and well-supported industrial trade unions. It was also limited: partly because the unions traded off wage rises for the total surrender of the pace of work to corporate management, and partly because the accord did not stretch out to include non-unionized workers outside the manufacturing heartlands. Those limitations then gave a sharply regional dimension to the emerging prosperity: visible in the north-east, Midwest and California, hardly visible at all in the rural centre and the old south. It also gave a distinctive racial and gender dimension to the emerging prosperity: restricting it in the main to white unionized working-class men, and to the women with whom they lived. But among those groups, however, living standards once beyond the hopes of a traditional middle class became ever more generalized: decent housing, available consumer goods, the spread of car ownership and of modest family vacations, even a shortening of the average working week.

This internal prosperity rested additionally on what had become by the 1960s well-embedded patterns of *external* trade and power. Early in the 1950s, the United States fought one war – in Korea – to hold communism at bay, and thereafter oversaw a series of small-scale invasions and military coups to maintain pro-American governments in power in both South America and the Middle East. Policing the new global order was not America's burden alone, however, although it quickly became a burden that was not equally shared. French, Dutch and particularly British imperial control was temporarily re-established after the Second World War in a string of colonial possessions across Africa and South Asia, in all of which this re-establishment was ultimately resisted and from which in the end colonial powers were unceremoniously expelled. But what remained in their place was largely political independence rooted in economic underdevelopment – the creation, that is, of a genuine third world, trade with which was undertaken on terms more favourable to the first world than to the third, and migration into and out of which reinforced northern white dominance there. Settlers from European colonial powers continued to hold key economic resources even in areas from which the colonial powers were now in retreat, such that non-white colonial peoples seeking a better quality of life had little option, in capitalism's golden years before the Vietnam War, other than to emigrate into the northern industrial heartlands, settling there at the very bottom of increasingly racially-fragmented working- and sub-working classes. In the United States, those immigration flows in the immediate postwar years were initially internal ones – the movement of African-American rural workers into the cities of the north-east and Midwest – but also increasingly over time external and Hispanic: guest workers in south western agriculture, construction workers into states along the Mexican border, Puerto Rican unskilled labour into the cities of the American north-east.

The resulting success of the US economy in the decades immediately after the Second World War, as measured in conventional terms, was remarkable. The annual growth rate of GDP averaged 3.8 per cent between 1948 and 1966, "rivaling in pace if not in duration, the fast growth of the last third of the nineteenth century".[4] The overall growth rate slowed thereafter, but was still averaging over 2.5 per cent in the troubled decade of the 1970s.[5] Behind that growth and on the supply side of the economy, as Robert Gordon has recently argued, were the long-term legacies of the full mobilization of economic resources during the war itself, what he described as "the productivity-enhancing learning by doing that occurred during the high-pressure economy of World War II", inspiring postwar America to exploit to the full "the great inventions of the late nineteenth century, especially electricity and the internal combustion engine".[6] On the demand side of the same economic equation, as Robert Reich put it, "the nation implemented what might be called a basic bargain with American workers. Employers paid them enough to buy what they produced" – "mass production and mass consumption" proving to be "perfect complements. Almost everyone who wanted a job could find one with good wages, or at least wages that were trending upward".[7] The result? "While poverty and inequality were not eliminated, the economic growth of the period was widely shared as real hourly wages grew rapidly and consistently (with only one year of decline in 1959) and the degree of income

31

inequality decreased over the period".[8] Labour productivity – average output/ hour – doubled between 1947 and 1977. So too did the median income. It was, as Reich put it, "30 years of Great Prosperity".

THE FALL

This initial period of American global economic leadership eventually disintegrated in the 1970s: first externally, and then from within. The major *external* consequence of the Cold War-inspired American decision to establish strong economic frontiers against the expansion of Soviet communism by overseeing the reconstruction of the economies of its former adversaries – West Germany and Japan – was that those two economies did exactly that. They reconstructed themselves: to such a point indeed that by the early 1970s the West German economy was exporting more manufactured goods into the capitalist bloc as a whole than was the United States itself; and that by the late 1970s rust-belts were beginning to open up in the Midwest heartland of US manufacturing as Japanese-made manufactured goods (particularly cars) began to capture a greater and greater share of the American domestic market. The US share of the manufactured exports of the six leading industrial countries stood at 25 per cent in 1955. By 1970, that percentage was down to 18.5 per cent, and falling.[9] From running a positive trade balance and a balance of payments deficit, the United States by 1975 was running deficits on both of its main international accounts, deficits that were made significantly worse from 1966 by the cost of financing a major Asian land war in South Vietnam.

That war was itself no accident. Rather, it was the direct consequence of the United States' Cold War willingness to take up the mantle of resistance to anti-colonialism that the collapsing empires of formerly hegemonic powers – the British and French in particular – could no longer sustain. The first sign of that willingness had come early in the postwar period, in the form of the Truman Doctrine: the US picking up the role of Middle Eastern anticommunist leadership from the UK as the Attlee Government made its own reluctant withdrawal from empire: first in Greece, then Palestine, and of course most visibly in Burma and in India. The defeat of a French colonial army at Dien Bien Phu in 1954 accelerated a parallel French retrenchment

and opened up a political vacuum that the United States moved quickly to fill
– a vacuum that eventually sucked the United States into the first of a series
of ultimately unsustainable regional wars. A global power whose industrial
might had enabled it to defeat both the German and Japanese empires by
1945 found itself, three decades later, entirely unable to make that industrial
capacity produce a similar military outcome in South-East Asia, in spite of
the Nixon Administration's willingness to carpet-bomb whole areas of Vietnam and to totally destabilize Cambodia and Laos in the process.

By the early 1970s, therefore, the basic and stable international framework of American postwar economic leadership was basic and stable no
longer. A global system built on low prices for basic resources that were provided by countries under direct/indirect colonial rule found itself by 1973
subject to powerful inflationary pressures: partly because the demand for
those resources began to rise (each major economy by the 1960s beginning
to expand and contract together); and partly because the most important
resource of all – oil – found its price increasingly fixed by a new cartel of oil
producers, namely OPEC. Moreover, a global system built on a system of fixed
exchange rates tied to the dollar found itself by 1971 awash with dollars that
were no longer in such great international demand; and because they were
not, their international value began to fall. The West German state, for example, faced with an ever larger influx of foreign capital, floated the Deutsche
Mark unilaterally in October 1969 and again in May 1971 – on each occasion
trying but eventually failing to maintain the parity of the DM against the dollar.[10] Faced with the inevitable, the Nixon Administration then allowed the
dollar to float and the Bretton Woods system to fall, leaving the capitalist
bloc as a whole with a system of fluctuating exchange rates (and the potential
for competitive devaluations) that throughout the 1970s slowed significantly
the growth rate of trade between the bloc's leading constituent economies.

The Bretton Woods system had worked well *internally* for the United
States when the best manufactured goods in the world were American made,
and when foreign economies wanting to buy them were short of the dollars
to do so. But in their years of easy global dominance – when major potential
competitor economies were still disrupted by the legacy of wartime bombing
and Allied occupation – key sectors of US manufacturing industry lost their
competitive edge. By 1983 Robert Reich was complaining that "America's

basic industries had lost the habit of competing", retreating into wage-cutting and protectionism in the face of the "first wave of low-priced Japanese steel, automobiles and television sets [that] hit America's shores in the late 1960s" – trying, as he put it, "to preserve its old industrial base at the price of a gradually declining standard of living for its citizens".[11] The MIT-based research team exploring the weakening competitiveness of goods "Made in America" was equally underwhelmed by the quality and character of the response of large American-based corporations to their eroding hold on global and domestic market share: pointing by way of explanation to "outdated strategies, short-time horizons, technological weaknesses in development and production, neglect of human resources, failures of cooperation and government and industry [being] at cross purposes".[12]

Things that worked well in the immediate past now worked less well or not at all – and became keys to failure rather than success – because the arrival of German and Japanese competition was said to have brought with it a new competitive paradigm: one in which economic success relied on things that American industry broadly lacked – patient capital, harmonious industrial relations, and investment (as Michael Porter told the incoming Clinton Administration) "not just in smokestacks and machines" but "also in less tangible assets such as research and development, training, supplier relationships, and the losses required to gain access to foreign markets".[13] Without those things, the strength of vital industrial clusters would weaken – and Porter's research suggested that they were weakening in the United States because of inadequacies in the US education and training systems, because of the short-term dividend requirements of US institutional investors, and because of government indifference to the health of US-based civilian-focused manufacturing. Throughout the Cold War years, the focus of federal-level industrial policy was primarily military, orchestrated through the Pentagon, and there was no parallel industrial policy aimed at strengthening civilian manufacturing output; rather, as Porter put it: "American policy was based on the assumption that U.S. industry had a commanding position. Today, for often self-inflicted reasons, that assumption is a shaky one".[14]

The assumption was shaky because beneath these emerging surface-level weaknesses, the tectonic plates underpinning the first postwar social settlement were moving out of line with each other by the 1970s. The growth rate of productivity across the manufacturing sector as a whole had by then slowed significantly, as the incremental advantage of adding more capital to already existing semi-automated production processes began to decline, and as the gap in labour productivity between the United States and its leading overseas competitor economies began to narrow. In the United States, "productivity had grown at a 2.8 per cent annual rate from 1947 until 1973. From 1973 to 1980, it grew at just a 1 per cent rate". That meant, among other, things, that real wages could not continue to rise "at the same rate as they had in the golden age" without firms passing those higher wages on "in the form of higher prices, or a squeeze in corporate profits". Both happened steadily in the 1970s "The inflation rate for the decade as a whole averaged 7.1 per cent annually ... at the same time, the profit share of corporate income was squeezed to its lowest level in the postwar era, falling to 17.1 per cent in 1979 from an average of 20.7 per cent in the sixties, a decline in profit share of almost 20 per cent".[15]

As the 1960s US triad of rising productivity, profits and wages began to break down, the resulting squeeze on corporate profits then obliged more and more large American corporations to re-examine the collective agreements struck with their unionized workers, and tempted ever more of them to relocate their production facilities: initially, mainly to areas within the United States where trade unionism was less entrenched; later, overseas. Simultaneously, both the exclusion of southern workers from any direct share in those northern collective agreements, and the underlying and unequal racial contract that the New Deal Democrats had left in place, came under challenge – first in the civil rights protests of the early 1960s, and then in the hot summers, the riots in major American cities, that were such a feature of the end of that decade – eventually helping to trigger a significant rise in federal welfare spending labelled by Lyndon Johnson as a long overdue "war on poverty". Any elite consensus on the desirability and effectiveness of that spending in particular, and of Keynesian demand management in general, then fell away as the 1970s progressed: eroded, year after year, by the simultaneous explosion of the two things – large-scale unemployment and rapid price inflation – that Keynesian demand management could only treat as alternatives.

The rise and fall of the neoliberal settlement

So it was that a global and domestic economic and social settlement which had looked so stable and set in stone in the immediate decades after the Second World War suddenly looked neither stable nor set; and because it did not, the United States experienced a decade of internal political turmoil, as both political elites and their electorates struggled to make sense of this unexpected set of highly unwelcome developments. The 1970s in the United States witnessed a set of deepening crises that signalled the total disintegration of the first internal settlement underpinning postwar US economic growth and prosperity – crises simultaneously of Fordism, of Keynesianism, and of a racially-charged system of welfare provision – that few had anticipated would occur and that none initially understood when they did occur. But, by the end of that troubled decade, at least one half of the interlocking networks of political and economic elites in America thought that it had found the understanding necessary to the crises of the age: namely a non-Keynesian, uniquely neoliberal, answer to why the 1970s had "gone wrong" in so unexpected and so dramatic a fashion. It was an answer – circulating initially only in conservative elite circles – that over time would call up another internal social settlement and period of external economic leadership. And in this second iteration of postwar American power, other things not anticipated in the 1970s would play an enormously important role: internally, the unexpected development of computers, with their enormous impact on labour productivity; and externally, the unexpected collapse of the Soviet Union and the opening up of China to foreign direct investment and trade, which together would eventually guarantee that the scope of American economic leadership this time around would be a genuinely global one.

THE RISE

The new neoliberal settlement inaugurated by the Reagan presidency in the United States (and by the parallel Thatcher premiership in the United Kingdom) ultimately rested on a new self-confidence and assertiveness in leading business circles on both sides of the Atlantic. As the 1970s progressed, "entrenched business interests such as the auto companies, the petroleum industry, defense firms and big financial institutions worked hand-in-hand with conservative political leaders to construct a 'free market' regime of accumulation designed to bolster business profits at the expense of all other social groups".[16] This was a genuine "employers' offensive": one consciously designed to "regain manufacturing competitiveness at the expense of both labour and its overseas rivals, while seeking to defend and consolidate its dominance of international financial services". It was an offensive which, as Robert Brenner later noted, "was marked by a two-decades long repression of wage growth, a secular fall in the value of the dollar, an accelerating shake-out of high-cost, low-profit means of production: and ultimately an important recovery of manufacturing profitability and investment".[17] It was an offensive, moreover, which in political terms aimed "to reverse almost all the key reforms of Roosevelt's New Deal".[18]

In consequence, an Administration came to power in Washington in 1980 determined to free American business of both federal government control and trade union-negotiated wage deals. It achieved the latter by challenging (and defeating) the union representing air traffic controllers, by facilitating the movement of productive capacity to union-free greenfield sites in the American south and west, and by quietly orchestrating the passage of legislation at state level that blocked trade union recruitment behind a libertarian rhetoric of defending the right to work. It achieved the former by steadily chipping away at the regulatory agencies created during the Keynesian years: filling them with appointees committed to free market ideologies, steadily underfunding the agencies they so inadequately led, and – by the 1990s – stripping away the divisions between different kinds of financial agencies that had been put in place after the bank collapse of the early 1930s. The deep cuts in income tax (and resulting large budget deficits) at the beginning of the Reagan presidency, and the scrapping of Glass-Steagall (and the attendant budget surpluses) at the end of the Clinton one, acted as the two bookends here to a fundamental resetting of the power-relationships between government, industry and labour in America. It was a resetting that left labour industrially weakened and government regulation of industry delegitimated. It was also a settlement that left large-scale American capital free to invest where and when it wanted, and able to reward its senior people as much or as little as it wished.

All this occurred against the background of a steady drumbeat of anti-statist rhetoric that incrementally but effectively shifted the centre of gravity of the common sense of the age: so that by the 1990s it was those wanting to use political power to manage private enterprise that had to justify their "interference" with free market forces that were everywhere presented as operating best when regulated least. Yet even so, the Reagan Administration continued to work closely with (and to subsidize heavily) key sectors of US industry that were central to its wider global mission: so the Pentagon continued to sustain US military engineering capacity; the Department of Energy continued to subsidize America's oil giants; and the Department of Agriculture continued to subsidize American agribusiness. But there was no such largesse either for US domestic producers of consumer goods, or for the recipients of what was already by leading international standards only modest levels of welfare provision. The "war on poverty" was declared lost by Ronald Reagan because "poverty won"; and poverty won because "government was not part of the solution. It was part of the problem". A new social settlement was thereby orchestrated into existence that blamed the poor for their poverty, denied workers the right to collectively bargain for their wages, and denuded regulatory agencies of their capacity to contain the worst excesses of unregulated market competition. It was little wonder then that the new social settlement, unlike its predecessor, broke the link between productivity and wages, and allowed poverty to rise and income inequality to widen once more – this time to levels last seen in the 1920s.

The new settlement – in place by the early 1990s – had its own internal and external face. *Externally*, the first decade of the Reagan revolution saw the United States boosting its military spending and offensive capacity significantly – this was the decade, after all, of the real "Star Wars" offensive – and using its still-unchallenged global clout to manipulate currencies in the interest of US-based manufacturers. The Plaza Accord of 1985, in which the United States forced a significant revaluation of both the Japanese yen and the German Deutsche Mark, marked the high-point of this initial move to protect US-based manufacturing industry as competition quickened and rust-belts opened up in the American Midwest. But by the mid-1990s, however, no such protectionism was necessary. The Plaza Accord so ripped the heart out of the rising home-based Japanese export machine that a decade later Japanese capital was pouring into the United States, as the main component of a flow of foreign direct investment that retooled much of US industry, and sustained a remarkable and unexpected explosion of American employment. For by then, it was not just that the Japanese postwar economic miracle had come to its end. By then, the Soviet Union had also unexpectedly collapsed, communist China was exploring its own route to a capitalist future, and the United States had unexpectedly found itself as the strongest major economy in a global economic order no longer divided into antagonistic blocs.

The first major *internal* consequence of the United States' unexpected emergence as the last global power standing was this explosion in the volume of foreign direct investment flowing into the safe haven of major American financial institutions. That influx simultaneously strengthened the political leverage of those institutions – facilitating their extensive deregulation at home in the glow of their increasing international status – and fuelled a stock-market boom. That stock-market boom in its turn artificially increased the paper value of all kinds of US companies, provided them with extra collateral for domestic borrowing, and so stoked a bubble of investment, employment and rising wages that peaked briefly in the last years of the old century. "Stock-market Keynesianism" was how it was described at the time: aggregate demand in the whole economy soared "as stockholders splurged on cars, vacations, and other luxuries".[19] And well they might: for the scale of foreign direct investment in the second half of the 1990s was unprecedented and remarkable. Indeed, it is striking just how far the recovery of the US economy in the 1980s and 1990s was based on a financial bubble, as a boom funded by borrowing foreign money.[20] "The net capital inflow of foreign capital increased from $59 billion in 1990–93 to around $140 billion in 1994 and 1995 and then increased again to $195 billion in 1996 and again to $264 billion in 1997. These amounts for 1996 and 1997 were roughly 20% of gross private domestic investment in the US economy during these years"[21], helping fuel an internationally recognized American "job-creating machine" that added 22 million new jobs to the US economy during the years of the Clinton presidency.

The original Reagan settlement had looked for a return to corporate profitability and rising labour productivity primarily by intensifying the labour process – having Americans work longer and harder while holding their real wages steady or falling. The necessary limits of that strategy were then unexpectedly eased in the 1990s by the development and dissemination of a new computer technology: a diffusion that first raised productivity in the industrial sectors creating the computers and then across the big-box retail sector in particular, where the spread of computerization helped offset the decline in productivity normally associated with the rise of service industries and the decline of manufacturing employment. In consequence, and for a brief period, profits and wages rose together again in America in the late 1990s – this time not on the basis of strong trade unions but on a rise in stock prices that created the illusion of wealth by progressively widening the gap between the paper value of the companies being traded and their actual competitiveness and profitability. It was a gap that narrowed briefly during the end of the dot.com boom in 2000, and which vanished completely eight years later. The gap that remained was that between productivity and pay. As Figure 2.1 indicates, between 1979 and 2013 productivity growth in the US economy outstripped wage growth by a staggering 800 per cent – a 72.2 per cent increase in productivity but only an 9.2 per cent increase in hourly compensation for all but the top 20 per cent.[22] Both gaps – the asset gap and the productivity-pay gap – served to differentiate the Reagan settlement dramatically from the postwar settlement that had preceded it.

For the underlying social settlement that emerged from the Reagan revolution did not rest ultimately on rising wages and the continuing industrial power of organized labour. It rested instead on exactly the reverse. The collapse of Russian communism, and the opening of the Chinese communist economy to foreign direct investment by multinational capitalist concerns, effectively doubled the size of the global proletariat between 1980 and 2000, and opened the way to its doubling again in the two decades that followed.[23] Weakened globally by the competition with cheap supplies of formerly peasant labour, and at home by a steadily rising flow of undocumented Hispanic workers across the southern border, the trade union-organized American labour force – the bedrock of the American "middle class" in the pre-Reagan years – found itself after 1980 progressively trapped in a "race to the bottom" as large US corporations increasingly relocated their production facilities to non-union low-wage sites: first within the United States as we have already seen (going south and going west); then slipping below the border into Mexico before eventually shifting further afield still – primarily into China but also, where appropriate, into a string of smaller Asian economies from Vietnam to Bangladesh. All that American workers could do by way of survival, in the face of this global onslaught, was to work longer hours for lower pay, to send more and more family members out into the paid labour force, and to meet their immediate consumer needs by borrowing against future earnings, maxing out their credit cards in the process.

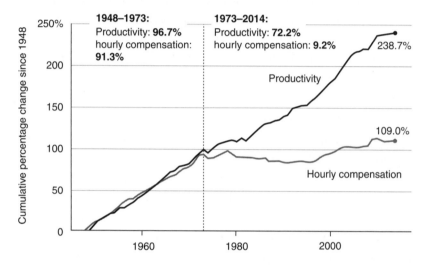

Figure 2.1 Disconnect between productivity and a typical worker's compensation, 1948–2014
(Source: Josh Bivens and Lawrence Mishel, "Understanding the Historic Divergence Between Productivity and a Typical Worker's Pay". Washington, DC: Economic Policy Institute, 2 September 2015, p. 4).

At the base of the new Reagan social settlement stood a middle class squeezed by foreign competition, unregulated immigration and a deregulated business community into a new mould. It was one in which "an enormous downward pressure on real wages ... led to the emergence of longer working hours, second (even third) jobs, and larger numbers of multi-earner households in an attempt to maintain overall family incomes".[24] It was a settlement in which real pay rates/hour stagnated for a forty-year period, and in which real income growth was largely concentrated in the top 20 per cent of income earners. (Taking the period 1979–2013 as a whole, middle-wage workers' hourly wage rose 6 per cent, the hourly rate for low-wage workers' fell 5 per cent, while high-wage workers saw their hourly rates increase by over 40 per cent).[25] It was also a settlement in which (at comparable points of the business cycle) the average hours worked on a yearly basis by the median American worker went up by 48 hours between 1952 and 1999: six extra days, or effectively an extra working week.[26] It was one in which, by 2000, a majority of the US labour force was female, with 60 per cent of women with children combining paid work with unpaid childcare. In 1966, that figure had been 20 per cent. And it was one in which levels of personal indebtedness reached new and unprecedented heights: by 2007, for example, "the typical American owed 138 per cent of their after-tax income".[27]

As David Brennan correctly notes: "In the final analysis, it is the shifting distribution of income away from median wage earners and towards top executives and the dramatic increase in workers' debts that most characterized the period after 1982".[28] Under the terms of the Reagan settlement, that is, inequality became policy.[29] The rich got richer, the poor poorer, and the middle class remained stuck; a middle class that then survived only by borrowing – to maintain/increase its private consumption – from the capital stocks and income holdings of the super-rich, in the process paying astronomical rates of interest on its credit cards for the privilege. It was a settlement that, as Fred Block said, was not only prolonged: it was also one that was "deeply flawed".[30]

THE FALL

Those flaws accumulated initially around the external face of the Reagan settlement, as the "peace dividend" generated in the 1990s by the collapse of the Soviet Union was entirely shattered by the attacks on the World Trade Center and the Pentagon on 9/11. Instead of a peace dividend and the space to reorient priorities towards internal economic and social reconstruction, the United States found itself instead immersed, from 2001, in a never-ending sequence of wars in the Middle East. The events of 9/11 – horrendous as they were – could be seen in part as a blowback from one aspect of the Cold War itself: the CIA funding and arming of the mujahideen in Afghanistan in the last days of the Soviet empire there. But the bulk of the military involvement into which the United States was subsequently sucked was not of that kind.

It was the product of the entirely independent decision to invade Iraq – to exercise American military hegemony under the cover of false claims about the origins of 9/11 – that then opened a Pandora's box of anti-Americanism and global jihad from which even now there is no quick and easy escape. The full ramifications of that fatal foreign policy error will be discussed in Chapter 6. What we need to note here is simply the scale of military spending with which, after 9/11, both civilian-focused public policy and the American economy had to deal. In 2000, US military spending absorbed 3 per cent of GDP. By 2010 that percentage was 4.8 and rising; as a base Pentagon budget of $287 billion in 2001 had expanded to $530 billion a decade later. If you add to that basic budget the costs of the wars in Afghanistan and Iraq, official military spending was by then absorbing between a fifth and a quarter of the entire federal budget. Additionally, add the cost of homeland security, the cost of the 16 intelligence agencies, the cost of veteran support and interest on war debt, and it is likely that by the time the financial crisis broke in 2008 military-related spending in all its forms was absorbing nearly half of the federal budget and perhaps 10 per cent of US GDP.[31]

The other external contradiction that eventually undid the Reagan-created social settlement was more directly economic in nature. The collapse of the Soviet Union triggered – in communist China – a determined if heavily managed opening to the West. The Chinese Communist Party began to allow foreign direct investment into specified areas of the territories it controlled, foreign direct investment designed to strengthen the Chinese export sector; and did so at precisely the moment when a combination of business deregulation and new communication technologies were combining to facilitate the global movement of capital on a scale, and with a speed, never before seen. American corporate capital was heavily involved in that global mobility: relatively slowly as China began the opening of its labour markets to foreign capital in the 1990s, and more rapidly after that opening was widened in the first decades of the new century. More and more large American companies – attracted by the availability of huge quantities of skilled, disciplined and cheap labour – relocated parts or the entirety of their production facilities offshore: in the process opening up (as we first noted in the Introduction) a large and growing American trade deficit with China. That deficit was just $10.1 billion in 1991. Twenty years later, it was $301 billion.[32] Any other country would have been obliged to cut back on domestic consumption in the face of such a short-fall: but not the United States. The US position as the last remaining super-power gave it a significant degree of financial arbitrage and deficit-tolerance: foreign funds flowing into Wall Street to help finance the deficit, and huge dollar surpluses building up in foreign central banks – particularly in Beijing.

But though cushioned in that fashion, the trade deficit set in motion two internal trends that ultimately eroded the economic superiority on which global hegemony ultimately always rests. It eroded the competitiveness (and indeed scale) of US-based manufacturing industry; and it pulled the rug from under the wage-structure of the American middle class, polarizing US labour markets increasing into a high-skill minority and a low-skill majority divi-sion, and exposing the latter to what elsewhere we have called "the Walmart effect".[33]

US-based manufacturing industry – which had been the bedrock of rising American prosperity in both the first postwar settlement and in the 1990s boom of this second one – shrunk in size, employment-capacity and inter-national competitiveness in the decade and a half that followed 9/11. As a proportion of GDP, home-based manufacturing contributed 18.7 per cent in 1980 but only 12.5 per cent in 2013, as its economic contribution was eclipsed by the rise of the service sector, particularly its financial division. As a source of employment (as again we noted earlier), US-based manufacturing industry shrunk: from 19.5 million in 1979 to 11.5 million in December 2011; and as a global leader, parts of the US-based manufacturing sector slipped even more dramatically, down into a second league. In 1991, the US economy led global competition in a swathe of manufacturing industries, especially those deploying the latest and most sophisticated technology.[34] By 2008, it led only in five: "hardware, software, biotechnology, aerospace and entertainment"[35] and by as early as 2002 a trade surplus in high technology goods with China had changed into an ongoing deficit of over $16 billion.[36] This mattered: it mattered because without a strong manufacturing base, a strong and inde-pendent foreign policy becomes ever more difficult to pursue. And it mattered, because high productivity in the manufacturing sector has been historically the source of strong wage growth, so that a shift into a predominantly low-productivity service economy weakened that productivity- and wage-dynamic at the very core of the American economic system.

So it should not be a surprise – although it was understood as such at the time – to discover that the remarkable job-creating capacity of the American economy in the 1990s slowed significantly in the years of the second Bush presidency,[37] and that the return of general wage stagnation forced more and more Americans into debt-financed personal consumption on an unprecedented scale. As the EPI reported in 2009, "the economic expansion from 2001 to the end of 2007 added jobs more slowly than any other expansion since World War II ... 0.9 per cent a year, about one-third of the 2.5 per cent posted in the average postwar expansion".[38] American workers on low wages, and those without work altogether, were particularly exposed to the Walmart effect. The big-box retailers forced their prices down by squeezing their suppliers, who survived only by outsourcing more-and-more of their production to cheap labour sites abroad. That undercut American wages at home, obliging more and more Americans to survive by buying only the cheap goods that the big-box retailers could offer because of this retail-induced outsourcing of manufacturing employment. The result, during the George W. Bush years, was a Walmart induced "wage race to the bottom", a race softened at the margins by the excessive use of credit cards (people consuming today by borrowing tomorrow's salary, and paying high fees for the privilege), and a race that left Walmart effectively acting as the American end of the Chinese manufacturing export drive. A drive that was so successful, in fact, that by 2011 the Chinese economy's production of manufactured goods had outstripped that of the United States in volume after a growth spurt of less than three decades in length, and Walmart had turned itself into America's largest single employer.

There was only one economic sector that proved initially immune to all of this systemic economic weakening, and that was the financial sector. There, the contribution to GDP flourished under the light regulation of financial institutions instituted first by the Clinton Administration and then by the second Bush one: financial activity growing, as a percentage of American GDP, from 2.8 per cent in 1950 to 8.3 per cent by 2006. With that growth came income growth too, and the pulling of the brightest and the best away from American manufacturing into American finance. Average salaries (with bonuses) in major US financial institutions in the 2000s ran 70 per cent higher than in the rest of the economy – a gap that as late as 1980 had not

45

existed at all;[39] and not surprisingly, therefore, the financial sector managed to recruit in 2006 a staggering 46 per cent of the Princeton graduating class and 25 per cent of the one from Harvard.[40] And with the money and the growth came the arrogance and the greed: arrogance that persuaded leading bankers that they required no regulation at all; and greed that locked the major institutions into fierce competition with each other for the market share (and flow of fees) that speculation in different forms of financial products could deliver. By 2008, indeed, maybe as much as 85 per cent of what Wall Street did was not functional to the rest of the economy.[41] It was simply speculative behaviour using other people's money as collateral; and it was speculation that in the end brought the whole edifice down.

The 2008 financial crisis that ended the social structure of accumulation designed in the Reagan years is best thought of as the monetary equivalent of a three-layered cake.[42] The top tier was a housing finance system that by the first decade of the new century was literally out of control. The middle tier was the regulatory system itself, effectively neutered by three decades of anti-statist free-market rhetoric; and the bottom tier was the all-pervasive presence by 2008 of debt in the American economic system: especially international trading debt and personal debt. It was the scale of US overseas indebtedness – anchored in the growing lack of domestic competitiveness of US-based manufacturing industry – that then flooded the global financial system with unwanted dollars, dollars whose reinvestment in US financial institutions both inflated the supply of credit available for house purchase and ensured that a housing collapse in America would race out (tsunami-like) into the wider global economy. And it was the scale of personal indebtedness in the United States – anchored in the stagnation of real wages for the bulk of American workers since the mid-1970s – that made subprime loans so attractive to so many Americans, and yet made them so difficult to pay off when their "teaser" period was over. Mix into that fragile concoction a sizeable slice of "recklessness, corruption, failure, greed and arrogance at the very heart of American finance"[43] and the result – in September 2008 – was the temporary collapse of the entire credit-creating system. Key financial institutions were by then so under-capitalized relative to their accumulated debt levels, the key players were so out of control and so overpaid, and the securitized financial products that they had sold to each other were so uncertain in value, that for a moment no one could tell which financial institutions were solvent and which were not. The Masters of the Universe on Wall Street, like the fabled emperor before them, had turned out to have no clothes: and in consequence a sustained period of economic growth based ultimately on faith in their capacity to generate an endless supply of credit came to an abrupt and a brutal end.

The nature of the current condition

And the end was brutal. The Reagan settlement crashed in a single month – September 2008 – a month in which a whole string of major US financial institutions either closed or teetered on the edge of bankruptcy, and a month in which the entire credit-creating system in the United States froze. It was a crash on a scale never seen since 1929, and a crash that was only ameliorated by swift intervention by a Bush Administration that entirely abandoned its deregulatory enthusiasms to literally order strong banks to underwrite weak ones, and used tax dollars to bail out first major Wall Street firms and then major auto companies.[44] The Bush Administration (and later the Obama one) had to bail out the latter because the crisis of Wall Street immediately threw the rest of the US (and indeed the global) economy into a deep and prolonged recession. In all previous post-Second World War recessions in the US economy, recovery was well underway by the seventh quarter after the recession's official beginning: normally, indeed, by that point the economy was running on average four percentage points higher than its pre-recession peak. But not this time: this time the US economy fell by 3.8 per cent in the last three months of 2008 – "the worst quarterly contraction in more than 26 years"[45]– and was still 3.2 per cent *smaller* after seven quarters than it had been at its 2007 peak.[46] There were more than a million job losses in the United States in November and December 2008 alone: and US companies axed more than 72,000 jobs on just one day (8 January) in 2009, to leave more than 15 million able-bodied US adults involuntarily unemployed by the middle of 2009. "Almost one in six workers" in the United States "reported having lost a job in the 2007–2009 period" as the US economy lost more than 7 million jobs in total in just 18 months, and as the unemployment rate jumped from 4.4 per cent before the credit crisis to 7.2 per cent immediately after it.[47] That rate later peaked at 10 per cent in the fall of 2009, with workers then reporting "very low rates of reemployment, difficulty finding full-time employment, and substantial earnings losses".[48] It was indeed the mother of all recessions!

However, not even a recession of this depth lasts forever, and this one did not. It was technically over by the middle of 2009: but its legacies remain, and the shadow it threw forward has yet to be fully shed. Those legacies, and that shadow, are evident in all the conventional measures of adequate economic performance.

GDP GROWTH, TRADE PERFORMANCE AND PRODUCTIVITY

The legacies are certainly visible in the long-term growth statistics. As late as 2013, overall economic output "was 13 per cent below its trend path from 1990 through 2007" with "2.2 per cent of that 13 due to slackness in the labour market, 3.9 per cent due to a shortfall in business capital and 3.5 per cent to continuing under-performance in total factor productivity".[49] Robert E. Hall, whose figures those are, put it this way in another jointly-authored paper: "Output grew substantially less in the recovery from the 2007–2009 recession than would normally have accompanied the healthy decline in the unemployment rate. It grew less than it would have given its normal relation to an index derived from many macro indicators. And it grew less than professional forecasters predicted, both at the time of the trough and throughout the recovery". The key question is why: and their answer focused in on two "key facts: productivity grew substantially less than its historical growth rate ... and labour-force participation shrank an atypical and unexpected amount".[50]

Partly that undershoot to trend was a product of sluggish overall rates of economic growth. Between June 2009 (the official end of the recession) and July 2015, the US economy grew on average about 2.1 per cent per year, a very low number when compared to the equivalent six years of the Reagan expansion (4.6 per cent), the first Bush-Clinton expansion (3.6 per cent) or even the modest expansion under George W. Bush (2003–06, at 3 per cent).* At the

---

* The rate improved slightly, to 2.9 per cent, by the third quarter of 2016, before dropping back, in the first quarter of 2017, to an annualized growth rate of 0.7 per cent. Second quarter growth in the US economy in 2017 expanded to an annual rate of 3 per cent again.

heart of that sluggishness was a significant fall in the number of new business start-ups;[51] and a parallel unwillingness on the part of existing businesses, in the face of uncertain levels of demand and in spite of unprecedently low rates of interest, to invest heavily in new plant and equipment, and in research and development. As the Council of Economic Advisers told the President in February 2016, "after being a bright spot early in the recovery, investment growth moderated in 2015": a cause for concern primarily because "investment net of depreciation is required to increase the capital stock. In 2009, net investment as a share of the capital stock fell to its lowest level in the postwar era, and the nominal capital stock even declined. Although net investment has rebounded somewhat in the recovery, its level as a share of the capital stock remains well below its historical average".*[52] In company with business sectors elsewhere in the advanced capitalist economies, US investment levels are currently running significantly below pre-crisis trends[53]– with US economic growth held back by what in 2016 the IMF cited as "insufficient demand and an overhang of debt" – and castigated as a self-perpetuating problem: "debt overhangs depress demand and weaken banks, creating deflationary pressures and discouraging investment, both of which perpetuate or worsen the demand shortfall and the noxious legacy of debt".[54] But how could it be otherwise with total non-financial private debt in the United States standing at $27 trillion and public debt at $16 trillion in 2016, the former having nearly tripled as a percentage of GDP: from 55 per cent in 1950 to 150 per cent today?[55]

The main immediate casualty of that dearth of adequate investment has been the current rate of US productivity growth. From 1995 to 2005, as the arrival of the Internet weaved its magic, labour productivity in the US economy grew by an average of 2.5 per cent per year: between 2010 and 2015 that rate dropped to 0.3 per cent per year (see Figure 2.2).[56] That would matter less if a dearth of private investment had been more than offset by an expansion

---

* It is worth noting that one important cause of underinvestment in post-recession America remains the high rate of corporate buy-outs and dividend distribution: the emergence, that is, in what was once the heartland of investment-based manufacturing, of a rentier-led capitalism that is now eroding long-term competitiveness by its zeal for short-term profit-taking. The US economy is now at such a point of concentration indeed that manufacturing, finance, utilities, and retail trade, are now all sectors where the top four firms account for at least 30 per cent of average industry sales – and so are under diminished competitive pressure to invest to capture a greater market share.

of public investment – particularly investment in basic social infrastructure – but no such expansion followed the initial stimulus package. Once that initial stimulus was gone, public sector investment plummeted too: to the point indeed, as Larry Summers noted in 2015, that "at this moment ... the share of public investment in GDP, adjusted for depreciation, so that's net share, is zero. We're not net investing at all" – just investing enough, that is, in bridges, roads, airports, rails and pipes to cover daily wear and tear![57] This, at the very time when the US economy needs an enormous injection of infrastructure investment to meet contemporary global competitive conditions – \$3.6 trillion to bring US infrastructure to a state of good repair by 2020, according to the American Society of Civil Engineers[58] – and when the US currently ranks only twelfth in global comparisons on the quality of infrastructure provision.[59]

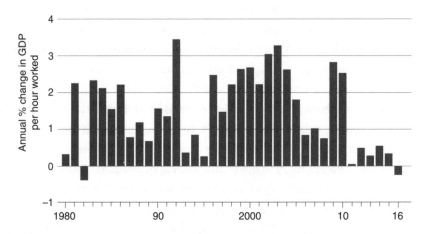

Figure 2.2: US productivity growth (annual percentage change in GDP per hour worked)
(Source: Sam Fleming and Chris Giles, "US productivity slips for first time in three decades", *Financial Times*, 25 May 2016, used under license from the *Financial Times*).

The other adverse consequence of under-investment, particularly in core US-based manufacturing industries, has been the continued shrinkage of manufacturing employment and the associated widening of the US balance of trade. As we noted in the Introduction, the number of US-based manufacturing jobs fell from 19.3 million in 1979 to 12.3 million in 2015 – a 37 per cent fall in a population that grew 43 per cent in those same years.[60] We saw too that the main immediate cause of this loss of manufacturing jobs has been the increased outsourcing of manufacturing capacity and employ-ment by large, shareholder-driven, US-based corporations. A whole string of scholars, indeed, has linked what Pierce and Schott labelled this "surprisingly rapid decline of US manufacturing employment"[61] to the opening of trade with China and to the increased outsourcing of manufacturing jobs that accompanied it. Estimates of the "China effect" vary between a quarter and a half of all manufacturing jobs lost in the US since 9/11 depending on the source adopted, but at least 2–2.4 million of those lost jobs can probably best be explained in that fashion.[62] And while there is some controversy about the scale of US deindustrialization linked to overseas trade, there is no equiv-alent controversy about the impact of that trade on America's overseas accounts. On that, there is general agreement: employment-outsourcing, and the growing import of manufactured products and components, have com-bined to further erode the US economy's already negative trade balance: negative with the rest of the world since June 1975, and at the end of 2016 still running at negative -2.7 per cent of US GDP.

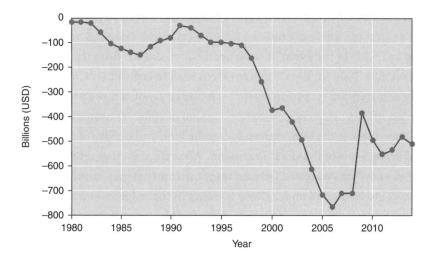

Figure 2.3 US trade balance, 1980–2014
(Source: US Census Bureau Foreign Trade Division).

EMPLOYMENT AND JOB CREATION

In line with patterns of recovery from previous financially-triggered recessions, it took a long time for employment levels to recover from the credit crisis and recession of 2008–09.[63] In this instance, it took a whole 74 months (to April 2014) for the economy's number of private sector jobs to reach the pre-recession peak of January 2008; and it did so because, as Alejandro Reuss later observed, the recession left America with a "triple-decker jobs crisis": an enormous jobs hole, high unemployment blocking wage growth, and a diminution in the flow of high-quality jobs.[64]

From late 2009, the economy did begin to create employment again; but since the potential labour force in the United States grows steadily each month simply by the arrival of new workers leaving the education system, this belated return to pre-recession numbers actually masked an overall drop in the pre-recession trajectory of job generation. Six years on from the start of the recession, "the total jobs gap – the number of jobs needed to return the U.S. economy to pre-recession health – [was still] 7.9 million jobs (3.6 million for women and 4.3 for men)";[65] and there were only enough new jobs on offer in the entire economy to meet the needs of less than 40 per cent of the Americans then seeking them. At that point in the slow recovery, indeed, "more than one in six men between 25 and 54 [was still] without a job"[66] and even as late as October 2015, the ratio of job-seekers to job-openings was still running at 1.5:1.[67] In the event, it took nearly a full decade from the start of the recession in 2008 for the US employment level to return to its "demographically adjusted pre-recession level"[68] – yet more proof, if more proof was still needed, of how uniquely severe the recession of 2008–09 turned out to be.

Then there is the important issue of the kind and quality of the jobs created in the wake of the Great Recession. What the data suggest is that many of these new jobs were ones paying wages so low that even covering housing costs could be a problem for those working in them. Job polarization within the American labour market intensified after the Great Recession, and continued to set different occupational groups on entirely different earning and work-experience trajectories. This was particularly so in the immediate wake of the recession, when employment in manufacturing and construction was slow to recover, while employment in restaurants, retail and routine

52

administration rebounded more quickly. The result overall, was that while "low-wage industries accounted for 22 per cent of the jobs lost during the recession from 2008 to 2010 ... they accounted for 44 per cent of the employment growth"[69] between 2010 and the middle of 2014. Indeed, on some accounts at least, "a stunning 94 per cent of the 9 million jobs created in the past decade" in the US economy "were temp or contract-based gigs".[70] So at least one thing is very clear: whatever else on the jobs front the Obama Administration may or may not have achieved, it entirely failed to stop during its eight-year tenure of office this ongoing polarization of the US labour market into a limited number of high-paying jobs and a plentiful supply of jobs that paid less well.[71]

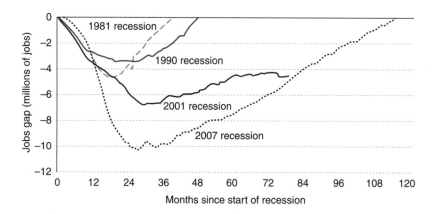

Figure 2.4 The closing of the jobs gap: recessions and recoveries compared (Source: Brookings, "The Closing of the Jobs Gap: A Decade of Recession and Recovery", 7 August 2017).

But a simple measure of job numbers does not tell us enough about the content and occupancy of the jobs themselves. One marked feature of post-recession America was the way in which many employers hung on to core workers, and increased their hours, rather than add to their labour force at a time of uncertain demand. American working hours, already long and disproportionately anti-social by comparative standards – more night-work, irregular scheduling[72] and weekend-working than in comparable western European economies – then lengthened and worsened still further as unemployment continued. Those fortunate to keep their job in post-recession America worked an average 47hours/week by 2014;[73] and probably worked with a higher level of intensity too[74] – certainly with a heightened level of job insecurity. And because (as we shall see), many jobs in the United States still did not pay a living wage, certain of the new jobs created after 2008 were occupied by the same person. The overall rate of workers holding multiple jobs is now falling – although recent Gallup data suggest that as many as 12 per cent of full-time workers have two jobs, and that 1 per cent even have three or more[75] – but those that remain are far more likely to be held by women than by men, and by young women in particular: 6.7 per cent of all working women aged 20–24 had multiple jobs in 2015.[76]

It was not all doom and gloom on the employment front, of course. Things definitely improved in the latter half of the Obama presidency, with the private sector chalking up 75 months of small but regular job expansion by the spring of 2016, so that the Obama Administration was able to close out its term of office pointing to six years of rising job numbers and to the creation of over 12 million new jobs on its watch.* But the Democrats could spin the Obama employment story in that way only by downplaying the slowness of the recovery, the job polarization (and erosion of job quality) that had accompanied it, and the fact that – if the Hamilton Project estimates were right – "we may not reach our former level of employment, when factoring in new labor-force entrants, until as late as mid-2017".[77] And although the official rate of unemployment fell to a ten-year low in April 2017, so too did the level of labour market participation: down to just 62.9 per cent as more-and-more eligible workers sidelined in the wake of the recession gave up the hunt for further job vacancies.

UNEMPLOYMENT AND PART-TIME WORKING

The Obama presidency ended, and the Trump presidency began, that is, with the long-term employment legacy of the Great Recession still unclear: with it still not obvious whether this particular glass was best thought of as being half-full or half-empty. But one thing that was clear by then was that as the

---

* August 2017 marked the eighty-second straight month of US job growth, the longest unbroken run on record.

job-creation numbers crept back up in the latter part of the Obama presidency, the official unemployment numbers did begin to fall. And on paper at least, this fall was real and significant: a 10 per cent rate of unemployment at the end of 2009 down to 4.6 per cent by the end of 2016 and to 4.4 per cent by mid-2017, so effectively re-establishing full employment if the normal calculations on the residual unemployable core of any modern labour force are to be believed. But in truth the unemployment numbers flattered to deceive too, in at least these three important ways.

Firstly, they obscured the *degree of involuntary underemployment* hidden away in the growth of part-time employment – people taking part-time work because no full-time work was available in an economy in which "particularly for middle- and low-wage earners, the key problem is often too few hours and/or too variable hours ... They would prefer to be working more hours, and to not have to navigate through erratic work hours or schedules".[78] There were still 6.5 million Americans trapped in this way as late as December 2016, as involuntary part-time employment embedded itself in certain key industries: most notably retail, and leisure and hospitality. Pre-recession, that number had been 4.4 million.[79] Some of that part-time work was chosen voluntarily, of course – often by working women juggling employment and childcare in a society still scarred by patriarchy and under-funded welfare support – but much of it was not. Historically, part-time employment in the United States made up about 17 per cent of total employment, and was heavily gendered. The post-recession spike in part-time employment, however, took that proportion up by at least two percentage points, and involved male workers in disproportionately large numbers. In 2012, only 49 per cent of those working less than 35 hours a week and seeking full-time employment were able to make the switch within the year. In 2006, that percentage had been twelve points higher.[80] And by 2015 the data was also showing "a significant rise in the incidence of alternative work arrangements in the US economy". "Alternative work arrangement" is a euphemism for lousy and insecure working conditions, for jobs that invariably come without associated benefits such as healthcare insurance or pension provision – arrangements that are now being experienced by over 15 per cent of the total US labour force, all of whom are currently working as "temporary help agency workers, on-call workers, contract workers, and independent contractors or freelancers".[81]

Secondly, as we noted earlier, the official unemployment figures also obscured the degree to which their fall was the product of *diminished labour market participation* rather than of genuine job creation: the numbers of the unemployed falling in part because people had given up searching for work, and in part possibly also – note this – from excessive opioid use!* The propensity of working-age adult men to drop out of the labour force entirely has long been a particularly US phenomenon: the president's Council of Economic Advisers told him in 2015 that "since 1965, the prime-age male labor force participation rate has fallen by an average of 0.16 percentage point each year", leaving the US with "the second largest decrease in prime-age male participation among members of the OECD since 1990".[82] The Great Recession and its aftermath then made that tendency worse. In early 2014, for example, 4.2 million of the 5.8 million American workers who would have been in the labour force if they could find work were aged under 55.[83] They would work if they could, but they didn't bother to seek work – primarily because the jobs available were so poorly paid that taking them still made supporting a family impossible.[84] By then indeed, the rate of labour market participation by potential American workers – in the 1990s the highest in the advanced capitalist world – had slipped to a level lower than even that in the UK: dropping from 66 per cent in 2008 to (as we just noted) 62.9 per cent seven years later.[85] Add those missing workers back in, and the official unemployment rate would have to rise by at least 3–4 percentage points.[†]

Thirdly, the official figures also obscured the full complexity of American employment patterns by drawing attention away from the *much higher levels of unemployment still in play for ethnic minority populations, for young workers and*

---

* Alan Krueger speculates that maybe 20 per cent of the fall in male labour market participation rates, and 25 per cent of the fall in female labour market participation rates, could possibly be linked to opioid use. On this see his *Where Have All the Workers Gone?*, published in draft form in the Brookings Papers on Economic Activity, September 2017.

† "US prime-age female participation fell from 6th to 17th of 22 OECD member countries between 1990 and 2010. Over the same period, the decline in the prime-age male participation rate was the second most severe of the OECD countries, and is now the third lowest among the 34 member countries. The US trends are particularly pronounced for non-Hispanic black men and less-skilled adults. There is now an 11 percentage point gap in participation rates between men with a college degree and those with a high school degree or less – whereas 50 years ago, the two rates were very similar." (Eleanor Krause and Isabel V. Sawhill, "What we know and don't know about declining labor force participation: a review", Washington, DC: Brookings, 17 May 2017).

workers over 55, and for the long-term unemployed: of the latter of whom in the middle of 2014 there were still at least 3.4 million, heading households that contained over 2 million children.[86] As researchers at Brookings put it in mid-2017, "even in the midst of prolonged economic expansion with a low national unemployment rate, jobs are not always available and not everyone who wants work can find it. Both job availability and demographics vary markedly around the country, yielding diverse populations wanting and/or needing work".[87] In late 2015, unemployment among teens, for example, was still 17 per cent, among young workers was still 12 per cent, and among African-American men was still twice that among equivalent white workers. Workers of colour, older workers, unskilled workers and former felons – all remained disproportionately vulnerable to job loss even as the economic recovery quickened; for it was a particular feature of the long shadow thrown by the Great Recession that during it "unemployment trickled down to poorer workers", as they were pushed out of the labour market by displaced "higher-incomes with more education [taking] jobs that [were] below their qualification level".[88] Job shortages in one kind of labour market – that for college graduates – then produced unemployment in another, that for high-school graduates. Workers in retail, and in leisure and hospitality, were also particularly exposed to involuntary part-time employment with erratic hours and poor/no benefits – and those workers were, of course, dispropor-tionately black and Hispanic.

The important thing that we must therefore note is that by the end of the Obama Administration none of these embedded labour market characteris-tics had fundamentally changed. Hispanic employment levels had by then returned to pre-recession levels – largely due to the revival of the construc-tion industry – but otherwise involuntary part-time employment, low rates of labour-market participation, and higher rates of unemployment for other key demographics, all continued apace.

WAGES AND WORKING CONDITIONS

Moreover, and broadly speaking, wages remained stuck for the vast majority of Americans throughout the long years of slow recovery from the Great Recession, and the gap between pay and productivity remained wide. Certain

Americans prospered excessively, most struggled to remain afloat, and (as we shall note in more detail later) poverty continued to restrict the life-experiences and potential of at least one American in seven. US workers went into the recession with virtually no trade-union protection across the bulk of the private sector, and that lack of protection left them disproportionately vulnerable to an intensification of their work processes as the recession eased. The combination of wage stagnation and eroding union power helped explain why the share of GDP going to labour, as opposed to capital, dropped from 68.8 per cent in 1970 to 60.7 per cent by 2013;[89] and why "between 2000 and the second quarter of 2015, the share of income generated by corporations that went to workers' wages (instead of going to capital income like profits) declined from 82.3 per cent to 75.5 per cent" – effectively reducing the US wage bill by $535 billion, or $3,770 per worker.[90]

As late as September 2015, the official labour-market data was showing that the median male US worker – the one working full-time and year round – earned no more in real terms in 2014 than his/her counterpart had in 1973: four decades of economic growth and recession that had left the wages of the median worker at the end exactly where they had been at the beginning.[91] Real wages then began to rise slightly – mainly because inflation fell away – but the benefits of that modest rise were not equally distributed. The rise was greater for skilled workers than for unskilled ones, for high-earning men than for low-earning ones, and for low-earning women than for those better paid.[92] The two significant things here are the slightness of the rise, and its distribution. As late as September 2015 "measured from the end of the Great Recession, real wages [had] barely risen – real compensation per hour only by 0.5 per cent, much less than at this point in past recoveries".[93] And at the same time, real wages had actually stagnated – or indeed fallen – for "the bottom 80 per cent of wage earners, including both male and female college graduates".[94] As *The New York Times* put it in September 2015, "for younger people, pay has actually declined. The average hourly wage for recent college graduates in early 2015 was $17.94, compared to $18.41 in 2000".[95] Only in September 2016 did the wage figures at long last begin to improve for the mass and generality of American workers – recording a robust 5.2 per cent increase in median household income in 2015 and a further 3.2 per cent in 2016 (leaving the bottom 80 per cent of US households with incomes still "just at or below those of 2007").[96] That was welcome if belated news to hard-pressed American families, but it still left the median household making 1.6 per cent less in 2015 than it had in 2007, before the Great Recession struck. And since the heaviest burden of inadequate pay continues to fall on young workers, lifetime earnings in the wake of the Great Recession continued to show a decidedly generational imbalance: with "the median male who turned 55 in 2013" reportedly earning "$136,400 less in lifetime income, measured in 2013 dollars, than a 55-year old sixteen years earlier".[97]

Low pay remained a major feature of many parts of the segmented US labour market throughout the recovery period. Over 4 workers in 10 nationwide still earned less than $15/hour in 2015: with that low pay heavily concentrated in low-skilled service industries.[98] A truly remarkable proportion of those working in food services – some 95 per cent of them – earned less than $15/hour, as did some three million cashiers and two million retail sales people.[99] Overall indeed, "for 12 of the 22 major occupational groups tracked by the Bureau of Labor ... average annual pay in 2014 was [actually] less than it was in 2004".[100] Among those groups were workers in education, healthcare support, transportation, farming, sales and personal care. And as we saw earlier, jobs that went into the recession paying high wages came out of it paying lower ones: with more than 60 per cent of the jobs lost during the recession paying between $14 and $21/hour, while more than half of all the new jobs created between 2009 and 2013 paid less than $14/hour.[101] In this regard, it is significant that the automotive industry went into the 2009 bailout paying existing workers $28/hour and more; but the industry returned to profitability paying new workers just half that rate, and less.[102] It is also significant that, as we shall explore more fully in Chapter 4, the United States has a larger percentage of its labour force – some 24.8 per cent – earning less than two-thirds of the median wage than do any of the other leading OECD economies. The equivalent percentage in Belgium is 4 per cent (number 2 in this unfortunate list, just behind the US, is the UK at 20.6 per cent).[103]

Throughout the recovery, the gap between the wages of white and non-white workers remained firmly intact. "In 2014, the median black and median Hispanic wages were only 75 per cent and 70 per cent, respectively, of the median white wage" and "all three groups [had] median wages in 2014 lower than in 2007".[104] Throughout the recovery too, a long-established gap between the median income of the two genders remained firmly in place. Low pay was a particular feature of industries employing largely female staff, often on a part-time basis. Hotel housekeeping was one such – an industry in which pay had not kept up with the price of the service being provided. "In the 1960s and 1970s", Monique Morrissey later calculated, "a housekeeper could afford a hotel room with her day's wages; by 2012 her wages only covered 78 per cent of the average ($83/$106)". Hardly surprising really, given that many of the housekeepers were women of colour or immigrants, earning in 2012 on average just over ten dollars a day.[105] Overall indeed, "women and people of colour" in contemporary America remain "over-represented in jobs paying less than a $15 wage" with "more than half of African-American workers and close to 60 per cent of Latino workers [making] less than $15".[106] EPI researchers in August 2017 estimated that black women workers had to work 7 extra months – well into July 2017 – to be paid the same amount of wages as the white men they worked alongside earned in 2016 alone.[107]

Finally, this: working conditions, in the absence of effective trade-union cover, remained difficult for the bulk of American workers throughout the recovery period. As we have seen, the typical working week remained long, the proportion of the workforce with unstable work shift schedules reached at least 17 per cent, the number of Americans working as "temps" reached a new record high (2.8 million in 2014), and the number of jobs requiring anti-social working hours continued to grow. So too, at state level, did the legislative assault on the ability of workers to unionize. The data on the union effect over both the long-term and the immediate period is clear. As the EPI reported in 2016, "private-sector union decline since the late 1970s has contributed to wage losses among workers who do not belong to a union. This is especially true for men, particularly non-college graduates" whose "weekly wages would be an estimated 8 per cent ($3016 a year) higher in 2013 if union density had remained at its 1979 levels"[108], while increases in the minimum wage in 16 states in 2016 raised the wages of more than 4.6 million Americans.[109] Yet in spite of this (or in truth, actually *because* of it) during the Obama years tougher right-to-work legislation, now aimed at public sector workers like teachers and firemen, was voted through by re-energized Republican legislators in states as disparate as Wisconsin – the scene of the biggest fight – Ohio and Indiana. This legislative onslaught has left the heartland of the country and the American south broadly union-free:[110] with residual pockets of effective labour resistance largely restricted to states on each of the country's coasts. The adverse effect of this on wages remain significant and intended – in 2015, wage rates in the so-called right-to-work states were running 3.1 percentage points lower on average than in states lacking such anti-union legislation.[111]

Preliminary conclusion

So rather contrary to the claims for American exceptionalism and economic superiority with which this chapter began, by mid-2017 the US economy was looking neither exceptional nor superior. Indeed, Donald J. Trump entered the presidency in January 2017 claiming that he had inherited a "mess", even though his inheritance was in truth better than that inherited by any of his three predecessors in the office, and in no way as severe as that inherited by Barack Obama.[112] But campaign rhetoric aside, the economy which the Republicans inherited in 2017 was in no condition to be credibly offered as a trouble-free model for others to follow; and if it was exceptional, some elements of that exceptionality were hardly desirable ones. Even before the crisis and recession, average annual hours worked in the United States exceeded those in Germany by over 350 a year (nearly 9 extra 40-hour weeks!) and manufacturing pay levels in the United States had fallen so low as to place the US as eleventh out of 20 countries in terms of their generosity.[113] The US also by then had "the dubious honor of being the only *no vacation nation* i.e. no legally required paid time off, and some weeks fewer actual days off per year than our European counterparts enjoy"[114] and because of its lax labour laws, was actually losing more people to death from work-related illnesses and injury (50,000 annually) than it was to death by gun violence (a mere 30,000!).[115] Americans do shoot themselves in excessive numbers by European standards, but to an even greater degree they also kill, poison and maim themselves at work with a depressing regularity.

The United States economy was also unable to be scored as totally "free" by Freedom House when that ultra-orthodox organization evaluated worker rights.* Forty-one countries were so scored in 2010: but not the US. Instead, the United States was relegated in the Freedom House survey to the subordinate category of "mostly free", putting it – in the Americas – in the same group as the Dominican Republic and Costa Rica and behind the Bahamas, Barbados, Canada, Chile and Uruguay. As Steven Greenhouse rightly wrote as the crisis began, these were and remain "tough times for the American worker" – times that mean "more poverty, more income inequality, more family tensions, more hours at work, more time away from the kids".[116]

The credit crisis created at the heart of the US financial system in 2008, and the deep recession to which that crisis then gave rise, only intensified these problems. Controversies remain about the causes of that crisis, and about the sluggishness of the economy's response to it – controversies to which we shall return in later chapters – but what is not in doubt is the fall-out from the crisis itself: stagnant wages, heightened job insecurity, and deteriorating working conditions for more and more Americans. The capitalism responsible for that fall-out is flawed indeed: so flawed in fact that the United States is visibly in need of both a new social settlement and a new growth strategy to deliver it. As Barack Obama came to the end of his second term of office, and writing to a predominantly British audience, he put it this way:

Decades of declining productivity growth and rising inequality have resulted in slower income growth for low- and middle-income families. Globalization and automation have weakened the position of workers and their ability to secure a decent wage. Too many potential physicists and engineers spend their careers shifting money around in the financial sector, instead of applying their talents to innovating in the real economy. And the financial crisis of 2008 only seemed to increase the

* In 2016, Freedom House recorded a "downward trend arrow" on the USA "due to the cumulative impact of flaws in the electoral system, a disturbing increase in the role of private money in election campaigns and the legislative process, legislative gridlock, the failure of the Obama administration to fulfill promises of enhanced government openness, and fresh evidence of racial discrimination and other dysfunctions in the criminal justice system." (The US was one of 15 countries so downgraded – a list that included Hungary, Turkey and Tajistan!) (*Freedom in the World 2016: Anxious Dictators, Wavering Democracies: Global Freedom under Pressure*, p. 23).

62

isolation of corporations and elites, who often seem to live by a different set of rules to ordinary citizens.[117]

This, from a president who had just spent two terms trying to create a more dynamic economy with a more equitable sharing of its records – but who had fundamentally failed in this transformative endeavour. The America he was leaving to his successors, so his note implies, remains flawed in important ways, and as such is still in need of serious and fundamental reform.

3

Chasing Hard and Standing Still: The UK Economy in the American Shadow

"Productivity is not everything, but in the long run it is almost everything (Krugman). The UK has a high-employment, low-productivity economy. The good news is that productivity levels are so low, relative to the UK's peers, that the potential for improvement is large. The bad news is that the UK is falling further behind."

Martin Wolf[1]

"Saying that productivity matters is not the same as saying we understand its determinants."

Andrew Haldane[2]

Great powers that stop being great tend to find their new and depleted condition both surprising and unwelcome. Indeed, a common first reaction – particularly among elite circles in such powers – tends to be denial, followed then by resistance and eventually by nostalgia. Certainly that pattern is overwhelmingly evident in the politics of the United Kingdom in the decades after 1945, as the country which had once stood alone in the face of Nazi expansion, and whose armies had ultimately prevailed, was forced to come to terms with its reduced standing in a postwar universe framed by the Cold War standoff between its two major wartime allies.

The depletion was both economic and political. It was economic in the sense that, well before the Second World War began, the United Kingdom had already lost its mid-nineteenth century status as the manufacturing capital of the world. In 1860 that dominance had been near total, with the UK then – as "the workshop of the world" – producing "53 per cent of the world's iron and 50 per cent of its coal and lignite", and consuming "just under half of the raw cotton output of the globe".[3] As the US Civil War began, the UK economy "alone was responsible for one-fifth of the world's commerce ... two-fifths of the trade in manufactured goods [and] over one-third of the world's merchant marine".[4] But that dominance did not last. From the 1870s, powerful economic competitors grew up in other areas of the emerging industrial capitalist "north" – with Germany at one end of the emerging industrial heartland and the United States at the other.[5] Moreover, a second industrial revolution in the 1890s eventually generated new sources of power (electricity), new commodities (not least automobiles), and new competitive capacities (based on the systematic application of science to production) in which the UK economy did not excel. With its existing capital stock, organizational structure and managerial expertise increasingly anchored in the "old industries" of the first industrial revolution, and lacking any strong political leadership demanding major industrial change, from the late-nineteenth century onwards British-based industry retreated more and more into the safe protected markets of empire, and allowed comparative economic advantage to slip inexorably away.[6]

This growing erosion of comparative economic strength was initially almost entirely hidden from public view. It was hidden between the two world wars by the temporary dislocation of potential competitors in Western Europe, and by the embedded isolationism of the United States – and also, it should be said, by the ubiquity of British inter-war imperial possessions and by the continuing size of its navy. It was temporarily hidden again after 1945 by an equivalent dislocation of wartime enemies – neither Germany nor Japan regained their economic edge until well into the 1960s – and by the unexpected rise in general living standards that slowly built up in the postwar United Kingdom as its economy did at long last begin to produce on a mass scale much sought-after consumer products like cars, televisions and fridges. But by the early 1960s at the very latest, recognition of the relative decline of the UK economy – its decline, that is, relative to the best of the rest elsewhere – could no longer be avoided: and in consequence UK politics settled into the ongoing debate about how best to reverse that decline that has consumed it ever since, and which consumes it to this day.[7]

At the heart of that debate, as we shall see, stood the question of the state: of its role, of its size, of its focus and of its responsibilities. From the 1960s onwards, right-wing critics increasingly focused their ire on the first and second of those, finding in the post-1945 UK state a behemoth in need of slaying: slaying because its welfare provisions were too generous and too burdensome to finance; and slaying because the UK state's weakness in the face of organized labour, and its propensity for over-regulation, left UK managers without the "freedom to manage" that conservatives hold to be so vital to the restoration of economic competitiveness. Left-wing critics of this same set of state institutions and practices increasingly focused in those same decades on just the reverse: on the failure of the postwar UK state to build a strong welfare-capitalism of the German or Scandinavian variety; and on the excessive preoccupation of successive UK governments with the maintenance of the UK's military and diplomatic role in the world. But what both sets of critics have been forced to confront is that, over time, the UK's economy has struggled to maintain the level of global competitiveness necessary to sustain a significant military and diplomatic capacity. It is not simply that the American economy has increasingly accumulated serious competitive flaws over time. It is also that the British economy – in so many ways its precursor and now its junior partner – acquired many of those same flaws earlier, and has struggled mightily but in vain to remove them ever since.

The rise and fall of the postwar settlement

The US economy emerged from the Second World War strengthened by the mobilization for war that the pursuit of military victory had made both necessary and possible. The UK economy did not. It emerged from the Second World War seriously depleted by the equivalent mobilization – with all the weaknesses of its previous investment patterns and levels fully exposed. The overseas investments built up in the late nineteenth century – the ones that had cushioned the impact of the UK's diminishing trade balance over time – were all but liquidated by 1945.* The UK entered the postwar world heavily in

---

* "The war had taken a heavy toll. The capital loss due to bombing and the inability to repair or renew machinery and plant meant that, at pre-war rates, it would take seven years to make good the damage suffered between 1939 and 1945. In the course of the war, financial assets of over £1,000,000,000 had been sold to finance the purchase of food and

debt, dependent for most of its foreign purchases on the continued existence of a sizeable flow of US aid – aid, in the form of the wartime lend-lease agreement, which the US Congress then abruptly cut off immediately that the war was over. The UK also entered the postwar years with a run-down coal industry as its main power source, with an over-stretched engineering industry still geared to wartime production, and with a population whose living standards, already low in the 1930s, had slipped further during the war and were now poised to fall yet again as lack of foreign aid reduced the ability of the UK government to finance the import of much needed basic resources, food and consumer goods. After the First World War, the UK had endured a twenty-year period of economic stagnation and depleted living standards. The fear in many quarters in 1945 was that the legacy of the Second World War would be similar. That it was not is testimony to the ongoing strength of the immediate postwar economic and social settlement put in place by the incoming Labour Government and then sustained by the Conservative ones that followed.

THE RISE

The economic and social settlement put in place in the UK by the Attlee Government immediately after the Second World War was a direct product of the war itself. Wartime mobilization had created full employment in the UK economy for effectively the very first time in its history, so that those managing that economy (and its individual units) could no longer rely on the threat of redundancy to keep wages down and workers in check. On the contrary, labour was now scarce, and had to be both retained and listened to. And those working in the factories and mines, and those returning to civilian life from the military, were in no mood to go back to the mass unemployment and generalized poverty of the 1930s. On the contrary, it is fairer to say that "as each year of hostilities gave way to the next, pressure built up for the creation, after the war, of a fairer and more socially egalitarian Britain, one in which the State would provide at least minimum levels of basic welfare for all".[8] As the

---

armaments, and this had cut net income from foreign investments from £175,000,000 a year in 1938 to less than £73,000,000 a year after 1940." (David Coates, *The Labour Party and the Struggle for Socialism.* Cambridge: Cambridge University Press, 1975/2009, p. 67).

British army demobilized the bulk of its men and women in uniform in 1945 and 1946, the soldiers returned to peacetime Britain expecting that this time – unlike in 1918 – politicians would deliver on their promise of a better Britain. They expected full employment. They expected better education and better housing. They expected basic healthcare. They expected to be treated with dignity and respect; and by an overwhelming majority they expected a Labour Government rather than a Conservative one to deliver on all those things. Winston Churchill had been acceptable to many of them as a wartime leader, but for peacetime they required politicians with a better track record than his on matters of social reform and economic justice.

The Labour Government that came to power in 1945 inherited, and maintained throughout its period in office, the wartime coalition's commitments to full employment, education reform, and the creation of a modern welfare state. Labour inherited, and maintained for a while, a full set of wartime controls over the private economy, and their own commitments to replacing part of that private ownership by nationalization: the taking of basic industries like coal, electricity, transport, shipbuilding and even steel into public ownership. A little over 20 per cent of the economy was in state hands by the time the Labour Party lost office in 1951, and 2,000,000 people were employed in the new state industries.[9] The incoming Labour Government also inherited the teachings if not the body – he died in 1946 – of John Maynard Keynes,* and spent their time in office replacing the direct control of investment and labour allocation of the war years by the Keynesian-inspired management of aggregate demand. The result – by 1951 – was an entirely new kind of political architecture around the struggling UK economy.

---

* "There is a considerable debate in the literature on postwar British politics about whether, and to what extent, there ever was a full-blown 'Keynesian revolution' in Britain. But this much at least is clear: that Keynes's thinking had a huge impact on the Labour Party in particular, because he explained why passivity before market forces could be self-defeating. His writings in the 1930s "advocated cautious and well-controlled anti-cyclical policies, allowing deficits to finance productive public works during depressions and paying back the debt during periods of expansion ... The Keynesian specification for the role of the State that emerged in the 1930s was one which required the government to manage levels of demand in the economy as a whole (by its instructions to banks, and by its own spending) in order to keep demand at a level that would generate high levels of employment. Keynes himself was quite cautious on how high 'high' could be without inflation setting in: some of his followers were less so." (David Coates, *The Crisis of Labour.* Oxford: Phillip Allan, 1989, p. 15).

At the core of that architecture stood a social-democratic state. It was one charged with the active economic management of the entire economy – expected, that is, to both run basic industries directly itself and staff a whole new set of public institutions (not least, a new national health service and a much expanded public education system). It was also expected to simultaneously direct investment into key areas of private-sector economic development, and maintain full employment across the economy as a whole by altering levels of its own spending – Keynesian style – spending more when the business cycle was down, spending less when it was not. Even when the Conservatives returned to power in 1951, those expectations and those practices remained intact: and Tory ministers, no less than their Labour predecessors, proved willing to liaise closely with organized labour, to sustain a system of progressive taxation, and to measure their success domestically by how far general living standards rose, the housing stock improved, and public service provision flourished.

This new internal postwar settlement in the UK was matched by an external one that was hardly new at all. The Attlee Government, like the wartime coalition government of which it had been a part, remained entirely committed to the maintenance of the United Kingdom as an independent global power. Less intransigently imperial than the Churchill wing of that coalition, the new government oversaw the withdrawal of the British from a newly divided south Asian continent – India, Burma and Ceylon were all abandoned, and Pakistan created, by 1948 – but otherwise proved to be a doughty defender of British imperial possessions. As one of the three main victors in the war just over, the Attlee Government demanded (and won) a British seat at the top table of all the new international agencies created in the 1940s under American leadership: and that included the IMF, the World Bank, the UN Security Council and ultimately NATO. In that military alliance, the UK struck an independent note, acquiring its own nuclear weapons capability by 1952; but otherwise settled in to an important but subordinate position as America's junior partner in the management of the capitalist side of the Cold War divide. A British army remained in place on the Rhine, and the British Treasury oversaw a sterling area within which the UK currency acted as a second reserve currency, supplementing the role played by the dollar across the capitalist bloc as a whole.

Because the British Treasury did play this oversight role, successive post-war British governments then took on, as a major policy commitment, the maintenance of the exchange rate of sterling against the dollar as *the* way of sustaining foreign confidence in London as a financial centre and in its currency as an international means of exchange. In the event, the first postwar exchange rate set between sterling and the dollar – modelled on the exchange rate that applied in the gold standard days of the 1920s – immediately proved too high to sustain, so that the Attlee Government was eventually obliged to devalue its own currency by 30 per cent in 1949, to a new and lower rate that subsequent governments then defended against overseas currency speculators right through to 1967, when yet another devaluation was forced upon a later Labour Government. This battle against devaluation would in the end cost UK manufacturing heavily. For defending the exchange rate of the pound meant keeping interest rates in London higher than would otherwise have been necessary; and the focus on sterling (and the City of London) pulled the attention of UK policy-makers away from the urgent need to strengthen the economy's export position behind a lower exchange rate in the manner later of both Germany and Japan. It was a lack of attention that the long-term health of the UK economy could ill-afford, especially given the fact that between 1950 and 1966 the UK was still spending "four to five per cent more of its gross national product on defence than were" either the Germans or the Japanese and that "almost all of this difference went into productive capital investment which, at compound interest, meant that their industry was able to overtake and surpass Britain's by the 1960s".[10]

But hindsight is, of course, a wonderful thing; and there is no escaping the fact that at the time – between, that is, the dates of the two devaluations (1949 and 1967) – UK governments continued to think of the United Kingdom, as did many overseas governments too, as the capitalist world's second financial power as well as its second military one: as a pale shadow of its former imperial self, that is, but still as a major and independent global player in the new American century. And for a while at least, that perception was not entirely illusory, as the United Kingdom enjoyed almost two decades of postwar internal economic growth and external superiority. The temporary dislocation of the economies of the major former Axis powers left the UK economy a brief competitive space. That space enabled both the old industries of Britain's Victorian past to enjoy one last hurrah, and the UK's new consumer-focused industries to consolidate themselves by developing a local version of American production techniques.

As late as 1961, there were still 200,000 British workers employed in the textile sector, and as late as 1956 there were more than 690,000 miners producing the coal that still powered 95 per cent of the UK economy. Yet by then the centre of gravity of the entire economy was on the move. It was on the move both spatially and sectorally as its heartland shifted south, away from the northern Victorian triangle of Belfast-Newcastle-Manchester (the home of coal and steel, textiles, and shipbuilding) into the English Midlands, the new home both of the capital-intensive and highly-productive light engineering industries of the postwar consumer boom, and of industries geared to maintaining the UK's global role as a major military power. In the 1950s and 1960s, in that midland belt, investment and employment moved into airplane production and munitions, and into industries producing washing machines, fridges, telephones, televisions, motorbikes and – overwhelmingly – cars. By 1966, these new manufacturing industries provided employment for over 9 million British workers – effectively, one British worker in three – half a million of whom worked in the car industry alone. And by then, that industry had become the economy's main source of exports, and the source of fully a third of the economy's entire economic growth in the 1950s and 1960s.[11] And there was growth – unbroken indeed for more than two decades – growth for the economy as a whole at a steady annual rate of 3.5 per cent between 1950 and 1955, 2.3 per cent between 1955 and 1960, 3.2 per cent between 1960 and 1965, and 2.0 per cent between 1965 and 1970.

However, it was not just employment in the privately owned manufacturing sector that flourished in the 1950s and 1960s. Employment in the public sector did too – employment in both the newly nationalized basic industries and in the UK's expanding health and education sector. Indeed, over 7 million workers were employed in the UK public sector by 1975, including 2 million in the nationalized industries and over 3 million in education, welfare and local government services. Employment growth on this scale and width then helped successive British governments sustain full employment for a generation, and in the process triggered the emergence of a new and entirely unexpected industrial compact between those who owned and managed British industry and those who worked inside it. It was a compact in which, because labour was scarce, national wage rates negotiated between employers' federations and national trade union leadership were regularly supplemented in core manufacturing industries by local bargains struck between the managers of individual firms and shop stewards representing the firm's own and particular workforce. The resulting wage drift at the heart of this emerging economy then helped raise living standards across the bulk of the UK workforce for an entire generation – helped trigger so substantial a rise in living standards, indeed, that by 1959 a Conservative Government could be re-elected for a third successive time on the slogan that "you've never had it so good". And they had not: the Conservatives were quite right. Per capita living standards that in the UK in 1950 had – in 1990 dollar terms – stood at only $6,847 were on their way by the late 1950s to doubling in a generation: on their way, that is, to $13,087 by 1979.

THE FALL

Sadly however, this newly found prosperity and self-confidence soon proved to be a false dawn – the glories of the past being no guarantee of equivalent glories in the future – so that, from at least the balance of payments crisis that hit the UK in the summer of 1961, the hunt was on for how best to modernize the economy and to reset the country's global role.

In fact, the need for a resetting of that role became obvious to those in charge in London slightly earlier, when Washington's refusal to back the British (and French) secretly planned invasion of Egypt in 1956 brought down a British prime minister, and forced from his successor both a humiliating withdrawal of British forces and the retention by the Egyptians of the ownership of the Suez Canal that the UK-led military operation had been designed to forestall. When almost immediately thereafter, the British government also discovered that Blue Streak – the missile system being developed by the UK's own armament industry for the independent deployment of the country's modest stock of nuclear weapons – was inadequate to the task, the die was totally cast. The UK government was forced to beg access to its US equivalent – Polaris – access which President Kennedy very reluctantly conceded to his British allies in 1962; and in consequence any pretence of great power status for the UK was finally gone. Instead of policing the world in alliance with the United States, UK governments by the 1960s were pulling UK troops back from east of Suez, and declining to give more than moral support to the US military operation in Vietnam. There was in fact a last hurrah for the UK as an imperial military power more than two decades later when, with tacit Washington support, Margaret Thatcher sent a naval force to retake the Falkland Islands from the Argentinians in 1983, and UK forces remained major contributors to NATO-led operations in the Balkans in the 1990s and in Afghanistan after 9/11: but this was all a pale reflection of what once had been the dominant and independent military presence of UK forces around the globe.

From at least the moment that the UK first applied for membership of the European Economic Community in 1961 (or the Common Market as it then was), the foreign policy question dominating British politics fundamentally shifted. It shifted away from how best could the UK be an independent global power acting in concert with Washington, towards how (if at all) to coordinate UK policy with a coalition of European nations among whom, at most, the UK could count itself as simply one of Europe's "Big Three" – France and Germany being the other two. The UK political elite (and a section of their wider electorate) took at least a generation to come to terms with the diminished status involved in that repositioning, and visibly they have not fully adjusted to it even yet. Hence the speed and enthusiasm with which Margaret Thatcher "hand-bagged" the first Bush president to mobilize a coalition in the first Gulf War, and with which Tony Blair moved to ally the United Kingdom with the second Bush president and to have UK troops invade Iraq alongside American ones. Hence too the speed and enthusiasm with which at least a section of the British Conservative Party campaigned for a British exit from the European Union in the referendum in 2016, a referendum that the "Exit" camp was strong enough to win.

Where the adjustment was made more easily – because the need for it became so visible as to become literally unavoidable – was on the internal policy agenda: triggering a set of sustained attempts by successive UK governments to reset the basic shape of the UK economy. The first attempt at that resetting, initiated by the same Conservative Government led by Harold Macmillan that withdrew troops from Egypt and negotiated the purchase of

Polaris submarines (and then carried to its logical conclusion by Labour Governments led by Harold Wilson and James Callaghan that Tony Blair would later label as "Old Labour") was ultimately a corporatist one. It was an attempt to incrementally strengthen the competitiveness of the UK's manufacturing base by negotiating small and steady adjustments with the major players involved in the industrial decision-making systems that were deemed in need of change: negotiations, that is, with major employers on the one hand, and with major trade unions on the other. Instead of breaking the industrial power of those players, as Margaret Thatcher would do when creating an entirely new social settlement later, first Conservative and then Labour Governments tried to retain the original postwar settlement while reforming it from within, and by actually strengthening the monopoly position of the private actors with whom the governments negotiated. The Conservatives gave a monopoly of labour representation to the TUC in 1962,[12] and the incoming Labour Government urged the creation of a powerful employers' organization, the CBI, in 1964. It was an attempt at corporatist deal-making that consumed British politics for at least two decades: from the 1959 election won by a government complacently asserting that its electorate had "never had it so good" to one lost by a government that had just endured "a winter of discontent" in 1979.

At stake was how to combine industrial modernization with ongoing job security, and how to combine full employment with price stability. The Macmillan Government sought the first of these combinations by building a structure of national planning modelled on French practice, creating a National Economic Development Council (NEDC) on which representatives of the business community and the trade union movement negotiated a set of economic plans under the supervision of politicians and civil servants from a newly created industry ministry. Later Labour Governments would supplement the main NEDC with a series of "little Neddies" – similarly constructed committees servicing separate industries – and with new government agencies of direct economic planning: particularly in the 1970s a National Enterprise Board charged with running a set of struggling industries and individual companies taken (or taken back) into public ownership to give them access to larger quantities of government-provided investment funds. By the mid-1970s those funds, and that scale of public ownership and investment in the

UK manufacturing sector, reached record heights. Labour returned to power in 1974 committed to a new social contract with what was by then a heavily-unionized and industrially-militant labour movement. It was a contract – enshrined in a new Industry Act designed to regenerate British industry – that proposed an extensive system of voluntary planning agreements, strengthened institutions of industrial democracy, and large quantities of publicly-provided industrial investment funds.[13] And yet, for all this activism, UK manufacturing continued to suffer from an incapacity to attract to itself the share of GNP for investment purposes characteristically attained by its key competitors. Gross non-residential investment as a percentage of GNP ran at 26.5 per cent in Japan between 1960 and 1973, and at 19.6 per cent in Germany. The equivalent UK figure never exceeded 14.6 per cent.[14]

The Macmillan Government sought the second of the corporatist goals – full employment without inflation – by trying to negotiate a limit on wage increases with national trade union leaders, so beginning (in 1961) eighteen years of incomes policies of different kinds negotiated annually between Treasury ministers and the Trades Union Congress. Over the years, the terms of those incomes policies toughened – pay settlements over the agreed norm eventually only being permitted in exchange for changes in working practices to boost productivity – and their use as a way of holding wage settlements below the inflation rate intensified. Time and again, governments tried to reinforce the power of national union leaders over shop stewards active at the local level, in order to slow the rate of wage drift then widely blamed for rising industrial prices. The Labour Government of the 1960s tried to do that by introducing a White Paper, *In Place of Strife*, whose implementation was blocked by opposition from backbench Labour MPs. The Tory Government of the early 1970s tried to effect a similar outcome via a direct legislative attack on the tactics used by those shop stewards – including unofficial strikes and flying pickets – only to be defeated (and ejected from power) by a general strike called against the legislation they passed. And the Labour Government of the late 1970s tried to get a similar grip on the rate of wage increases by holding wages down in the public sector as an example to private employers. It was that strategy that – for all its success in "bringing down inflation while holding employment essentially stable"[15] – eventually triggered mass industrial unrest among low paid public sector workers, produced the 1978–9 "winter of discontent", and eroded completely public confidence in the corporatist route to economic modernization in the UK.[16]

But if industrial unrest on the surface of British politics was the backdrop to the final collapse of the first postwar economic and social settlement in the UK, what ultimately brought that settlement to its bitter and debilitating end was the general and underlying crisis of Keynesianism experienced across the advanced industrialized world in the 1970s. As we briefly noted earlier, that crisis was partly triggered from outside, as the unequal terms of trade on which the developed world exchanged goods with the less developed one at the start of the postwar period was challenged – first by the oil producers of the Middle East in response to western support for Israeli military expansion, and then by the general rise in demand for basic commodities produced by the increasing impact of one "economic miracle" after another: first the German, then the French, then the Japanese, and even the Italian. The UK broadly speaking missed out on those miracles, but not on the economic price-pain caused by the resulting shift in global terms of trade. So much pain in fact that by late 1975, and again in the summer of 1976, foreign confidence in the trade performance of the UK economy, and in the value of its currency, was so fragile that the UK was obliged to twice call in the International Monetary Fund, twice take a loan, and twice suffer the indignity of having its domestic economic policy dictated to it from outside.[17]

But the main source of the crisis of Keynesianism in the UK in the 1970s was largely *internal*: the result of the slowing down of the rate of productivity growth in one part of the manufacturing sector after another as the full implementation of Fordist methods of production was achieved, and so could not be easily and regularly replicated. The introduction of Fordist production methods always gave workers on the semi-automated production lines greater bargaining power, so always involved a trade-off between the productivity gains made and the greater wages won. In the United States, that trade-off gave prosperity and job security to northern and midwestern unionized white workers for a generation, as we saw. But there, the unions were weaker, and the productivity gains greater, than in the commensurate UK case. The UK really experienced what commentators later called a more "flawed form of Fordism".[18] UK factories were smaller, the UK market was more limited, and UK workers more unionized and entrenched than their American counterparts.

The result was a more acute form of Keynesian crisis in the UK than in the US: but still a crisis that in its essentials was the same in both places.

Keynesian demand management of a capitalist economy worked best when the choice on offer for both politicians and their electorates was one between unemployment and inflation. Keynesians attacked the first by increasing public spending and the second by reducing it. What Keynesianism had no answer to, however, was the simultaneous experience of unemployment and inflation. But that was exactly what hit the UK in the 1970s. Governments in power in the 1970s faced an economy scarred by stagflation, and had no effective policy solution to those incompatible imperatives; and because they had not, the political credibility of a non-Keynesian answer to dwindling economic competitiveness grew and grew. It grew so quickly and so well, indeed, as to sweep a Keynesian-inspired Labour Government out of power in 1979, and to open the way to the construction of an entirely different social and economic settlement – a neoliberal one.

The rise and fall of the neoliberal settlement

The wave of strike action that immobilized public services in the UK in the winter of 1979 gave Margaret Thatcher her opportunity for power. It was an opportunity that she then took, and used – took to close her Labour Party opponents out of power for three elections under her leadership and one under her successor, and used to entirely reset the distribution of power in British industry and the public perceptions of the role of government that underpinned it. In the process, Margaret Thatcher proved herself to be not simply a new kind of politician. She also became, like Ronald Reagan in the United States quite quickly afterwards, a major redesigner of her country's political and social landscape, and as such a truly hegemonic force in national politics.

THE RISE

The Thatcher argument on entering office in 1979 was that the trade union movement in the UK had simply become too strong, and had used that strength to encourage Labour governments to pursue the wrong kind of economic programme. Trade union strength had been used in corporatist Britain to encourage the state management of the private sector, to its long-term detriment. Reducing that strength would, therefore, free up the space for the private sector to flourish without that management. It was Margaret Thatcher's view that the UK's processes of wealth creation had been weakened by three decades of Keynesianism, and that the economy's investment performance had been eroded by the effect on labour costs of over-full employment, and by the impact of high rates of government borrowing on the cost of raising capital. It was axiomatic to Thatcherism that the economy's entrepreneurial capacities had been undermined by the high marginal rates of tax made necessary by excessive government spending and by the state's propensity for egalitarian social engineering, and that the work ethic of its labour force had been corroded by the dependency mentality/culture created by extensive welfare provision. The Thatcher wing of the Conservative Party entered government in 1979 convinced that the growth in state bureaucracies had tipped the balance of advantage in the labour market away from private capital, and had exposed particularly small- and medium-sized businesses to stifling levels of regulation and form-filling. And they believed strongly that the persistent willingness of politicians to take credit for post-war economic growth had fuelled the illusion that economic growth was something you could talk into existence, rather than something you actually had to create by investment, competition, hard work and the taking of risks.

The best route to economic competitiveness, from Margaret Thatcher's point of view, was a market one: allowing market forces to run their course, and allowing unregulated competition to weed out the uncompetitive. The job of the government was not to oversee that process or to micro-manage it – let alone to act pre-emptively to soften its impact. The proper job of the UK government was different and more limited. Its job was to bring prices under control by cutting back on its own scale of economic ownership, spending and intervention, and by closing down the corporatist structures that previous Labour Governments had used to artificially balance inflation and unemployment. Margaret Thatcher entered office as a committed monetarist, convinced that if the government simply managed the money supply, private enterprise would quickly generate the growth and employment that corporatism had failed to bring. She left office more than a decade later less convinced of the simple and direct relationship between the money supply and economic growth, but even more convinced than she had been at the outset of the vital role of unregulated market forces in the generation of a prosperous economy and a harmonious society.

Between those two dates – 1979 and 1990 – Margaret Thatcher effected what Stuart Hall perceptively recognized from the beginning as "the great moving right show".[19] She shifted, that is, the entire centre of British politics away from corporatism and towards neoliberalism; and she achieved that shift by what her government did, by what it stopped doing, and by what it said it was doing and why. It was a shift that involved a fundamental resetting of domestic economic policy, a complete redesign of major economic institutions, and a total sea change in prevailing modes of political discourse. Margaret Thatcher's programme was a genuine political revolution, one that – as John Major's first Chancellor of the Exchequer said in the House of Commons on the day of her resignation – put the concept of "the market" back at the heart of UK political discourse and public policy-making. Indeed it was a measure of her impact as a truly hegemonic politician that Norman Lamont could legitimately make that claim: at the end of a decade dominated by her attempt "to articulate to her hegemonic principle (of unbridled individualism) all the important ideological elements in the society, and to establish a certain definition of reality as the common sense of an entire age".[20] If Antonio Gramsci had ever been a conservative, he would undoubtedly have singled her out for special adulation. Her supporters certainly did!

During her period in office, Margaret Thatcher effectively "rolled back" the British state – and did so consciously, and on principle. Her governments, unlike their predecessors, did not claim to guarantee full employment: in fact unemployment peaked at over 3 million in the UK during the first Thatcher Government. Instead, her governments focused on controlling inflation, which was running at an annual rate of over 13 per cent when she first entered office: initially by slashing public spending to restrict the money supply; later by cutting taxes and easing business regulations to trigger economic growth. Thatcher governments no longer negotiated incomes policies or consulted with national trade leadership: on the contrary, the Thatcherites moved quickly to shut down the corporatist institutions they had inherited from Labour, and to keep their distance from peak organizations of both capital and labour. Her governments closed both the National Enterprise Board and the Manpower Service Commission, and downgraded the NEDC. They closed industrial training boards, and they sold off a whole swathe of publicly-owned institutions and companies – starting with British Aerospace, and going through to the water companies, to electricity supply and eventually even to what was left of the coal industry after the year-long miners' strike. They also passed a whole series of new labour laws – five in total in the 1980s[21]– that curbed the rights of workers to join unions and the rights of trade unionists to take industrial action without penalty.[22]

Then when (and only when) they were ready, the Thatcherite Conservatives took on the strongest of the unions (the National Union of Miners), endured and won a year-long dispute with the NUM that for a while brought the UK nearly to the status of a police-state, and then rapidly ran down the coal industry over whose wages they and the miners had fought. And although Thatcher governments retained public ownership of (and so direct responsibility for) the major welfare services – Margaret Thatcher was never able to privatize the National Health Service – they systematically exposed public sector workers and their managers to internal market forces, by recommodifying those services wherever they could: obliging local authorities to tender for services rather than to provide them directly themselves, obliging colleges and universities to bid for students, and requiring hospitals to charge for patient care. Privatization, deregulation and recommodification were all key Thatcherite principles of government; and when implemented steadily for a decade, entirely redrew both the boundaries of the British state and the electorate's expectations of that state.

That is not to say that Margaret Thatcher's governments were weak ones. They were not. They matched their "freeing of the market" with the "strengthening and centralization of the state powers" that were retained, effecting less a full-blooded rolling back of the state than presiding over a redrawing of its boundaries, and a pulling of power back towards the centre in whatever area of state regulation remained. Domestically, that meant – among other things – taking direct control of what was taught in UK schools, increasing police powers, keeping up strong ideological pressure on the national media, and shutting unions out entirely from sensitive security agencies and sites like GCHQ. And of course in foreign policy terms, Margaret Thatcher was neither a libertarian nor a shrinking violet in any form. On the contrary, her foreign policy made no break with what had gone before. In foreign policy at least, there was no Thatcherite revolution.

Instead, Margaret Thatcher combined her domestic resetting of UK policy from corporatism to neoliberalism with a reinforced commitment to the role of the United Kingdom as a major global force and as the leading ally of the United States in the fight against communism. In the area of foreign policy, Margaret Thatcher was indeed the "Iron Lady" – fighting socialism at home and communism abroad as she would put it. It was Margaret Thatcher who led the fight inside the European Union both for the extension of the single market and against any French-designed plans to build a stronger political union based on that market. It was Margaret Thatcher who took the high-stakes gamble of sending a modest UK naval task force to the South Atlantic to retake the Falkland Islands. It was Margaret Thatcher who supported the Reagan Administration's firm stance against (and then welcomed the embrace of) the Soviet Union as it began its internal reform; and it was Margaret Thatcher who pressured George Herbert Bush into leading a coalition of forces against Saddam Hussein in the first Gulf War. No less than Winston Churchill before her, Margaret Thatcher did not seek to redesign the UK internally only to weaken it externally. On the contrary, one of the great drivers of her internal agenda was her steadfast determination to protect and extend the independent role of the United Kingdom as an international player.

THE FALL

The big problem for Margaret Thatcher's neoliberal revolution, however, was that for all the fine rhetoric and brief period of sustained economic growth that accompanied it, in the end the policy changes failed to deliver. The UK economy after 1979 experienced periods of growth interspersed with first steep (1980–82) and then prolonged (1989–1992) recession, which kept levels of manufacturing output and investment *below* 1979 levels until the end of the 1980s and left the growth performance of the UK manufacturing sector well below that of key competitors. In fact, that first Thatcher-induced recession "was the deepest in UK industrial history: one characterized by a 20 per

cent loss of manufacturing capacity, and a destruction of 1.7 million manufacturing jobs",[23] and as late as 1992, the volume of manufacturing output in
the UK had only crept to a level one per cent higher than it had been in 1973,
at the height of Edward Heath's three-day week. Moreover, whatever slight
rise in labour productivity the Thatcher decade saw in this now reduced
manufacturing sector was not the result of any expensive industrial modernization. It was far more the product of "an intensification in the length and
rate of work in the context of large-scale unemployment and the widespread
closure of the least efficient plants".[24]

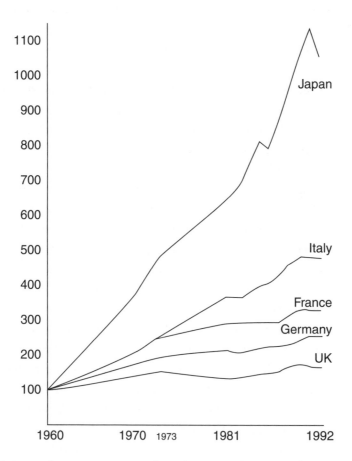

Figure 3.1 Manufacturing output in the UK, 1962–92 (1960 = 100)
(Source: Trade and Industry Committee, *Second Report: The Competitiveness of UK
Manufacturing Industry.* London: HMSO, 1994, p. 16).

As we noted in earlier work, it was "true that investment, as a percentage of GDP, had by the end of the Thatcher decade risen beyond its 1979 level, and that investment in manufacturing did rise – by some 12.8 per cent – over the decade 1979–89; but that figure looks paltry when set against comparable investment in Western European manufacturing industry, and positively minuscule when set against the 320.3 per cent growth in the volume of investment in financial services in the UK in the same period".[25] In 1970 UK-based manufacturing industry had contributed over 30 per cent of the economy's GDP. By 1995 it contributed just 22 per cent, and by then both its share of total world exports of manufactured goods and its employment levels had actually halved: from 16.8 per cent to 8.4 per cent of world exports, and from 8.5 million workers employed to just over 4 million. As the Select Committee on Trade and Industry reported to the House of Commons in 1994, "taking the last two decades as a whole, the UK is the only major industrial country whose manufacturing output has remained virtually static".[26] This "huge shakeout in manufacturing had the effect of strengthening those sectors of the economy based around the financial and service core of the South East and the major MNCs in oil, electrical engineering, pharmaceuticals and defense".[27] So, areas of competitive strength remained – in 1990 the management guru Michael Porter finding them still in UK-based finance, retailing, chemicals, aircraft production and defence goods among others – but even he thought few of them to be unusually strong relative to their German and Japanese competitors,[28] and none of them were strong enough to meet the UK's ever developing appetite for high-quality consumer goods, more and more of which were made abroad.

So, Thatcherism both worked and didn't work. It worked in the sense of leaving private capital free to manage and to move. But it didn't work in the sense that much of the capital that was deregulated did indeed then choose to move. It chose to move out of industrial investment, and it chose to move abroad. Steadily through the 1980s, large-scale British manufacturing moved offshore, and the pattern of UK-based investment increasingly shifted into finance and into general service provision, as the industrial part of the Thatcher economy increasingly became simply a production platform for foreign capital: one from which transnational corporations could sell products assembled in Britain into a more prosperous European-wide market

– with them choosing the UK as an investment site not because of its prosperity, but because its labour codes were the weakest and its level of corporate
taxation the lowest in all of northern continental Europe. Yet even this inflow
of foreign direct investment, which did partially regalvanize the UK car
industry in the last two decades of the century, could not prevent the UK
from opening a substantial deficit on its balance of trade – a deficit in manufactured goods starting in 1983 which was unprecedented except in wartime
and which is now apparently permanent. For as we noted in earlier work, "the
scale of foreign direct investment (and its impact of employment) was actually tiny during the Conservative years, when set against the total movement
of capital in and out of the UK. Between 1979 and 1992 the total flows of capital out of the UK exceeded those coming in for every year except 1987; and
the employment effect of Japanese in-plants in particular (with 25,000 new
manufacturing jobs created in the 1980s) were drowned by the destruction of
200,000 equivalent jobs by the top 25 British-owned transnationals".[29]

For what the unregulated financial flows so powerfully advocated by Margaret Thatcher singularly failed to do, in spite of a decade of unabashedly
pro-business public policy, was to regenerate British industry across the
totality of its sectors. Instead those flows helped fuel an increasingly debt-
based consumer boom in the 1980s, and a full-scale housing boom (of escalating house prices, followed by negative equity) in the early 1990s.[30] And
throughout it all, UK productivity remained low by comparative standards,
UK living standards continued to trail those in the best of the UK's European
competitors, and a widening gap opened up between Britain's rich and Britain's poor. This, despite the fact that the Thatcher period as a whole saw a
significant *increase* in the length of the working day (with the typical UK male
worker putting in two extra hours a week, and the typical female worker an
extra three hours a week, in the last ten years of Tory rule). The result was
a steady fall in the UK's position in key league tables of wages and living
standards. In 1960, per capita income in the UK had exceeded that in West
Germany, France, Italy and Japan: in the latter case by a factor of nearly three.
By 1998 per capita income had slipped below that delivered by each of these
key competitor economies, particularly the German. And at the century's
end, it remained the case that – for all the talk of Britain's productivity miracle under Thatcherism – "British workers still worked the longest hours in

northern Europe" and that the bulk of the jobs being created still "remained predominantly low paid, and low skilled, and in the service sector".[31]

Indeed, it was a measure of how far short of economic success the Thatcher revolution eventually fell that many of its core assertions – on money supply, business deregulation and limited state involvement in industry – began to be quietly abandoned even by a Conservative Government just as soon as Margaret Thatcher herself had been forced from office. The Major Government that followed hers was far more active on the industrial front than her governments had been, far more socially concerned, and ultimately far more welfare-minded. But by then, the political gloss had entirely rubbed off the basic Thatcherite product. The years of power had corrupted parts of the Tory political class; and even in Margaret Thatcher's heyday, UK public support for extreme pro-market views had never been total. On the contrary, strong residues of support for social democratic values remained for Thatcher's opponents to tap into and to develop; so that as enthusiasm for the Tory Party wilted, a political opening reappeared for a new kind of Labour Party. It was one that Tony Blair's New Labour took in style in 1997, returning from the political wilderness with a parliamentary majority of 179 seats as the Conservatives went down to their most traumatic electoral rejection since 1846.

But the stress here has to be on the "newness" of New Labour. Tony Blair's arrival at Number 10 marked a political landslide, but not a fundamental break with Thatcher's neoliberal settlement. On the contrary, New Labour was at most "Thatcher-lite". The Blair years in opposition had been used to reset the party's institutions and policies in ways closer to a Thatcherite vision. Gone were the close personal, organizational and programmatic linkages between the Labour leadership and the trade unions. There would be no new corporatist "social contract" from New Labour.[32] Gone too was "Old" Labour's tolerance of tax-and-spend social democracy. The incoming Labour Government – whose domestic policy was set by a Chancellor of the Exchequer as "iron" and "prudent" in his way as Margaret Thatcher had been – chose to operate initially within pre-set Conservative spending limits, eschewed any notion of more progressive taxation, and had no plans to tighten regulations around, or nationalize parts of, a privately-owned economy that New Labour proposed to energize by an enthusiastic adoption of market-strengthening policies.[33] New Labour entered office fully committed to the new growth theory then becoming fashionable in policy-making circles – post neoclassical endogenous growth theory – the one that prioritized the transformation of the existing welfare state into a social investment state, and the transformation of education policy from a tool of social reform into one for strengthening human capital.[34] As Tony Blair once put it, "the key to survival in the modern world is access to knowledge and information ... information is the currency of our economies".[35] Hence his mantra at the 1997 Labour Party conference: "education, education, education".

New Labour bought entirely into the neoliberal version of globalization: the one that rendered a Keynesian focus on the management of aggregate demand no longer nationally viable, advocating instead the development of public policies designed to attract foreign direct investment by improving local factors of production – reskilling labour, easing business regulations, and lowering levels of personal and corporate tax. And in true neoliberal fashion, the vision of economic success underpinning New Labour was simultaneously both post-industrial and post-Fordist. So, it was a New Labour Government after 1997, and not just the Thatcherite ones before it, which eulogized the new technology-based industries and did nothing to regenerate the UK's remaining textile mills, coal mines or steel works. It was a New Labour Government after 1997, like the Thatcher ones, which maintained the independence of sterling, and the autonomy of the City of London, by remaining outside the Eurozone. It was a New Labour Government which regularly lectured other member states of the European Union on the need to deregulate labour markets and to lower rates of corporate taxation; and it was a New Labour Government, and not just a Thatcherite one, that regularly deployed UK military forces overseas in a series of initially minor (and ultimately major) set of "Blair's Wars".[36]

What New Labour brought to the table, that Margaret Thatcher's governments had not, was a willingness to underpin market forces with extended welfare services: with a national system of childcare provision from 1997; with more spending on healthcare and education from 2001; and throughout, with tax credits to ease the financial pressure on the UK's poor (particularly on pensioners and those on low pay). This was not old-style social democracy. Rather, it was neoliberalism with a softer face. For New Labour welfare policies were as market-oriented as Thatcher's had been: hospitals were to be built with private finance, schools were to compete via published league tables, single mothers were increasingly pressured to rejoin the paid labour force as their children reached school age, and so on. And New Labour was just as keen as its Conservative predecessors had been to keep levels of business and labour-market regulation lower than those common in Western Europe, the better to attract to the UK foreign direct investment designed to increase the productivity of labour – a productivity goal to which Gordon Brown (first as Chancellor and later as prime minister) attached particular importance. And it was a focus that initially paid off: in that the UK narrowed the productivity gap with the United States to 33 per cent under New Labour, continuing a trend first begun under New Labour's Conservative predecessors. The gap had been 43 per cent in 1979.

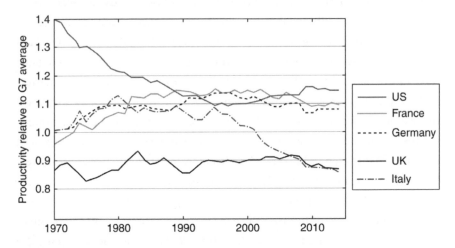

Figure 3.2 UK labour productivity relative to the G7 average
(Source: Richard Jones, "Innovation, Research and the UK's Productivity Crisis". Sheffield: SPERI Paper No. 28, April 2016, p. 3).

For a while, the whole strategy seemed to work. From late 1992 to early 2008, the UK economy experienced 66 quarters of unbroken economic growth. That pattern was not even disturbed by the end of the dot.com boom, or by the events of 9/11, as was its US equivalent. So steady was that growth indeed that Gordon Brown, in launching his last budget before becoming prime minister, could boast of the UK Treasury, on his watch, having beaten the cycle of "stop-and-go" economics once and for all. But this complacency was seriously misplaced, as events were soon to demonstrate. The economic growth over which New Labour had presided between 1997 and 2007 turned out to be based on the insecure foundation of excessive credit-debt, low wages and a dwindling manufacturing sector – on foundations no more stable than those prevalent at the same time in the United States of George W. Bush. As early as 2004, the volume of consumer debt in the UK broke the £1 trillion barrier for the first time, with 80 per cent of it in the form of loans secured against mortgages and remortgages – at the very moment when real incomes were falling under the impact of higher taxes, inflation and low salary settlements. The UK went into the financial crisis of 2008 immersed in a consumer boom underpinned by soaring housing prices, at the very moment when the UK wage gap between CEO pay and factory wages was the highest in Western Europe, and when those wages were lower, not simply than those in the United States and Japan, but also than those in Sweden, Germany and France.

So, when Gordon Brown spoke of taming the business cycle, telling the House of Commons that "we will never return to the old boom and bust",[37] he spoke too soon. Within six months of his declaration, "boom and bust" economics was back with a vengeance. For by September 2007, Northern Rock had triggered the first run on a UK bank in over a century – had become the first domino to go down – and the instability that its fate illuminated then swept the entire US and UK financial systems: sending the UK economy into a recession no less deep than its US counterpart, and making unavoidably clear the limits of a social and economic settlement based on light regulation, weak trade unions, and systematic deindustrialization. Far from lifting the UK economy onto a new, higher and more sustainable growth path, New Labour's tolerance of light business regulation and Thatcher-like labour laws culminated in 2008 and 2009 in the worst economic recession the UK had seen since the 1930s, and by 2010 in the return to power of a Conservative Party keen to redesign a Thatcherite project for a post-Thatcher age.

The nature of the current condition

The Faustian pact that New Labour made with the UK's financial institutions left Gordon Brown as prime minister unable to contain the fallout from the collapse of Northern Rock in 2007 and of Lehmann Brothers a year later. For by then, as we have just seen, it was increasingly clear that the surface prosperity of the UK economy under his stewardship had ultimately been constructed to an excessive degree on debt: on international debt, on private debt and, in the wake of the financial crisis, on government debt as well. Even before the crisis struck, the UK trade deficit was running at a record high (£93.1 billion in 2008), primarily with Hong Kong, France, Germany, Norway and China; and debt levels in the UK banking system had risen by more than 150 per cent in less than a decade.[38] Although mortgage lending for consumption purposes was less of a factor in the UK crisis than in the US one, personal debt levels in the UK had also grown exponentially in the immediate run up to the financial crisis: rising another half trillion pounds from 2004 to 2009 in an economy that by then had more than 50 million credit cards in daily circulation. And by 2010 and in response to the financial crisis, public debt, at £185 billion (up from £30 billion in 2005/6) was taking up almost 11 per cent of GDP.[39] That made UK public debt at the end of New Labour's years in office the highest of any economy in the European Union: higher even – as a percentage of GDP – than that of Greece. For like the United States, the United Kingdom, as the other home of only lightly-regulated finance, took the full brunt of the recession that City speculation had triggered. New Labour's lightly regulated UK economy experienced that recession on a scale and to a degree that economies like Canada's, where "boring bank" had remained the norm, managed to avoid, and so in consequence New Labour was obliged to respond with public spending on a commensurate scale.

As Craig Berry later noted, "the deepest recession since the Great Depression officially began" in the United Kingdom "in the second quarter of 2008, with the economy shrinking by 0.9 per cent, then 1.4 per cent and 2.1 per cent in subsequent quarters. Results initially worsened in 2009 (-2.5 per cent growth in the first quarter) before finally stabilizing towards the end of the year".[40] By April 2010 – New Labour's last full month in office – the official level of unemployment hit 8 per cent (2.5 million people out of work), wiping out all the job gains of the New Labour years by taking that number back to its highest point since the very start of the "Great Moderation"[41] in 1994. The number of people economically inactive – those involuntarily unemployed and those not seeking work – was even higher that month: 8.16 million people in total, 21.5 per cent of the population as a whole. New Labour was already planning £6 billion of austerity cuts of its own – and hence more short-term unemployment – as it went down to electoral defeat: but those reluctantly designed cuts were as nothing compared to what actually was to follow in the deliberately-adopted austerity budgets of the Conservative-led coalition government that followed New Labour into power. For here was one key difference between the fallout from the failure of neoliberalism in the two economies: the immediate political legacy of the financial crisis in the UK was exactly the reverse of that in the US. The crisis in each case cost the governing party power – that much the two economies shared – but whereas the casualty in the US was the Republican Party, in the UK it was Labour.

As we shall see in more detail in Chapter 7, the coalition government elected in the UK in 2010 went in for austerity politics with enthusiasm and zeal. Its emergency budget in June 2010 cut planned public spending by £40 billion by 2014–15 (77% by cuts, 23% by tax hikes) – in what the Institute for Fiscal Studies called at the time, "the longest, deepest, sustained period of cuts to public services spending since World War II"[42] – on the promise that the UK's £149 billion public sector indebtedness would have largely disappeared by 2015. The coalition government then followed its initial budget with others on the usual annual basis – staying fiscally neutral in 2011, but planning a further £15 billion worth of cuts for 2016–17 – and then cutting £2.5 billion from public spending in 2013 as it proposed seven more years of austerity to bring government revenues and spending into balance. It persisted with this austerity strategy even though its initial projections failed to materialize, even though the UK economy over which it presided eventually lost its Triple-A credit rating, and even though august bodies such as the IMF repeatedly called on it to ease back on its austerity programmes.[43] It was not, after all, as though the UK government *had* to cut spending to the degree chosen. Alternative policies were available to it – and were known to be available to it – including higher taxation, greater borrowing and a slow rate of programme-pruning.[44] But finance minister George Osborne and the Conservative wing of the coalition proved to be both committed and persistent pruners of public programmes: so committed in fact that IMF projections had UK public spending – which in 2009 had been at German levels – dropping to levels lower even than in the United States by 2017.[45] Ideology, not economics, drove the story in London at least as much as it did in the increasingly gridlocked politics of Washington, DC; and it was an ideology which many welcomed[46] and of which Margaret Thatcher would undoubtedly have been very proud.

The results thus far, however, have not been impressive.

GDP GROWTH, TRADE PERFORMANCE AND PRODUCTIVITY

The conventionally-used figures on recent UK economic growth suggest gathering strength: gathering strength both in comparison to the economy's performance in the years immediately following the 2008 financial crisis, and strength when compared to other leading (particularly European) economies over that same period. Prior to the 2015 general election that the Conservatives won outright, George Osborne could legitimately claim (as he did) that the UK economy grew faster in 2014 than any other advanced economy – slower, obviously, than China but way better than the growth performance of either the Eurozone economies or even the United States. That growth caused the IMF in 2014 and 2015 to publicly withdraw its critique of Osborne's austerity strategy[47] but that withdrawal was itself premature, because in truth the surface appearance of economic success in Osborne's Britain only flattered to deceive.*

It was not that the return to economic growth came because austerity persisted. It was far more that growth came as the pressure of the austerity pedal was significantly eased. The Osborne pitch for the success of his growth strategy downplayed the extent to which the UK's rate of recovery from the recession was actually impeded by his early and heavy culling of public spending. Far from growing rapidly as it came out of the 2008–9 recession,

---

* Craig Berry correctly characterized this as only "a pseudo recovery", arguing that "some indicators of economic performance are pointing in the right direction – notably, overall output growth ... But others, such as levels of pay and investment, provide evidence of very worrying trends that have yet to be addressed. Furthermore, growth appears to have been driven by a recovery in the economic activities which fueled growth under the pre-crisis growth model. This indicates the failure of rebalancing [and] is also suggestive of a precarious future for the British economy, because some of the key features of the previous growth model, such as the ability of the mainstream banking sector to offer cheap consumer credit, seem unable to reclaim the role they previously played". (SPERI Paper No. 7, "Are We There Yet?", p. 1).

the UK economy experienced a double-dip recession in 2011–12 (its first since the oil crisis of the 1970s) and teetered on the edge of a triple one early in 2013 after making the slowest recovery from any recession in the last three centuries;[48] and by 2014 was only growing by 3 per cent per annum, as UK GDP at last passed its pre-recession level. As late as mid-2013, the UK economy was still 3.3 per cent smaller than it had been in 2008, with its rate of gross fixed capital formation some 25 per cent lower than immediately prior to the financial crisis.[49] Any balanced view of recent UK economic performance data, therefore, makes it abundantly clear that the rate of recovery quickened again in 2013 and 2014 only *after* the Coalition Government eased back on the austerity pedal;[50] and that the initial adverse effect of the Brexit vote was softened by the May Government rapidly putting Osborne's further planned austerity measures on hold.[51] What the Osborne pruning of public services did instead was to move the UK into an unprecedented period of general deflation or stable prices; and deflation – if the Japanese experience is any guide – guarantees a lower than normal trajectory of growth as consumers hold back on purchasing and as saving rates disproportionately rise. As this volume goes to press, the National Institute of Economic Research's projected annual growth rate for the UK economy for 2017–18 period remains stuck below 2.0 per cent – 1.7 per cent in 2017, 1.9 per cent in 2018[52] – as in April 2017 UK growth slowed to its lowest pace for a year, just 0.2 per cent over the first quarter (and then by July, 0.3 per cent for the second quarter[53]): opening up the prospect that *secular stagnation* may be the UK's new normal as far as economic growth is concerned.[54]

Moreover, the economic growth achieved towards the end of the Coalition Government's tenure in office proved to be built on as equally fragile a basis as that achieved by New Labour. Despite the Chancellor's 2011 assertion that the UK economy stood poised to be "carried aloft by the march of the makers", and the desire of the Coalition Government to rebalance the UK economy by strengthening the role of manufacturing relative to finance, the UK manufacturing sector did not improve either its size or its international competitiveness in any significant fashion in the years that followed the ejection of New Labour from power. On the contrary, "the manufacturing sector is now a smaller component of overall economic output – 9.7 per cent of total gross value added – compared to 10.9 per cent before the financial crisis",[55] and UK manufacturing output was actually *down* 5.7 per cent in the third quarter of 2016, as against the third quarter of 2007.[56] The energy, pharmaceutical and agricultural sectors all continued to struggle as late as 2015; although there were bright spots, of course: not least the government-sustained aerospace industry (the second biggest after the US one), and the UK automotive industry, now almost entirely foreign-owned, where output hit a 10 year high in 2015, with 80 per cent of that output exported.[57] And because manufacturing did not improve, the UK's balance of trade did not improve either. On the contrary, the UK's export sector continued the steady loss of market share of export goods visible from the late 1990s, a trend that was particularly marked from 2013, as the exchange rate of sterling began to strengthen against both the euro and the dollar. Because of the Brexit vote, that strength against the dollar has now gone: but the trade deficit remains undented. Taking all four quarters of 2015 together, the UK's current account deficit – at £96.2 billion or 5.2 per cent of GDP – was the largest since 1948.

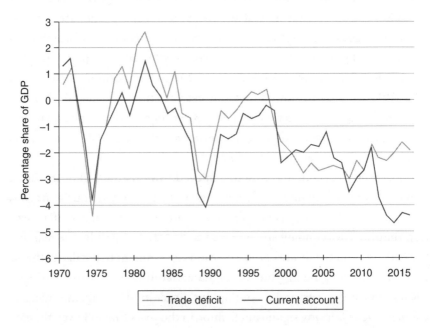

Figure 3.3 UK current account and trade deficit as a percentage of GDP, 1970–2016 (Source: Industrial Strategy Commission, "Laying the Foundations", SPERI July 2017, p. 11).

Nor did the Osborne austerity medicine in any way ease the deepest underlying weakness of the UK economy inherited from the years of neoliberal ascendancy: its less than competitively adequate level (and growth rate) of labour productivity. The UK productivity puzzle, first noted in the Introduction, remained fully in place. In fact, the Coalition Government presided over an economy with the weakest productivity record of any government since the Second World War: as the Office of National Statistics put it, "the absence of productivity growth in the seven years since 2007 is unprecedented in the postwar period",[58] locking GDP/hour in the UK on a trend line 15 per cent lower than that established from 1979 to 2008.[59] Quite why productivity performance is so low and so entrenched is a matter of huge controversy, but clearly one factor in play since 2008 has been the hoarding of labour made cheaper by the fall in real wages that has accompanied it. What productivity growth per worker has occurred since 2014/15 has been the result of working longer hours, not of working more effectively per hour: with the result that the productivity gap between the UK and its major competitors remained firmly in place.

EMPLOYMENT AND JOB CREATION

The employment data for the UK under George Osborne's guidance also flattered to deceive. Sarah O'Connor put it this way: "the labour market's strange behavior remains the defining puzzle of the British economy. Whether you choose to call it a 'jobs miracle', a 'productivity disaster' or a 'cost of living crisis', you are describing the same phenomenon: very strong employment gains relative to economic output, with the corollary of dreadful productivity and wage growth".[60] For although on the surface, the employment record looks strong and improving, behind the figures serious structural weaknesses remain. Although the UK moved its unemployment rate down from 7.9 per cent in 2010 to 6.8 per cent in 2014 and to 4.9 per cent by the end of 2016 – when it reached an eleven-year low* – the TUC estimated as recently as 2012 that involuntary part-time work kept that official rate at only 50 per cent of its true value;[61] as one in seven of those in work at the start of the recession

---

* It is even lower as we go to press: 4.1 per cent, a 42-year low.

lost their employment at some point in the years that followed. Those fortunate enough to retain their full-time job were now likely to work the third
longest hours in the EU – 42.7 hours per week, behind only Austria and
Greece[62]– while as many as 1.4 million of the part-timers working alongside
them were on zero-hours contracts. In 2012, as the UK economy went into a
second brief recession, the unemployment rates among 16–24 year-old workers in the UK stood at 22 per cent and among black and Asian migrants at a
staggering 44 per cent.[63] And although UK labour market participation rates
have held up better than in the US since 2008, and at 63.6 per cent now exceed
US rates for the first time,[64] two features of this employment record remain of
particular concern.

Firstly, recent employment figures have been improved in part by an
unprecedented growth in "self-employment" – self-employment which
accounts for a third of the increase in employment since the recession,[65] now
accounts for more than 15 per cent of the labour force, and is shifting the
overall UK labour market in an eastern and southern European direction.*
Some of this growth is genuinely entrepreneurial: but most is not, acting
instead as a cover for "people working part-time and paid a fraction of the
wage enjoyed by full-time employees".[66] On the eve of the June 2017 general
election, indeed, the GMB union calculated that "up to 10 million Britons or
nearly a third of the UK workforce" currently lacked secure employment,
remaining trapped in "the gig economy, on zero- or short-hours contracts", or
surviving as "temporary workers, the underemployed, and those at risk of
false self-employment".[67] That staggering 10 million figure included the rising number of officially-registered part-time workers who wanted but were
unable to obtain full-time work. (Their number reached nearly 1.4 million in
2013,[68] – as the rate of underemployment in the UK economy rose from 7 per
cent before the recession to 10.5 per cent by the end of 2012[69]– to by then
match the numbers of those working on zero-hours contracts.)† What many

---

* The *FT* put it this way in October 2016. "A focus of concern is the gradual shift from the
traditional model of employment, on full-time permanent contracts, to more precarious
forms of work – including temporary and zero-hours contracts, part-time jobs and the systemic use of self-employed staff by companies such as Uber and Deliveroo." (*Financial Times*,
19 October 2016).
† "Since 2011, the number of people on zero-hours contracts has increased fivefold ... the
type of people who find themselves on these contracts. Typically, it is women, young people,

employers did in the immediate wake of the recession was keep workers on the books but reduce their hours,[70] and yet paradoxically the number of UK workers recording unpaid overtime also rose to record levels over the same period. There were 5.4 million of them in 2013, including one part-time worker in five[71] and probably every schoolteacher and junior hospital doctor in the land: at the very time when long-term unemployment persisted for over five per cent of the total labour force and had risen sharply for 16–24 year-old workers from ethnic minority backgrounds.[72] And remarkably, it was the OECD's view in 2015 that "in the UK, non-standard work including zero-hours contracts accounted for *all* net job growth since 1995".[73] All!

Secondly, what made it worse was that the Coalition Government, as the centre-piece of its austerity drive, deliberately cut public-sector employment – by over 630,000 jobs with more in the pipeline[74]– without total employment growth doing more than keeping pace with the growth of the UK population in total. The scale and impact of those cuts are of historic proportions. If fully implemented as planned by 2018/19, there will be over one million *fewer* teachers, health workers, police officers, firemen and general civil servants employed than were in post at the end of the Great Recession. In addition to the attack that this represents on the quality of the UK's welfare services, it also constitutes a serious erosion in the scale and job security of the UK's public sector-based middle class. This restructuring of the entire UK labour force would be employment-neutral, of course, if all that slack was then easily absorbed by a revitalized private sector. But so far, that revitalization remains modest, and what job creation we have seen in the UK private sector simply gives cause for greater concern. It is true that some parts of the private sector have been recent net job creators – the tech sector, for example, now employing over one million workers out of the UK's 28 million total, rather than the 915,000 it employed out of 27 million in 2010[75] – but that simply points to a labour market polarization of the kind also visible in the United States. The UK manufacturing sector's general shedding of labour is gutting the English private sector middle class just as effectively in the UK as

and foreign nationals" (New Economics Foundation, 17 March 2017). Maybe now the number has peaked: a slight fall in the number of people confirming that their main job did not offer them a guaranteed minimum number of hours (883,000) was reported in September 2017, down from 903,000 a year earlier. (*Financial Times*, 20 September 2017).

outsourcing is doing in the US, leaving a growing gap between high-paid, high-productivity, tech employment for the fortunate few, and for the rest, increasing exposure to what the TUC General Secretary Frances O'Grady has called "bad jobs",[76]– jobs that pay badly, and jobs whose pay does not rise in line either with growing productivity or falling unemployment. In fact, even before the financial crisis, the UK economy was shifting more rapidly towards low-skill jobs and less towards high skilled jobs than was common elsewhere in Europe, a squeezing of the middle that employment trends post-recession can only have intensified.*

WAGES

If the post-2010 employment numbers were available to the Conservatives in 2015 as part of their defence of their record in power, the wage numbers most definitely were not. As we first noted in the Introduction, in the UK at the end of the period of coalition government average wages were still at 2004 levels, with no likelihood of their returning to their 2008 peak until well after 2020.[77] It is true that, as the UK moved towards its second post-crisis general election, real wages which have been falling in the UK for six years did begin to rise faster than inflation again: but in the event, that rise was sufficiently modest and slow as to still leave the average UK family £1,600 worse off in 2014 than they had been in 2009. Things did then ease a little more: so that by the time of the third post-crisis general election (in June 2017), family incomes in the UK had "recovered to pre-crisis levels and done better in growth terms than wages, largely due to the tax and benefit system"[78] that protected pensioners in particular (most notably through "the triple lock"† guarantee that the May Government would have ended, had that third election result turned out better from the Conservatives' point of view!). But even then, there were features of the wage settlements left in place in the UK at the end of the neoliberal settlement that remain particularly concerning: two in

---

* "For every 10 middle-skilled jobs that disappeared in the UK between 1996 and 2008, about 4.5 of the replacement jobs were high-skilled and 5.5 were low-skilled. In Ireland, the balance was about eight high-skilled to two low-skilled, while in France and Germany it was about seven to three." (*Financial Times*, 19 January 2015).

† A guarantee to raise the state pension annually by the *higher* of either the rate of inflation, the rate of wage increases, or 2 per cent.

particular – the *depth and longevity* of the fall in earnings in the wake of the recession, and its *differential distribution* between different parts of the UK labour force.

The inverse relationship between employment and wages in the post-2008 UK economic recovery was truly remarkable. If the TUC was right, as late as 2014 British workers were still "suffering the longest and most severe decline in real earnings since the mid-Victorian era". The TUC data suggested that we have to go back to the 1860s "for a pay freeze as deep and as long as this one".[79] Certainly, living standards went through a severe and prolonged squeeze in the UK after 2008, the longest since records began, according to the Social Market Foundation.[80] Compared to 2007, the average worker saw an 8 per cent decline in real weekly-earnings by 2014; and for the self-employed in the same period, real incomes fell 22 per cent. And if real wages then began to recover, as they definitely did in both 2015 and 2016, the improvement only represented the beginnings of a clawback to pre-recession levels. As a recent Resolution Foundation report put it, "average incomes in the low to middle income group were no higher in 2014–15 than in 2004–05, reflecting not just the turmoil of the post-crisis period but also a sharp pre-crisis slowdown in income growth".[81] And as late as December 2016, the TUC was finding emergency workers earning less at Christmas than they had five years before: nurses' salaries down on average by £2,000, midwives' by £3,300, police officers' by £1,300, ambulance drivers' by £2,200 and firefighters' by £3,200.[82] Little Christmas cheer there.

This prolonged fall in real wages helps throw light on the otherwise puzzling difference in the relationship between wages and labour productivity after 2008, when the UK experience is compared to that of other leading economies (including the American one). After 2008, the US "saw real wage stagnation and rising labour productivity". The UK did not. It combined falling wages with slow productivity growth, in part at least because of a significant shift of "the labour supply curve ... to the right" – because, that is, of the presence in the UK's increasingly deregulated labour markets of "more individuals willing to work at any given wage". As Blundell and his colleagues noted at the time: at the height of the recession in 2010–11, among workers who stayed in the same job one-third experienced nominal wage cuts and 70 per cent experienced real ones; and they tolerated this (no doubt reluctantly) because their heightened sense of job insecurity left more and more of them willing to "attach more weight to staying in work (because their expected time to find another job was longer than in the past) than on securing higher wages".[83] Young workers and the self-employed were especially vulnerable here, with the burden of wage adjustment falling particularly heavily on them. The typical weekly earnings of self-employed workers in 2014/15, for example, "were about £240 a week. After adjusting for inflation, that is less than in 1994/95, as far back as the data goes".[84] And "young workers have been the ones most affected since the crisis, experiencing a sharp fall in real weekly wages (of the order of 16 per cent for workers aged 18–21), linked to lower hours, part-time work and self-employment arrangements".[85]

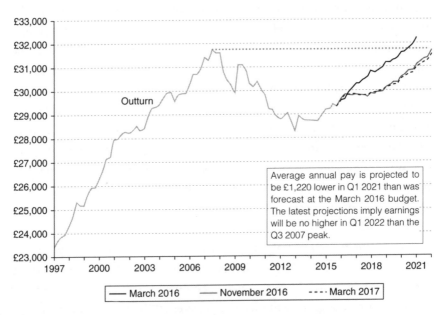

Figure 3.4 Real-terms average annual earnings outturn and projections, 1997–2021
(Source: Stephen Clarke *et al.*, "Are we nearly there yet?". London: Resolution Foundation, March 2017, p. 25).

Little wonder then that, surveying the UK labour market towards the end of the Cameron-Osborne era, SPERI's Craig Berry could treat the low unemployment numbers to which the Government attached such importance as, at best, a "Pyrrhic victory", concealing "significant problems in terms of under-employment, precarious employment, stagnating wages, regional inequality and polarization between high-skilled and low-skilled workers".[86] As Theresa May's government took over from that of David Cameron in mid-2016, the UK labour market was combining low levels of unemployment with, at best, modest rates of real wage growth. Since the two do not normally combine, it is the novelty that needs to be explained. Likely candidates included the growing number of non-UK born job-seekers (immigration accounted for about half the increase of total UK workers in 2015), the fact that the bulk of the jobs being created were in low-paying sectors (not least retail and hospitality), the persistence of large-scale involuntary part-time employment, and the tight squeeze on pay rates in the public sector (which still accounts in the UK for 18 per cent of total employment*). The growth in Uber-like self-employment might well be a fifth candidate; as overall, as Larry Elliott recently put it, "Britain specializes in low-wage, low-skill, low productivity jobs. That is why earnings growth is so poor".[87]

Preliminary conclusion

This then is the economy that the Conservative Government must now somehow disconnect from its major market, the European Union. The long-term economic consequences of Brexit are still hard to establish, given the preliminary nature thus far of the negotiations on separation terms. But the immediate signs are not encouraging. Inflation is quickening again in the UK – more rapidly indeed in the UK than elsewhere in the G7 – and so already eroding the value of any significant gains in real wages; and transnational corporations are already beginning to relocate out of the UK and into the heart of continental Europe (even in the financial sector where historically London has been so strong). There was no immediate Brexit-induced collapse

---

* "The restrictions on pay for Britain's 5.4 million public-sector workers are particularly controversial. All but the lowest-paid public servants had their salaries frozen between 2011 and 2012. Their pay rose slightly in the following three years. Then the government announced that it would cap annual public-sector pay increases at an average of 1 per cent until 2020." (*The Economist*, 8 July 2017). In July 2017, the headline rate of inflation in the UK was running at 2.6 per cent.

of business confidence or consumer spending, as the leaders of the "Remain" camp feared before the referendum,* but their pessimism about the long-term viability of a UK economy positioned outside the European Union remains a legitimate one: not least because, even before the referendum result was known, the UK economy was seriously scarred by what Martin Wolf recently called "longstanding supply-side failures". His list included "low investment, particularly in infrastructure; inadequate basic education of much of the population and the numeracy of much of its elite; a grossly distorted housing market; over-centralization of government; and a corporate sector whose leaders are motivated more by the share price than by the long-term health of the business".[88] That list could no doubt be extended – we have just seen long-term underperformance on wages, living standards and the creation of well-paid employment; but for the moment, it is less the length of the list that is important than its similarity to equivalent lists addressed to the United States.

For what we are seeing here are not just inadequacies and weaknesses in one isolated national economy – or indeed in two. What we are seeing are the local manifestations – first in the US and now in the UK – of weaknesses produced by the establishment in each of a distinctive model of capitalism and an associated strategy for economic growth: one in which "domestic consumption is sustained by escalating asset prices and private debt, predicated upon the continuation of low inflation, low interest rates and deregulated financial institutions".[89] The impact of that model on key aspects of social life – not least in the UK case, housing – will occupy us in later chapters, as will the politics and mind-set that such a model helps to consolidate. What we need to recognize here, however, before we move to those later topics, are the defining features of the model itself – the features that the two economies broadly share. Colin Hay recently labelled the model as *Anglo-Liberal* and singled out the following characteristics:[90]

---

* By mid-2017, the validity of those fears was becoming ever more evident, however, as Brexit uncertainty impacted negatively on investment levels, employment prospects and consumer confidence across a swathe of UK economic sectors, from manufacturing and construction to financial and other services. (See, for example, Phillip Inman, UK services sector growth hits four-month low amid Brexit fears," *The Guardian*, 5 July 2017).

- The hegemony of an assertive neoliberal ideology;
- An elite policy community increasingly trapped in its own thinking within this narrow ideological framework;
- Substantial deregulation of markets and privatization of financial management;
- Huge dependence on the supply of cheap hydrocarbons, with seriously damaging environmental consequences;
- The systemic build-up of debt incurred principally to fuel consumption;
- An accumulation of risk within the economic system, with growth over time increasingly associated with accelerated exposure to that risk;
- The absence of a coherent theory of society, or social well-being, beyond the sum of individual, supposedly rational goal-setting;
- The consequent embedding of inequalities between and within countries;
- A limited view of global governance as requiring little more than rules to manage competition between national economies.

There is great virtue in treating both economies in this common fashion, because in both cases it is the underlying weaknesses of the model that now outweigh its strengths, and helps explain why the trajectory of GDP growth in both since 2008 has been so poor by recent historical standards. In the UK case, that underperformance has been, and remains, particularly striking: with the result, as Martin Wolf also rightly noted, that right now "this is no world-beating economy. It is not even a European-beating economy, except on creating what are too often low-paid jobs".[91] No less than in the United States, therefore, we are dealing in the UK with an economy that in its core defining institutions and practices is deeply flawed, and as such is in need of fundamental reform.

PART II

Divided Societies

4

The Fading of the American Dream?

"The reason they call it the American Dream is because you have to be asleep to believe it."

George Carlin[1]

"I know enough about this country to know that Donald Trump is not a fluke ... that nothing will change until America reckons with race."

Kali Holloway[2]

"The American Dream is back."

Donald J. Trump[3]

Unlike any other major industrialized economy, the American one sits on top of a consciously-created society, one put together after 1620 by a mixture of voluntary and involuntary migration – the trans-oceanic movement of immigrants and slaves – into a land mass whose native inhabitants were an early casualty of that migration. Carefully editing US history to downplay the ethnic cleansing and forced slavery elements within it, contemporary American apologists regularly assert that – precisely because of its unique design – the society so consciously created turned out to be morally, socially and economically superior to the societies that the first generations of American transplants had left behind. As the American national anthem has it, the United States understands itself to be "the land of the free and the home of the brave" – understands itself, that is, as a country that possesses a unique trio of advantages: a unique set of dominant values focused around individualism and personal freedom, a uniquely prosperous economy based on private ownership, and a uniquely open social order in which individuals can

107

progress entirely through their own merit. The continuing influx of immi-grants seeking precisely those freedoms, prosperity and social mobility then only serves to reinforce the conviction – visible across the entire US political class, but particularly well-embedded in the belief systems of American con-servatives – that the United States remains "the shining city on the hill" which all other countries and peoples seek to emulate.[4]

The reality behind such claims is much more complicated than their advocates imply: but in one regard at least the claim for American superiority has, until recently, had enormous force. For over the postwar period as a whole, living standards in the United States have been significantly higher than those enjoyed by the mass and generality of people living in other major industrial economies – not to mention higher than the living standards of those unfortunate enough to be marooned either in former communist coun-tries or in the underdeveloped world. That economic superiority was not there in the 1930s. As we saw earlier, the American consumer boom of the "roaring twenties" completely collapsed after 1929: with horrendous social consequences. But in the immediate aftermath of the Second World War, America did see an explosion in general living standards of a kind not easily replicated elsewhere. For one generation at least, white male workers based in US manufacturing industries on either coast and in the Midwest attained a standard of living that had never been experienced before by working-class people. Well-unionized American workers gained access to consumer goods (televisions, fridges, telephones), to a quality of housing, and to a scale of leisure time that put them one generation and one class ahead of their equivalents in north-western Europe (including in the United Kingdom). What passed for a blue-collar north-eastern standard of life in the 1950s and 1960s looked middle-class to European eyes, and would not be matched by most working classes in Western Europe or Japan until the 1970s and 1980s.

But that gap in consumption patterns was never total. It was never total in part because it did not apply to everyone even in the United States: cer-tainly not to African-Americans or to other minority populations, or to non-unionized white workers in the American south: and small-town America was never that affluent.[5] And the gap was never total because, from the 1970s, there was a convergence of living standards on either side of the oceans: a convergence triggered by catch-up growth in Western Europe and Japan, and by stalled real-wage growth in the United States as the Reagan revolution embedded itself in US employment practices. There is now considerable controversy surrounding that stalling of real wages in post-Reagan America.[6] There are plenty of economists challenging the claim that it occurred, and even more noting that – even if wage rates stalled – what those wages bought has become ever more high-quality and sophisticated. The cars bought by US wages in the 1970s, and their equivalents four decades later, were not the same; and four decades later, wages were also being spent on consumer goods that were literally unimaginable in the 1970s. They were being spent, for example, on sophisticated electronic goods that added to the quality of daily life even if financed by the running up of unprecedented levels of personal debt.

That controversy will no doubt continue. But certain things remain without dispute. One is that the United States is no longer the outlier here – standards of living and levels of social mobility are now higher in a set of other countries than they are in America, a list of countries that actually includes America's neighbour to the north – Canada.[7] A second is that much of the working-class income gains and wealth accumulation – the gains that enabled the bulk of white Americans to start talking of themselves from the 1970s as middle-class rather than blue-collar – were wiped away in the crisis of 2008 and in the recession that followed.[8] A third is that the main legacy of the crash and its recession has been the growing recognition, by both politicians and their electorates in the United States, that key things are not as good at home as we all once thought. A decade away now from the financial crisis of 2008, deep fissures in American society remain – and remain visible. Five at least are worth exploring in detail here: the growing insecurity of the American middle class; the persistence of widespread poverty and cycles of deprivation at the base of American society; the embedded nature of racism that leaves class trumped by race in unique ways in the United States; the persistence of gender inequalities that block easy access to a proper work–life balance for the vast majority of both male and female American workers; and the generalized depletion of US social capital that threatens to intensify all these social vulnerabilities in generations to come.

As we first noted in the Introduction, mortality rates are currently *rising*

for white non-Hispanic middle-aged men and women – non-college educated whites, aged 45–54.[9] Death rates among similar working-class groups
in other affluent economies, including those of Canada, Sweden, the UK and
Australia, are actually falling, as they are in the United States for other groups
of workers, including middle-aged African-Americans and Hispanics. But
right now, as Figure 4.1 indicates, a key part of the white section of the American working class – and not just its men, but also its women – is literally
smoking, drinking, eating, and drugging itself to an early death, in a society in
which death rates per age group among non-whites continue to be higher
than among their white counterparts. Anne Case, whose data this is, put the
issue this way in a recent article in *The Washington Post*:

> Policy makers often speak as if the epidemic will be over as soon as we
> tackle both legal and illegal opioids. Better control of opioids is essential,
> but even without opioid deaths, there would still be as many or more
> deaths from suicide and liver diseases. Opioids are like guns handed out
> in a suicide ward; they have certainly made the total epidemic much
> worse, but they are not the cause of the underlying depression. We sus-
> pect that deaths of despair among those without a university degree are
> primarily the result of a 40-year stagnation of median real wages and a
> long-term decline in the number of well-paying jobs for those without
> a bachelor's degree. Falling labour force participation, sluggish wage
> growth and associated dysfunctional marriage and child-rearing pat-
> terns have undermined the meaning of working people's lives as well.[10]

Race, gender, class, and early death all go together in contemporary
America: which is why this particular data set – of growing mortality rates in
the midst of one of the most affluent countries on earth – though shocking,
should not surprise us. For as we shall now see, the contemporary United
States is less a social model for everyone to emulate than a time-bomb for
others to avoid; and avoiding that explosion will require a fundamental resetting of some very basic US social structures and practices, for they too are
currently seriously flawed.

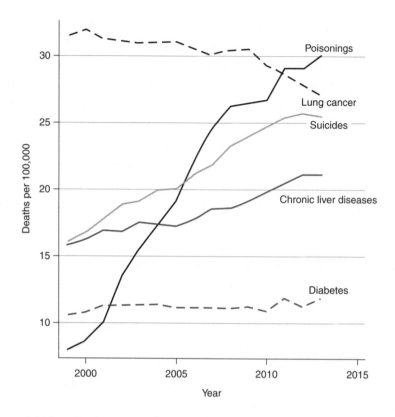

Figure 4.1 Mortality by cause, white non-hispanic, ages 45–54
(Source: Anne Case and Angus Deaton, "Rising Morbidity and Mortality in
Midlife Among White, Non-Hispanic Americans in the 21st Century," *PNAS*,
September 2015).

The growing insecurity of the American middle class

Definitions of the American middle class abound – and your view of its fate
turns critically on the definition you deploy. In the 2012 Presidential campaign, Mitt Romney famously defined the middle class as anyone earning
less than $200,000 a year, making 96 per cent of the entire US electorate
middle class. The Pew Research Institute, by contrast, defines middle-income
households as "those with an income that is two-thirds to double that of
the US median household, after incomes have been adjusted for household

size".[11] That definition put the US middle class in 2013 at 51 per cent of the entire population. Now if a class is to carry the label of "middle", it certainly needs to be located between two social formations that carry different labels, which is why for purposes of comprehension here it seems more sensible to go in the direction of Pew than of Romney: by characterizing the American middle class as one that is socially located above the American poor and below the super-rich. Boundary problems will always remain – for members of the middle class as well as for those analyzing them – but focusing on people occupying income-positions between the fortieth and sixtieth percentile of the American income ladder does seem the appropriate place to start.

When you focus in on those income-earners, several things stand out. One is that the American middle class is shrinking relative to the classes both above and below it – so that the 120.8 million current middle-income earners are now matched by the 121.3 million adult Americans who are above or below them in income terms. Middle-class Americans no longer constitute the overwhelming economic majority in the contemporary United States: on the contrary, the approximately 50 per cent of Americans now in that middle position stands in sharp contrast to the 80 per cent there in 1971, a change reflecting the growth of both high-income earners and the American poor. Moreover, this shrinkage is occurring in every part of the United States: more than 80 per cent of metropolitan areas in the United States experienced some form of this middle-class shrinkage between 2000 and 2015, as median household incomes in 203 of 229 cities actually fell.[12]

Overall, the median income of this shrunken middle class was four percentage points lower in 2015 than in 2000, and its median wealth (assets minus debts) 28 per cent less.* One result? What the Pew research team labelled "the hollowing out of the American middle class" and the opening-up of an ever-widening gap "in income and wealth between middle- and upper-income households in the past three to four decades".[13] As Richard Reeves recently put it, "the American upper middle class [the top 20 per cent of income earners] is separating, slowly but surely, from the rest of society"; and

* The income figures for 2016 corrected that shortfall slightly, but even though most families are now nearly back to 2007 income levels, inequality continues to grow, with the top fifth of earners taking more than half of all overall income in 2016 – itself a record.

"the separation is not just economic. Gaps are growing on a whole range of dimensions, including family structure, education, lifestyle and geography".[14] A second result? The United States slipping to twenty-seventh in the international league table on median wealth. In the calculus of assets less liabilities, the US average of $38,786 in 2013 was $150,000 lower than the top (Australian) figure, and even $77,000 lower than that for the UK (which ranked sixth).[15] This is what Robert Samuelson called "the true middle-class squeeze" caused by the financial crisis of 2008 and its aftermath. "The Great Recession", as he put it, "hurled incomes all the way back to the late 1980s and early 1990s" and dealt with assets in a similar way. The result: "people's expectations about their living standards were set in the early 2000s, while their incomes and assets are stuck at levels 15 to 20 years earlier".[16]

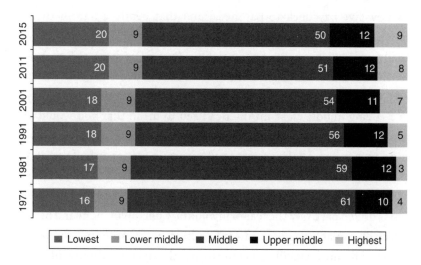

Figure 4.2 Share of adults living in middle-income households in the US (%) (Source: Christopher Degryse, "Digitalization of the Economy and its Impact on Labour Markets". Brussels: European Trade Union Institute, Working Paper 2016:02, p. 42).

A second feature that stands out from the data on the current state of the American middle class is that so many members of that class now suffer anxiety and stress levels that were previously the monopoly of the American poor. Report after report makes this abundantly clear. When the Pew

Research Center, for example, surveyed the middle class in 2012, it found "fully 85 per cent of self-described middle-class adults [saying that] it is more difficult now than it was a decade ago for middle-class people to maintain their standard of living". Pew called that report, *The Lost Decade of the Middle Class*.[17] Research data gathered by academics at Rutgers reinforced the Pew findings: reporting in 2014 that 42 per cent of their sample had less savings then than in 2009 and that 25 per cent had a *lot* less. They called their report, "Unhappy, Worried and Pessimistic: Americans in the Aftermath of the Great Recession".[18] And JPMorgan Chase, sampling the bank accounts and spending patterns of their own customers, concluded in May 2015 that the typical American "household did not have a sufficient financial buffer to weather the degree of income and consumption volatility observed in our data".[19] But this too should not surprise us, given that at least two-thirds of all adult Americans now live paycheck-to-paycheck, and that nearly a half of them are recently on record as believing that an unexpected bill of only $400 would actually tip them into acute financial difficulties.[20] For them, as Robert Reich recently observed, "a downturn in demand, or sudden change in consumer needs, or a personal injury or sickness, can make it impossible to pay the bills".[21] Being middle class in America used to mean that you would know financial security for life; but clearly it does not mean that now. Just the reverse, in fact. Financial insecurity and anxiety is, for nearly half the US adult population, currently the dominant condition of the day.*

This is a financial insecurity – Neal Gabler called it "financial impotence" – that is driven partly by the fear of involuntary unemployment and by a general lack of available savings. Edward Wolff recently estimated, for example, that were a family on median income to lose that income, they would be able to continue their normal spending pattern for just 6 days![22] But it is also a financial insecurity rooted in the rising costs of the things that the American middle class habitually consume – what Patricia Cohen recently referred to

---

* Echoing findings we will see later for the UK, the Consumer Financial Protection Bureau's first national survey on the financial well-being of US consumers – released in October 2017 – found "more than 40 per cent of adults struggling to make ends meet ... 43 per cent ... struggling to pay bills. Additionally, over one-third – 34 per cent – of all consumers surveyed reported experiencing material hardships in the past year ... (examples include running out of food, not being able to afford a place to live, or lacking the money to seek medical treatment)." (CFBP, 4 October 2017).

as "the traditional bedrocks of middle-class life: adequate healthcare, college for the children and retirement savings, generally with a car and a regular summer vacation thrown in".[23] Three of those costs stand out as currently particularly burdensome: the costs of housing, education, and health care. All have recently been rising dramatically, as median income has stagnated. Indeed, between 2000 and 2012, "the costs of key elements of security rose dramatically, including childcare costs – which grew by 37 per cent – and healthcare costs – both employee premiums and out-of-pocket costs – which grew by 85 per cent". As the Center for American Progress's aptly named report, "The Middle-Class Squeeze", from which these figures are drawn, concluded: "investing in the basic pillars of middle-class security – childcare, housing, and healthcare, as well as setting aside modest savings for retirement and college – cost an alarming $10,600 more in 2012 than it did in 2000. Put another way, [the median family] household's income was stagnant – rising by less than 1 per cent – while basic pillars of middle-class security rose by more than 30 per cent".[24] Add to that the way in which inflation-adjusted tuition costs at public universities have risen by at least 250 per cent since 1982 – leaving an average student debt level of currently $25,000, making the class of 2015 the most indebted ever[25] – plus the continuing presence in the US housing market of negative equity for still one homeowner in five, and it is little wonder that the Center for American Progress felt obliged to title its follow-up report in 2015, "The Middle Class at Risk".[26]

This increasing sense of insecurity among members of what was once America's core middle class is itself a product of at least three deeper processes at work in the economy and society surrounding that class, two of which we explored in some detail in Chapter 1 and one of which requires deeper examination here. The middle class in America is currently financially stretched because of the gap that opened up – in the Reagan and post-Reagan years – between the trajectory of labour productivity growth and that of middle-class wages (Larry Mishel and Heidi Shierholz recently and rightly labelled this decoupling of pay and productivity "as one of the most glaring failures of the American model").[27] The financial pressure created by that gap is now being compounded by the much lower trajectory of productivity growth which with the US economy has been burdened since the financial crisis of 2008 and its ensuing recession – a lower trajectory that the

President's Council of Economic Advisers estimated in 2015 to have lowered median income by as much as $30,000. Both these features of US productivity performance surfaced for analysis in Chapter 2.*

So too did the second driver of contemporary middle-class stress in the United States, namely the outsourcing of well-paid manufacturing jobs to labour forces abroad who were willing to work for less pay. As we saw in Chapter 2, that outsourcing both took middle-class jobs and wages away, and where manufacturing jobs remained, also helped to reduce the wages that employers now feel obliged to pay. The result, if the recent National Employment Law Project research report is accurate, is that manufacturing wages in the United States now rank "in the bottom half of all jobs". "In decades past", as the report put it, "production workers employed in manufacturing earned wages significantly higher than the US average, but by 2013 the typical manufacturing production worker made 7.7 per cent below the median wage for all occupations".[28] It may be – as Harry Holzer has recently argued[29] – that this "hollowing out" of well-paid employment in manufacturing and construction is being offset to a degree by the rise of a new middle class based in healthcare and other services. But if it is, that new middle class is still insufficiently large or well-paid to entirely fill the gap left by the shrinkage of manufacturing employment. Indeed, and to the contrary, it is the rise of low-productivity service sector employment that is currently helping to pull American middle-class wages down, and the steady erosion of middle-skill jobs† that is triggering what Tüzemen and Willis recently called "the vanishing middle" – the polarization of an entire economy into a mixture of high-skilled *and* low-skilled jobs.[30]

---

* This analysis is echoed in the introduction to the 2010 "Report of the White House Task Force on the Middle Class" that drew the president's attention to the existence of "two very different growth regimes over different periods of history. Between 1947 and 1979, for example, real median family income grew at an annual rate of 2.4 per cent, which amounts to about a doubling of real income over this period. After 1979, however, this trend decelerated significantly, as real median family income grew only 0.4 per cent a year, for a total increase of 14 per cent ... in the later regime, since 1979, the growth of family income has become increasingly disconnected from the broader growth of output and productivity. While productivity has continued to grow robustly, middle-class families are no longer getting their share of that growth." (p. 3).

† These middle-skill occupations include sales, office and administrative support, production, construction, extraction, installation, maintenance and repair, transportation, and material moving.

What both those drivers – the productivity-wage gap and the outsourcing-wage cutting one – reflect is a changing balance of power between capital and labour in the US economy, one intimately linked to the deliberate erosion of trade union powers and worker rights under the Reagan settlement from the 1980s. But the main manifestation of that changing balance of power, as it effects the American middle class, is neither of those things: neither technology nor capital-export. It is the deliberate escalation of inequalities in wealth and income that accompanied rising productivity and the global relocation of production by American companies both before and after 2008. The inequality figures for the contemporary USA are truly staggering, are now higher than anywhere else in the advanced industrial world, and are reflective of a level of personal greed and sense of entitlement among America's privileged top earners that has only one precedent in American history – that of the greed and vandalism of America's late nineteenth-century Gilded Age. Right-wing figures are forever condemning the entitlement culture of the so-called welfare queens; but if they want to see an entitlement culture operating in all its glory, they should redirect their attention (and ours) towards the American super-rich, not the American super-poor.

In terms of wealth holding, in 2015 just 160,000 families (0.1 per cent of US households) "owned nearly as much as everyone from the very poor to the upper middle class combined – 90 per cent of the country, some 145 million families in total".[31] In both 2013 and 2014, the top 14 of those wealth-holders made more from their investments than the entire federal budget line for food stamps[32] and the top 100 CEOs had as much retirement wealth waiting for them in old age as did the bottom 41 per cent of American families taken together.[33] In terms of income, the latest data set available to us suggests that between 1970 and 2014, the real income of the 117 million Americans stuck in the bottom half of the income-ladder experienced virtually zero growth, even after allowing for taxes and benefits, while that of the top 1 per cent exploded. Similar Congressional Budget Office (CBO) data released in 2011 showed the average real after-tax household income of the top one per cent of US income earners rising by 275 per cent between 1979 and 2007, while the income of the bottom 20 per cent rose by only 18 per cent.[34]

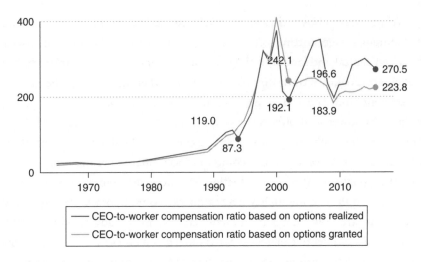

400

242.1

196.6

● 270.5

● 223.8

200

192.1

183.9

119.0

87.3

0

1970   1980   1990   2000   2010

——— CEO-to-worker compensation ratio based on options realized

——— CEO-to-worker compensation ratio based on options granted

Figure 4.3 CEO-to-worker compensation ratio, 1965–2016
(Source: Lawrence Mishel and Jessica Schieder, "CEO pay remains high relative to the pay of typical workers and high wage earners". Washington, DC: Economic Policy Institute, 20 July 2017).

The ratio of CEO pay to average wages in America's largest companies reached 270.5:1 in 2016[35] – many times higher than in the United States in the 1960s and 1970s (the ratio was 20:1 in 1965) and many times higher than in Germany, for example, even though Germany has the stronger manufacturing and trading economy. This uniquely American scale of inequality is the product of a staggering 997 per cent rise in inflation-adjusted CEO compensation between 1978 and 2014. That was "a rise [that was] almost double stock market growth and substantially greater than the painfully slow 10.9 per cent growth in a typical worker's annual compensation over the same period".[36] Greed on this scale leaves less in the salary fund for those lower down the corporate pecking order – and that includes the mass and generality of the American middle class. As the Pew Report on "The Squeezed Middle-Class" found: "fully 49 per cent of US aggregate income went to upper-income households in 2014, up from 29 per cent in 1970. The share accruing to middle-income households was 43 per cent in 2014, down substantially from 62 per cent in 1970".[37] But how could it be otherwise when "in the vast majority of US states, the top 1 per cent of earners captured at least half of the income gains during the first three years of the economic recovery" and "in seventeen states, the 1 per cent raked in *all* of the income growth".[38] And how could it be otherwise when, as incomes began to rise across the board (as they did in 2015), "the latest IRS data show that incomes for the bottom 99 per cent of families grew by 3.9 per cent over 2014 levels ... but incomes for those families in the top 1 per cent of earners grew even faster, by 7.7 per cent over the same period".[39]

The first result of this intensified and embedded income inequality has been that the United States now occupies an outlier position on "the Great Gatsby curve" showing the interplay of inequality and the intergenerational elasticity of income[40] – an outlier on intergenerational social mobility not because social mobility is greater and easier in modern America than in other leading industrial economies (those with more egalitarian distributions of economic rewards) but because these days American social mobility is, relative to them, lower and more difficult. The other result has been and remains, as we saw earlier, depleted levels of personal consumption, and associated reductions in rates of capital investment and economic growth – what Larry Summers and others have labelled "secular stagnation". A proper response to both these underlying weaknesses in the US model awaits us in the last chapter of this volume. All we need note now is that, although the American middle class is still a protected class – it remains a major beneficiary of America's hidden welfare state,[41] through the tax benefits that flow to it via mortgage tax relief and tax relief on healthcare premiums – those protections have not been sufficient to sustain its median living standard relative to the best of the rest abroad.

US upper middle-class living standards are still world beaters, but for those at the bottom of the American middle class (those in the 20 and 30 percentage bands of US income earners) standards have recently slipped badly in international terms. Far from being secure and prosperous, those occupying the bottom rungs of the American middle class now live, on a daily basis, just one personal financial crisis away from falling through the low-income trapdoor into the ranks of the American poor. It is this fear of downward social mobility, and despair at ever attaining the American Dream, that feeds support for right-wing populism of the kind captured so successfully by Donald Trump in 2016. It is a fear anchored in the reality of a receding American Dream for successive generations of Americans. Those born in 1940 had a 92 per cent chance of eventually earning more than their parents. The equivalent figure now for those born in 1980 is just 50 per cent.[42]

The persistence of widespread poverty

How much poverty exists in contemporary America is also – to a degree – a matter of definition. As late as 1963, the United States did not even possess an official measure of poverty. It took Michael Harrington's book, *The Other America: Poverty in the United States*, with its estimate of 50 million Americans living in penury, to trigger the US Government into action.[43] The result, as Lyndon Johnson announced his war on poverty in his first State of the Union Address, was the adoption of Mollie Orshansky's calculations of the minimum food budget for families of different sizes and her assumption that food bills made up about a third of a typical family budget.[44] The result was a measure of poverty as an absolute income number, varying by size of family. Later, in Europe, the official poverty level came to be set at 60 per cent of median income, and therefore went up as incomes rose: but not in the United States. Poverty in the United States remains measured the Orshansky way, with the figures varying by size of family and being adjusted year by year only in relation to inflation.

Needless to say, so crude a measure has its critics, many of which point out that as incomes rise, the proportion spent on food characteristically declines; that government programmes directing money to the poor are not counted by the Orshansky method; and that living costs (not least that of housing) vary enormously across the United States, making a one-size-fits-all definition all but meaningless. Even sterner critics, doubting the scale of poverty recorded and rarely being poor themselves, regularly point to the supposedly "affluent" life style of the contemporary American poor when compared either to poverty in America's past or to middle-class living standards in large parts of the still developing world.[45] And partly for all these reasons, the US does now have a supplemental poverty measure, issued by the Census Bureau annually since 2011 alongside the official figures – a supplemental measure that allows for regional variations in costs, for the impact of government policies on the incomes of poor households, the extra costs involved in taking a job and travelling to it, the impact of rising health costs, and the changing shape of the American family.

But measured in either the old way or the new, the same storyline comes over each time: that the US official rate of poverty was cut from its 1959 level of 22 per cent to 11.1 per cent by 1973 while the war on poverty was being seriously fought in the pre-Reagan years; but that since the war on poverty was abandoned by the Reagan Administration, the US poverty rate has largely stabilized at a higher percentage – anywhere between 13 and 15 per cent depending on the year, or at around one American in seven and around one American child in every five.* In 2014, "the nation's official poverty rate ... was 14.8 per cent, which means there were 46.7 million people in poverty". Using the supplemental measure, the rate was 15.3 per cent and the total was 48 million.[46] In 2015, things did improve slightly, as at long last the poverty rate dropped 1.2 percentage points, its largest one-year drop since 1999: primarily because – seven years out from the recession – the US economy did begin again to create a flow of new if low-paid jobs that enabled more of the unemployed to find work, and those caught in part-time employment slightly to increase their hours.

These are, sadly however, still world-class poverty figures: bigger by far than those in any other major industrialized economy. And yet even so, by focusing on the *scale* of poverty, the official count can help mask the *degree* of abject poverty in contemporary America – deep poverty measured by an income, before welfare benefits are factored in, of less than $2/person/day – a deep poverty that in 2011 affected 1.65 million US households containing 3.5 million children.[47] These "very poor" Americans made up half of the official poor in 2011 – some 20.5 million Americans in total – living on an annual income of "$5,570 or less for an individual and $11,157 for a family of four".[48] They were central to the five per cent of American households who in 2015 experienced "very low food security, meaning that the food intake of one or more household members was reduced and their eating patterns were disrupted at times during the year because the household lacked money and

---

* Using the European 60 per cent of median income definition of poverty, the proportion of American children living in poverty rises to one in every three – putting the US behind 35 other leading economies. The equivalent Norwegian figure, for example, would be one child in every twenty.

other resources for food". Overall in 2015, 12.7 per cent of American house-holds knew some degree of food insecurity at some point in the year, and 87.3 per cent did not.[49]

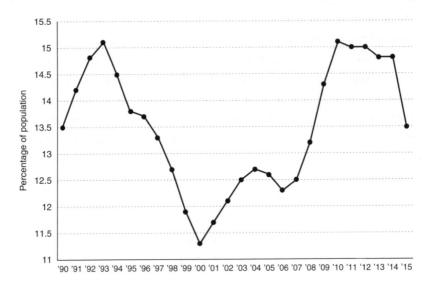

Figure 4.4 Poverty rate in the US, 1990–2015
(Source: US Census Bureau).

As overall totals, the official poverty figures mask two other things too. They mask the remarkable extent to which Americans move in and out of poverty, so underestimating the numbers of those who are regularly on the edge of poverty, threatened by poverty, or struggling daily just to avoid it. As data from the Census Bureau made clear in 2014, "a much larger subset of people slip in and out of poverty all the time. For instance, between 2009 and 2011, nearly one-third of the country – 31.6 per cent – fell below the official poverty line for at least two months. By contrast, only 3.5 per cent of the US population remained poor for the entire period".[50] Even before the finan-cial crisis, when only one American in eight was officially poor, the Center for American Progress reported that "one third of all Americans [would] expe-rience poverty within a 13-year period" and that "in that period, one in 10 Americans [were] poor most of the time, and one in 20 [were] poor for 10 or more years".[51] Likewise, the Economic Policy Institute calculated that a working family of four (two parents, two children) needed an income of over $48,000 in 2008 to meet standard family expenses (housing, food, medical bills, child care and other necessities), and that "over three times as many families fall below family budget thresholds as fall below the official poverty line", particularly "young families, families with a low degree of education, and minority families".[52] In 2008, the official poverty threshold for a working family of four was just $21,834.

The overall figures on US poverty also mask the different ways in which Americans currently become poor. It is not just that the US welfare net is thin and ungenerous, so that to be "on welfare" is to be poor, although (as we shall soon see) that is certainly the case. It is also that at least one-third of all Americans currently trapped in poverty are poor even though they work full-time for wages; and at the height of the recession caused by the financial crisis of 2008, that another one-third of the American poor were in poverty because they were involuntarily unemployed. There is thus no single arche-type for America's poor: "they are low-wage workers, single mothers, disabled veterans, the elderly, immigrants, marginalized factory workers, the severely mentally ill, the formerly incarcerated, the undereducated and the fallen middle class".[53] In that medley of poverty sources, the big three (apart from incarceration*) are low pay, job-loss and welfare dependency. These three currently combine in contemporary America to create a semi-permanent underclass of citizens locked in poor housing, facing poor public services, cut off from anything but poorly-rewarded employment, and so denied full access to the high-quality consumption lifestyles that, from outside the United States, are often understood to be available to the entirety of the US population.†

---

* The US prison population, at 2.3 million, is the world's largest; 11 million Americans cycle through jails and prisons each year, and a full 75 million Americans have a felony on their record and so are vulnerable to employers' background checking. "Men with criminal records account for about 34 per cent of all non-working men ages 25 to 54, according to a recent New York Times/CBS News/Kaiser Family Foundation report." (*New York Times*, 25 February 2015).

† The Hamilton Project found, for 2014, that 13 per cent of those living in poverty were in full-time employment, and that just over a quarter of the American poor were in work but unable to find full-time employment. Eighteen per cent – a third of the non-working poor – were disabled; 26 per cent – just under half of non-workers – were either care-givers or students, and 6 per cent were retirees.

Low pay – both its paucity and its volatility[54] – is a huge problem in contemporary America, and a major source of contemporary poverty. As Peter Edelman, the premier journalistic source for work on US poverty, recently put it: "we've been drowning in a flood of low-wage jobs for the last forty years".[55] Low-wage work – understood as full-time employment generating no more than twice the official poverty level for the relevant type of family – is now the condition for 103 million working Americans: "fully one-third of the population", that is, "has an income below what would be $36,000 for a family of three".[56] And the core working poor – those actually earning less than the official poverty level while being fully employed – rose by 1.4 million between 2007 and 2014, to grow beyond 10 million in total and to 6.9 per cent of all workers employed; as wage earners in the bottom 20 percentile of the US income distribution spent those seven years experiencing wage erosion in 45 states of the lower 48.[57] Poverty wages are a reality in industry after industry in contemporary America: in retail, in fast food production, in restaurants, in transport, in farming and among housekeepers and cleaners, to name but a few. When the Working Poor Families Project last surveyed the US economy as a whole – in 2013 – they found 10.65 million families on poverty wages, families that included almost three children out of every five in the United States.[58] This used to be a high-wage economy. It is not any more. On the contrary, and as we saw in Chapter 2, the United States now "leads the industrial world in the percentage of its jobs that are low-wage. Nearly 25 per cent of the workforce make less than two-thirds of the nation's median wage – ahead of Britain (where just 21 per cent hold such low-paying jobs), Germany (20 per cent) and Japan (15 per cent)".[59] Raising the federal minimum wage in the United States to just $12/hour would bring salary relief to a staggering 37.7 million Americans – to 27 per cent, that is, of the entire employed labour force.[60]

If low pay was, and remains, one main source of poverty in the contemporary United States, *involuntary unemployment* remains another. That source of poverty was particularly potent immediately after the financial crisis of 2008, when eight million jobs were lost in a two-year period (January 2008 to December 2009) and unemployment peaked at 15.6 million Americans. For so too did poverty, increasing by 2.6 percentage points between 2007 and 2010,[61] softened only by the extension of unemployment benefits beyond the traditional 12 weeks to a full year or even two. The big problem that the

long-term unemployed have is getting back into full-time work at all. That is
true in all recessions, but was particularly so in the recession that followed
the 2008 financial crisis. In 2010, 2011 and 2012, "the share of the unemployed who had been out of work for 6 months or more averaged more
than 40 per cent" and even as late as the spring of 2014, those out of work for
more than 28 weeks represented fully a third of all unemployed persons.[62]
The long-term unemployed this time were older and more African-American
even than the short-term unemployed, as involuntary unemployment locked
excluded workers into a poverty that was first based on unemployment insurance and then on food stamps and charity. For although Congress initially
extended unemployment insurance to up to an additional 13 to 20 weeks,
that emergency legislation from 2008 was allowed to run out in 2013 (and
at least nine states had simultaneously cut the maximum duration of unemployment insurance recipiency), so that at the end of 2014, the share
of unemployed workers receiving unemployment insurance had fallen to a
record low: to less than one unemployed worker in four.[63] There are conservative economists, of course, who argue that providing unemployment
insurance to the long-term unemployed only encourages them to remain jobless longer. But the bulk of the available evidence suggests otherwise: that
"workers won't magically find jobs if their unemployment insurance gets
cut".[64] What they will "magically find" is genuine poverty. Indeed, in 2014, the
Hamilton Project found that 27 per cent of those in poverty were working-age
adults unable to find full-time work.[65]

Being "*on welfare*" is the other great way of ensuring that you are, and will
remain poor, in contemporary America. You will *be* poor, because the welfare
payments are kept deliberately modest to ease the tax burden on the more
affluent, and to encourage recipients of welfare to seek gainful employment.
You will *remain* poor because the gainful employment available to you, if it is
available at all, will itself be low paid; and as you move towards it, not only will
your costs rise (for transport, clothing and, of course, childcare) but your benefits will be cut.[66] The American poor often find themselves in a classic welfare
trap, effectively paying a rate of tax (losing benefits as they begin to earn) that
is far higher than the rate of income tax that Republicans regularly cite as a
disincentive to enterprise by the more affluent. This conservative "welfare to
work" strategy, the one that was adopted by the Clinton Administration after

the signing of the Personal Responsibility and Work Reconciliation Act of 1996, is often claimed to have worked. Bill Clinton himself defended it as such in 2006, when the policy was a decade old.[67] But even the Clinton version of welfare-to-work did not lessen US poverty so much as move the poor around – off welfare-based poverty and into poverty wages – so that the poor remained with us even as the welfare rolls declined.

This is not to deny, however, the importance of that welfare safety net. It is only to bewail its inadequacy. For there is no doubting the fact that without it the level of poverty in the United States would be even higher, and by quite some margin. Earned Income Tax Credits, for example, lifted 6 million low-paid workers out of poverty in 2011. Those tax credits, when combined with child tax credits, took 2.9 percentage points off the 2013 poverty level, and 6.4 percentage points off the rate of child poverty.[68] Food stamps (SNAP) "kept nearly 5 million people out of poverty in 2012 alone, and without it, the child poverty rate would have been three percentage points higher".[69] Even Social Security – normally thought of in the US as simply a payment to retir-ees – acts additionally "as one of the federal government's largest antipoverty programs for children", with its payments to the surviving dependent of a parent or guardian who had died/been disabled actually directly helping 3.2 million children in 2014 and indirectly helping 3.2 million more – helping, that is, some 9 per cent of all American children in total.[70]

Temporary Assistance to Needy Families (the cornerstone of the 1996 reform) was and is less potent as a poverty-reducer. Indeed, it is a feature of the post-1996 US welfare net that straightforward cash payments to the poor have largely been squeezed out of the system. Leaving California and New York to one side – as the two states that do make such payments (nearly half of all TANF payments, 1.4 million of them, are concentrated in those two states alone) – the other 48 states dispense cash these days to just 1.7 million Americans in total. In 1996, 68 families out of every 100 in poverty got cash assistance. By 2016 that figure is down to just 23 per cent.[71] Certainly during the 2008–9 recession, while unemployment benefit spending rose by 139 per cent and food stamp spending by 29 per cent, spending in TANF programmes rose only 6.8 per cent.[72] So this is not an overly generous welfare net. It is one that helps the temporarily unemployed, and the low paid, more than it helps the long-term welfare-based poor, and its main vehicle for that latter task these days is SNAP (food stamps). The average monthly food allowance/participant under SNAP in 2014 was a miserable $125.35 – somewhere between $4 and $5 per person per day. Some welfare net!

Yet for all these limitations, a systematic and careful review of the impact of the full set of US welfare programmes concluded in 2011 that those programmes had "a major impact on poverty rates, reducing the percentage of the poor in 2004 from 29 per cent to 13.4 per cent, estimates which are robust to different measures of the poverty line"[73] – 50 million Americans in poverty rather than 90 million.[74] A parallel study using the supplemental poverty measure (SPM) – the one that includes the impact of welfare programmes – estimated for 2012 "the deep poverty rate (the share of the population with incomes below 50 per cent of the poverty threshold) under the SPM to be only 5.3 per cent, while if no transfers were included the deep poverty rate would be 19.2 per cent – over three times higher".[75] Overall, the welfare net lifted 40 million Americans across the admittedly very low official poverty thresholds in 2010 – "about half because of Social Security and half due to the other programmes".[76] By the end of 2010, indeed, nearly half of all Americans (48.6 per cent) lived in a household receiving one or more welfare benefits; with the generous state benefits (and associated higher taxation) in blue states (Democratic ones) and the less generous (and the lower taxes) in red states (Republican ones).[77] In the latter states in particular, conservatives like to claim that the welfare net reproduces poverty, with the implication that in its absence the poverty figures would go down. It is a measure of their flawed thinking, as well as of the flawed nature of the unregulated capitalism which they espouse, that the data run entirely otherwise. Without welfare payments, levels of poverty in the United States would likely be as high as nearly one American in three;[78] but with welfare of the kind now provided, that ratio continues to be stubbornly high. The level of poverty is high in the United States because the welfare safety net is thin, not because it is thick: but the level is lower than would be the case if that safety net was not there at all.

Two final thoughts on the state of poverty in contemporary America. The first is this: that the consequences of poverty – either based on low pay or on welfare dependency – are everywhere the same, and are strongly negative. There is now a life expectancy gap based on income in the United States, and it is a widening one. Comparing men born in 1930 to those born in 1960, the

National Academy of Sciences, Engineering and Medicine recently found a 7.1-year increase in life expectancy for the richest 20 per cent (to 88.8 years for those born in 1960) and a 0.5-year fall in life expectancy for the bottom 20 per cent (to 76.1 years). "The higher your income, the longer you live".[79] And before they die, the rich and the poor differ in the degree to which they experience food insecurity, mental stress, and exposure to depression and even to drugs. Currently, people living in poverty in the United States are twice as likely to be depressed as those who are not, perhaps in part because one household in seven was food insecure in the United States in 2014 – meaning that at some point in that year they lacked the resources to feed all their members.[80] Such households were also more likely (by a gap of 7.3 percentage points in the Alternative Healthy Eating index) to be surviving on foods with low nutritional value; and they are also likely to be paying more than more affluent Americans for the poor food they buy and the limited amounts of money they borrow. If they are working, they are even more likely to experience higher commuting costs than better paid workers.[81] Poverty is, in that sense, both entrenched and self-perpetuating in the contemporary United States. Breaking out of it, although possible, is extraordinarily difficult – particularly for the children of the poor – who find themselves the innocent victims of cycles of deprivation created for them by the adults with whom they live: cycles of deprivation created by the cumulative interplay of poor diet, inadequate schooling, lack of easy access to well-paying jobs when the school years are done, and social isolation in areas of intense material deprivation.[82]

The second final thought on the state of poverty in the United States is that it is intimately bound up with the issue of race: so bound up, in fact, that the racial dimension of America's contemporary social crisis now needs separate examination of its own.

The ubiquity of race in America

Middle-class insecurity, and the fear and experience of poverty, are to be found everywhere in contemporary America; but neither the insecurity nor the fear is evenly distributed either by region, or by generation, or by ethnic

group. On the contrary, wherever the US economy and society underper-
forms, you can be sure that your experience of that underperformance will be
greater, the more that your skin colour is non-white. America, as it grew over
time to economic and global greatness, always grew at the expense of its least
favoured citizens and non-citizens – and those least favoured ones were
invariably black, brown and red: much less often, white.

The data on this are very clear. It is widely conceded now that America's
slave past is and must remain a source of shame and regret – the only disagree-
ment there being whether that shame needs, even now, to be accompanied
by reparations. It is also widely conceded that ending slavery did not termi-
nate the racism that slavery initially created and then sustained. Formally
and officially now, after the civil rights campaigns of the 1960s, we are in a
"post-Jim Crow" period in American history. But the legacies of a century of
post-Civil War Jim Crow remain enormous, and indeed remain so potent that
the struggle is still on to defend something as basic as the right of African-
Americans to vote. The fact that the United States is "post-Jim Crow" means
that outright statements of a racist kind are now widely condemned; but quietly and ubiquitously, deep-seated white racism is alive and well in America.
Indeed, so alive and well is it that divisions of class are regularly overlaid with
divisions of colour, to the point at which the latter obscure the former over
and over again.

Take the unemployment data, for example. The recession that followed
the 2008 financial crisis drove the unemployment rate up for all sections of
the US labour force, as we saw: but the burden of increased unemployment
fell particularly heavily on African-American and Hispanic workers at the
bottom of the American income pile. Hispanic workers were burdened in part
because of their heavy involvement in the construction industry – 14 per cent
of all Hispanic workers were employed there in 2007, some 3 million people
in total. Black workers were disproportionately burdened because African-
American employment is skewed towards public sector jobs at both the federal and state level – roughly one in five black adults are so employed – leaving
the African-American community hit twice: first by the recession, and then
by the cutbacks in public spending that came with the austerity policies
insisted upon by Republican legislators in Washington, DC and in a string of
state capitals from 2012.[83] At least half a million public sector jobs were lost

129

between 2007 and 2014, and another million which might have been created in more normal times were not. As the economy then slowly recovered, and the construction industry with it, Hispanic Americans saw their employment rate return to 2007 levels by 2014: but the unemployment rate among African-Americans was much slower to follow suit. As late as the last quarter of 2015, white unemployment rates varied from 1.5 per cent in South Dakota to 6.7 per cent in West Virginia. Those for African Americans varied from 6.7 per cent in West Virginia to 13.1 per cent in Illinois. So even though, early in 2016, unemployment among African-American workers slipped under 10 per cent for the first time in a decade (the equivalent white rate being 4.7 per cent), it remained the case that even then "the *lowest* black unemployment rate in the country (West Virginia) [was] the same as the *highest* white unemployment rate (also West Virginia)".[84] For there is no escaping the fact that, in the US economy as it is presently constructed, "the black unemployment rate has been [consistently] twice as high as the white unemployment rate for 50 years"[85] or more – and in that sense, that black unemployment rates are always at levels that for white workers would be called a matter of crisis.

Nor is it simply a matter of the ethnic structuring of exposure to unemployment. Disparities remain equally entrenched in the spheres of income and wealth. In fact, in those spheres, prevailing trends are currently making an already marked disparity even worse. This was a disparity that was already moving against African-American families *before* the 2008 recession: "on all the major indicators – incomes, wages, employment, and poverty – African-Americans were worse off in 2007 than they were in 2000". The tight labour markets of the 1990s had "led to the largest decline in African-American poverty since the 1960s", but those gains were then reversed in the jobless recovery between 2002 and 2007 when "African-American median family income *fell* by $404 or 1%".[86] Come the 2008 crisis, the resulting recession and the only slow recovery, and the income data then deteriorated further. As of 2013, "42.2 per cent of Hispanic workers and 35.7 per cent of black workers, compared with less than one-fourth (22.5 per cent) of white workers, earned poverty-level wages";[87] in the process helping to create currently a nearly $28,000 gap in median income between white households ($71,300) and black households ($43,300).[88] "Among the 10.6 million low-income working families in America" in 2013, "racial/ethnic minorities constitute 58 per cent, despite only making up 40 per cent of all working families nationwide".[89] Indeed, it is a measure of the depth and embedded nature of racism in contemporary America that, for all the decades of civil rights agitation, "black–white wage gaps are larger today than they were in 1979".[90]

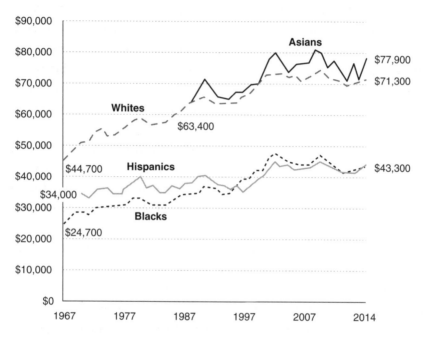

Figure 4.5 Racial gaps in household income persist
(Source: Pew Research Center, "Demographic Trends and Economic Well-Being", 27 June 2016, p. 4).

The Pew Report, "The American Middle Class is Losing Ground" cited earlier in this chapter did see, in the data it gathered, one spark of improvement in the pattern of ethnic inequality in modern America: namely the emergence, from the 1970s, of a slightly larger black middle class whose creation increased the proportion of black families in both the upper-income tier and the middle one. But even Pew was obliged to concede that "this progress notwithstanding, blacks are still significantly less likely than adults overall to be middle income or upper income".[91] And the earlier Pew Report on the distribution of wealth between different ethnic groups underscored that modesty of progress. For by 2011 the bursting of the housing bubble – the one that had triggered the 2008 financial crisis – had also helped widen the wealth gap between whites, blacks and Hispanics to record levels. Between 2005 and 2009, inflation-adjusted median wealth fell, by "66 per cent among Hispanic households and 53 per cent among black households, compared with just 16 per cent among white households:" to leave "the median wealth of white households ... 20 times that of black households and 18 times that of Hispanic households – lopsided wealth ratios [that were] the largest since the government began publishing such data a quarter century ago".[92] As things stand now, "the average black household will need 228 years to accumulate as much wealth as their white counterparts hold today. For the average Latino family, it will take 84 years".[93]

The housing crisis of 2006–7 fell particularly heavily on African-American middle-class families because so much of the very modest amounts of wealth accumulated by black families is invested in the houses they have struggled so hard to earn. The bursting of the housing bubble left 10 per cent of black middle-class families facing foreclosure by 2011 and 2012 (the figure for white middle-class families was just 7 per cent), and it wrecked the college-planning of so many black parents who saw their wealth (and indeed their credit-worthiness) dramatically reduced by falling house prices. And yet tragically, even in the wake of the destruction of so much black wealth in America, and the associated struggle of black parents to finance higher education for their children, it remains the case that so many of the young black Americans who do make it through college then still run into the silent wall of job discrimination. The unemployment rate among young black college graduates (age 24–29) was still 9.4 per cent in May 2016. The equivalent rate among black high-school graduates was then 28.4 per cent – in both cases, rates that were far higher than their white equivalents.[94] Those same black college graduates also run into a wall of debt, and again a wall steeper for them to climb than that facing their white counterparts. In fact, "the moment they earn their bachelor's degree, black college graduates owe $7,400 more on average than their white peers ($23,400 versus $16,000 ...) but over the next few years, the black-white disparity triples to a whopping $25,000"[95] due to differential interest accrual and graduate school borrowing.

So being black and middle class is tough in contemporary America: being black and poor is even worse. The black poor were the greatest beneficiaries of the war on poverty in the 1960s – but then that was only to be expected, since poverty rates amongst black Americans have long been so much higher than among whites. "Black poverty fell quickly between 1959 and 1969, from 55.1 per cent to 32.3 per cent, but after that the drop was slower and more uneven".[96] By 2013 the poverty rate for the United States as a whole was 14.3 per cent but for African-Americans it was still 25.8 per cent (only native-Americans and Alaskan natives, at 27 per cent, had a higher rate of poverty that year). For as the war on poverty was replaced by the philosophy of welfare-to-work, deepening residential segregation – so-called "white flight" – reduced the number of mixed income neighbourhoods,[97] effectively terminated the move towards desegregated schools,[98] and increased the growth and spread of extreme-poverty neighbourhoods.[99] The resulting heavy concentration of the American poor in large metropolitan areas then compounded the difficulties of leaving poverty behind, by exposing more and more African-American and Hispanic Americans to what, in 2016, Brookings researchers labelled as the five interlocking evils that give poverty in contemporary America such a multidimensional face: "low household incomes, limited education (less than a high-school degree), lack of health insurance, low income area, and household unemployment". In 2014, "more than 3 million black and 5 million Hispanic adults suffer[ed] from at least three of these disadvantages",[100] with poor Hispanic Americans disproportionately likely to suffer from limited education and black Americans from unemployment.

It is at the bottom of the US class structure that race, income, housing, and education all come together in a daunting mixture of interlocking deprivations. Poor African-Americans, and poor Hispanic Americans, experience the highest level of spatial concentration and social segregation of any group of the American poor – isolated from their more affluent counterparts by being trapped in poor sections of towns and cities: sections that lack adequate social capital or the tax base to create it (so poor schools, run-down housing and inadequate transport networks) and sections from which white flight has removed well-paying jobs and the consumer economy that good jobs alone sustain. Add to that the resulting unemployment, particularly of young men, and the "black" economy that comes in to fill that space (an economy of drugs, petty-crime and prostitution). Mix into the cocktail too both a federally-funded and extensive war on drugs that we now know was initially designed specifically to weaken urban black radicalism,[101] and a criminal justice system with a long and deplorable record of racial discrimination – and the result is the new Jim Crow: "more African-American adults under correctional control today – in prison or jail, on probation or parole – than were enslaved in 1850, a decade before the Civil War began".[102] The US now possesses a system of mass incarceration that has over 2 million inmates, having quadrupled in size since 1980 to currently lock-up nearly one adult American in every hundred. It is a system of mass incarceration that – among its other crimes – now takes one of every nine African-American men between the ages of 20 and 34 out of the ghetto and into the largest prison system in the non-communist world,[103] and in consequence leaves one in nine black children with a parent in or newly out of prison.[104]

It is this extraction of young black men from civic life in the United States that makes a mockery of conservative claims that if only young black women would marry, they would avoid poverty. Because it is an extraction that, on the contrary, locks those women ever deeper into that poverty, as they are left alone to rear their children and organize their housing in urban communities denuded of adequate employment, childcare, and schooling of quality: and trapped in urban communities with a higher rate of male absenteeism (and therefore male role models for their sons) than the United States as a whole had between 1941 and 1945 when it had sent its young men away to fight fascism and racism abroad. "1.5 million missing black men" was how *The New York Times* labelled its 2015 discovery that early death and long prison sentences is now denuding African-American communities of one in six African-American men aged 24 to 54, and leaving a gender ratio there of just 83 men per 100 black women – the gender ratio for white men and women being broadly at parity.[105] As Michelle Alexander recently noted, "a black child born today is less likely to be raised by both parents than a black child born into slavery ... due in large part to the mass imprisonment of black fathers".[106]* The latest consequence of this state-induced destruction of the African-American family to capture national attention, has been the rate of eviction from their homes of single African-American mothers unable to pay their

---

* "Across the United States, [those same] black infants die at a rate that's more than twice as high as that of white infants." (Zoe Carpenter, "Black Births Matter," *The Nation*, 6 March 2017).

rent. As Matthew Desmond's *Evicted* leaves us in no doubt, in a city like Milwaukee with less than 105,000 renter households, "16,000 adults and children were being evicted every year ... especially ... in black neighbourhoods, where female renters were nine times as likely to be forced from their homes as women in poor white neighbourhoods".[107] "Poor black men were locked up," Desmond wrote, and "poor black women were locked out".*

Gender inequality and work–life balance

So being black and being female in the contemporary United States is to carry two heavy but distinguishable social burdens; and to be poor is additionally to carry a third. Which of those burdens is the heaviest, and most determining of both health and happiness, remains a matter of huge controversy – in both the academic community and the public square – but one thing at least is clear. It is that whether you are poor or rich, white or black, being a woman in modern America invariably restricts and diminishes the life-chances that you will enjoy, relative to those enjoyed by men of a similar social class and ethnic background. America may be the land of the free, but in practice male freedom and female freedom are still very different things.

There is nothing new about gender inequality, of course. It is as American as apple pie. Women did not even get the vote in America until 1919. But unlike apple pie, gender inequality has lately been challenged as un-American by what are now two generations of mobilized social campaigners – by the

---

* This also. "The irony is that the scourge of eviction is a function of inequality. As Desmond notes, in 2008, [the year of the evictions he studied] tax benefits for middle-class and affluent homeowners exceeded $171 billion. This figure dwarfs the $22.5 billion that he estimates would be needed to give every poor renter in the country a housing voucher." (Press). As *The Washington Post* put it: "the geography that we live today – where poverty clusters alongside poverty, while the better-off live in entirely different school districts – is in large part a product of deliberate policies and government investments. The creation of the Interstate highway system enabled white flight. The federal mortgage interest deduction subsidized middle-income families buying homes there. For three decades, the Federal Housing Administration had separate underwriting standards for mortgages in all-white areas and all-black ones, institutionalizing the practice of "redlining." That policy ended in the 1960s, but the patterns it reinforced didn't end with it. "Exclusionary zoning" to this day prevents the construction of modest or more affordable housing in many communities." (14 April 2014).

first wave of modern feminism in the 1970s, and by the children of those campaigners three/four decades later. That recent challenge remains a particularly important one because in relation to gender, as in relation to both class and race, embedded social inequalities remain. The feminist upsurge of the 1970s made blatant gender discrimination illegal in the United States, left blatant sexism socially unacceptable, and ate away at various kinds of glass ceilings blocking female advancement – that much progress is now a matter of record – but as the campaign rhetoric of Donald Trump made only too clear, systemic sexism is still alive and well in America, generating as it does so social problems that need urgently to be both recognized and addressed.

Gender inequality is particularly evident in the world of paid work, even though in the United States, as in most other advanced industrial economies, the last seventy years has seen a remarkable transformation in the social role and position of women. The US, like the UK, came out of the Second World War consciously reconstituting the "male breadwinner model" as the normal relationship between the world of work and that of home. Single women, ethnic minority women, and women without children, were still members of the paid labour force, as they had been before the war – almost always in subordinate positions and invariably concentrated in highly segregated occupations close in character to the domestic roles played by married women. But after 1945, married women (particularly white middle-class women with children) were encouraged to retreat from war work and remain at home, and as such to become entirely dependent on the wages brought back to them from the public world of work by the men to whom they were married. The associated changes in the welfare systems that also accompanied immediate postwar reconstruction – not least the expansion of secondary and higher education – then helped eventually to erode that male-dominated model: incrementally in the 1950s and 1960s, then more rapidly thereafter; so that by the turn of the century a full 50 per cent of the US paid labour force was female, and most married women with children returned to paid work at some stage in their children's early years. That return then made a significant contribution to overall US economic growth and prosperity. CAP economists estimated in 2014 that "between 1979 and 2012, the increase in hours worked by women accounted for 11 per cent of the growth in GDP", and that without that extra work "families would have spent at least $1.7 trillion less on goods and services a year – roughly equivalent to the combined US spending on Social Security, Medicare and Medicaid in 2012".[108]

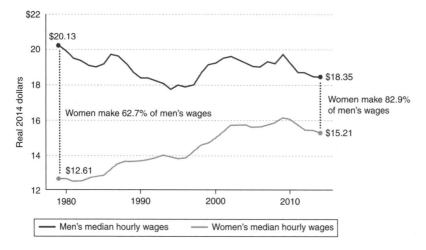

Figure 4.6 The gender gap persists, but has narrowed since 1979 (Source: Alyssa Davis and Elise Gould, "Closing the Pay Gap and Beyond". Washington, DC: Economic Policy Institute, Briefing Paper #412, 18 November 2015, p. 5).

Even now, however, the legacies of sexism and patriarchy remain as potent barriers to the full and equal participation of American women in the labour force of an increasingly deindustrialized America. Responsibility for childcare and unpaid domestic work still remain predominantly theirs, eased as a burden only by the slight increase in male participation in the traditionally female side of domestic life – childcare, cooking, cleaning and the care of the old.[109] Technological changes and the greater commodification of household tasks have also helped. The contraceptive pill, the fridge and the automated washing machine must stand as three of the great triggers to female advancement in the modern period; but not even that trinity has removed fully the double-burden (of unpaid and paid work) now carried by most working women, nor brought women's pay up to that of the men with whom most of them still cohabit. The excessive concentration of women in low-paid service and public sector employment, the breaks in their career path occasioned by childbirth, their resulting preference for part-time work compatible with school calendars, and residual male attitudes of superiority and resistance to role-sharing, all combine to leave most women in contemporary America still earning just 80 cents on the male dollar and still systematically underrepresented in senior positions across the bulk of the corporate world.[110]

The interplay of gender and pay in the modern period is a complex one, made more complicated still in the United States by the overlay on both gender and pay of race, education and age. So, for example, although "women consistently make less money than men of their race ... white and Asian women" in contemporary America still "out-earn black and Hispanic men".[111] Moreover, while in 29 of 73 major college subjects recently analyzed, young white female graduates actually slightly out-earned their white male equivalents, in all 73 subjects taken together female graduates nearly achieved parity: 97 cents on the male dollar during their twenties. But the same research data also showed that this parity does not last: for college graduates by mid-career the pay gap is back to 85 cents on the dollar,[112] and for all women (including non-college educated ones) the gap is wider still. In contemporary America, women earn less than men in all but five low-status occupations,* and the gaps are greatest for women of colour. In 2014, "Hispanic and African-American women working full time earned just 55 cents and 60 cents respectively, for every dollar earned by white, non-Hispanic men".[113] And it is a gender wage gap that persists *within* all racial and ethnic groups. Again taking 2014 as our data point, Asian women earned 81 cents for every dollar earned by Asian men, African-American women earned 82 cents for every dollar earned by black men, Hispanic 88 cents, and white non-Hispanic women 75 cents, on their equivalent male workers. Indeed, the older a woman is, the greater the gender pay gap she is likely to experience; and that expanding gap cannot be fully explained by her job choice or by her decision to pull out of paid-work for a while to have children (there is a substantial cost there: "women's earnings are reduced by about 7 per cent per child"). The Center for American Progress recently estimated that "38 per cent of the [gender pay] gap is unexplainable by measurable factors" such as these, and that accordingly "gender-based pay discrimination is still a

---

* Wholesale and retail buyers (except farm products); police and sheriff's patrol officers; bookkeeping, accounting and auditing clerks; general office clerks; and data entry keepers.

significant cause of the discrepancy in pay between men and women" in contemporary America. It is a discrepancy that over a 40-year career costs women on average $430,000, and costs women of colour even more – over $1 million in the case of Latinas.[114]

If women in the United States do still retain the edge on their men in any one key aspect of the contemporary income distribution, it is their disproportionate exposure to poverty and to low pay. The much-discussed transformation of the traditional American family[115] is now at least two generations old, and one of its most striking features is the increase in out-of-wedlock births from one child in 20 in 1970 to one child in three today. So it is not simply the case that by 2012, 63.3 per cent of American mothers were the sole, primary or co-breadwinners for their households.[116] It is also that there are now more single women than married women in the United States, that there are at least 12 million families (containing over 17 million children) that survive with only one breadwinner and care-giver, and that 80 per cent of those single-breadwinner families are headed by a woman.[117] It is also that race factors in here too – and does so in a significant way. Today, as Valerie Wilson has recently reported, "more than two-thirds of all African-American working mothers are single moms, making them the primary, if not sole, economic providers for their families. By comparison, 29.6 per cent of white working mothers and 47.9 per cent of Hispanic working mothers are single".[118]

It is not that the act of marriage *per se* is the best defense against poverty in modern America. It is rather that families protect themselves best against poverty by having two full-time income earners living together, married or otherwise. For 2012, two in every five of those female-headed single-breadwinner families in the United States were living below the poverty line, with half of those families living in extreme poverty (with incomes below half the federal poverty level),[119] as single women with children in contemporary America continued to be disproportionately exposed to low pay, and disproportionately dependent on welfare support at the very moment when that support has been eroded away under the welfare-to-work regimes put in place since 1996. And even the single/married mothers who avoid that level of welfare dependency have still found themselves on a wage/salary trajectory lower than the one they were on before childbirth, and at the end of their working lives less well positioned to live well on an adequate pension. The latest pension data suggests that currently older women in America "live on just three-quarters of the retirement income of men" and that "as a result are 80 per cent more likely to be impoverished than men". Women over eighty are even more vulnerable to poverty. For them, the median income gap has recently widened to 70 per cent.[120]

Finally in this section, this: if greater exposure to poverty in their child-bearing years, and then again in old age, is still the lot of far too many lower-class American women, their more prosperous contemporaries face other burdens as well. Two burdens in particular are of great contemporary relevance: the absence of adequate public support for their balancing of work and life – the balancing of their responsibilities as paid workers with those linked to their unpaid roles as parents, and (often) as care-givers to their aging relatives as well – and their growing inability to combine saving for their own retirement with the costs of higher education that kick in for middle-class American families as their children graduate from high school.

The United States is the only major industrial economy that does not have a nationally mandated and funded paid-maternity leave, let alone paid leave for the fathers of the children concerned.* The United States is also an outlier on legislation to allow flexible working and job security while pregnant. "Nearly 40 million American workers – 39 per cent of all employees – still lack access to a single paid sick-day", and "workers with young children or elder care responsibilities are no more likely to have access to paid leave than comparable workers without the same family obligations".[121] The United States is an outlier in the other direction too, in that American workers (lacking a strong trade union base) are currently disproportionately exposed to irregular scheduling at work that makes the planning of childcare so difficult,[122] and exposed to childcare in the United States that is – by the standards of the best of the rest abroad (in this case, Scandinavia) – woefully underfunded and inadequately supervised.

Good quality American childcare is, in consequence, hard to find, patchy

---

* At the state level, only California, New Jersey and Rhode Island currently have fully-implemented family leave policies. New York's new legislation is scheduled to begin in 2018, and now at least 23 cities and five states have statutes on the books that give some rights to paid sick leave.

in availability, and extremely expensive when available. The White House Task Force on the Middle Class reported in 2010 that "since 2000, child-care costs have grown significantly faster than inflation and twice as fast as the median household income". It found that those costs still varied by state, but that in 2010, 126 million Americans lived in states where the annual cost of childcare exceeded $10,000. It also found that in every state of the union "monthly child-care fees for two children at any age [were] higher than the median cost of rent".[123] The resulting cross-pressures created by the necessity, yet difficulty, of combining paid work with high-quality childrearing is now acute across the entire millennial generation; but this being America, it is particularly acute for black families which, relative to their white counterparts, "work more, earn less, and face difficult childcare choices".[124] It is, after all, women of colour who provide the highest number of female breadwinners, the highest number of single-parent families, and yet are less equipped than white families with the income (and access to support) vital to the creation of an adequate work–life balance.

Given the costs of childcare* even where it is available, it is hardly surprising that the Center for American Progress felt obliged to report in 2015 that many US families – and particularly the women within them – were having to choose "between spending a sizeable portion of their paycheck on child care, finding less expensive – and possibly lower quality – unregulated childcare, or leaving the workforce to become a full-time caregiver".[125] (And not just to children too, but to be care-givers to elderly relatives also, as the cost of long-term care for the old continues to soar.) Nor is it surprising that the burdens of that choice still fall most heavily on families with the lowest of incomes – "families living below the poverty line who pay for childcare spend an average of 36 per cent of their annual income on childcare"[126] – or that the rate of labour market participation by American women, a rate that as late as 1990 was the sixth highest in the OECD, had by 2010 fallen back in rank to seventeenth out of the OECD top 22.[127] Pulling those two themes together

---

*   "At nearly $18,000 per year, the average cost of centre-based care for an infant and a pre-schooler amounts to 29 per cent of the median family income. Analysis by the US Bureau of the Census shows that the average weekly cost of childcare for families with employed mothers is about 30 per cent higher than it was 15 years ago." (Center for American Progress, "Child Care Deserts". Washington, DC, 27 October 2016).

– high childcare costs and low family income – CAP recently estimated that "in 2016 alone, nearly 2 million parents of children age 5 and younger had to quit a job, not take a job, or greatly change their job because of problems with childcare".[128]

When in November 2015, Pew researchers explored stress levels among two-parent households in which both parents work full-time (which is currently nearly half of all such households) they found that "for many mothers who work full-time, feeling rushed is an almost constant reality" and that "among all working parents with children under age 18, more than half (56%) say it is difficult to balance the responsibilities of their job with responsibilities of the family".[129] And of course they do, for America has a hidden and submerged childcare crisis of a significant scale, one that is only now beginning to become an electoral issue even though it is currently lived every day as a source of pressure on hardworking and financially-pressed parents – a daily source of stress for young adult men and women trying to make ends meet while striking a proper balance between their duties at work and their responsibilities at home.

Then add this – a uniquely American addition to the costs of family life and to the daily pressures associated with it for both slightly older and slightly younger Americans – the exploding costs of higher education in the United States and the linked growth in the volume of student debt. That debt now exceeds in scale the credit card debt carried by the students and their parents, and is the one major new addition to family expenditures experienced by American families in the second half of their typically 20–40-year period of childrearing responsibilities. For as the cost of college continued to rise faster than the general rate of inflation, in the context of broadly stagnant wages for a generation, total student debt in the United States rose to fill the gap. Total student debt in America exceeded $1 trillion for the first time in 2012 (it reached $1.5 trillion by April 2017), with the average student leaving college then owing $25,000 in unpaid bills and with one in ten owing more than twice that amount.[130] The rate of debt default among students in the United States, at over 11 per cent, is now running three times higher than the rate of default on mortgages; in a federally-regulated debt-system in which student debt is the only debt that cannot be removed by bankruptcy and under which "the average monthly payment for borrowers in their 20s is

$351. If you're making minimum wage, that's 48 hours of work for your loans alone".[131] Since the bulk of both the debt and the default is currently falling on the shoulders of Americans under 40, this particular indebtedness is having a seriously negative effect on the ability of an entire generation to buy homes and to begin families.* So, this too will need to be factored in as a major issue when, at the end of this volume, we take a full stock-taking of our contemporary condition and of the routes to its adequate resolution. Student debt is not the only burden carried by many contemporary American families, but it is a very real and very recent one nonetheless.

The crisis of the American family

Taken together, this chapter's review of middle-class stress, of embedded poverty, and of entrenched discrimination by both ethnicity and gender, paints a very bleak picture of modern American society. Both its tone and content certainly run counter to the social optimism invariably associated with claims about American exceptionalism and the potency of the American Dream. It also runs counter to histories and analyses of recent social change that prioritize progressive developments, of which of course there have been many. Gender divisions may remain, but blatant sexism is now widely criticized across the entirety of the United States. Racial divisions and tensions still run deep, but the original Jim Crow is over and multicultural demographic change in contemporary America is now both rapid and irreversible. Poverty and stagnant wages still constrain the life chances of all but a few privileged Americans, but the absolute standard of living of the vast-majority of contemporary Americans is now so much greater than it was a generation ago. That progress is not being denied here. On the contrary, such positive changes need to be recognized, celebrated, and then defended, for

---

* But not only on their shoulders. The fastest growing group of student-loan defaulters are actually defaulters over the age of 60: a trend that "not only reflects borrowers carrying student debt later into life, but also the increasing number of older consumers that have borrowed or co-signed student loans for the children and grandchildren. A recent government report found that an increasing number of older Americans ... have been subject to offsets of their Social Security benefits in-order-to repay this debt." (http://cardtrack.com/wp-content/uploads/2017/01).

social trends can be reversed if the forces driving them are systematically reconfigured. And that is the argument here: that such a reversal is possible; that because of its flawed economy, America is now at a social as well as at an economic tipping point – one at which public policies on a long set of social issues are likely to be fundamentally reconfigured. And because we are at such a tipping point, that the question which now looms in the United States is primarily one of "reconfigured in which direction?"

There is a very real danger – as the Administration of Barack Obama fades into memory, replaced in power by that of Donald J. Trump – that the crisis of the family will be resolved in the American case in a conservative rather than a progressive manner (unless the American Democratic Left takes that crisis on board and responds to it in its totality) because of two features of that crisis that are uniquely American. Not every dimension of this crisis is unique in that fashion – and the features that are shared with families elsewhere in the advanced capitalist world, including families in the UK, will be added next. But what needs to be recognized here, before turning to those UK parallels, are the dimensions of the growing American social crisis that are specific to the United States. Those specificities include, at the very least, unique American community divisions and unique American cultural concerns.

The very fact that America is a composite nation – one consciously created by welcoming waves of immigrants – means that the growing economic pressures experienced by American families are invariably understood by those families as falling on them as members of ethnically distinct communities. The large degree of cross-community marriage down the years means that, particularly for Caucasian Americans, their family lineage is often a complex one, taking several minutes to explain ("Italian and Greek on my father's side, Irish and Polish on my mother's", and so on). But that mixing rarely stretches across the oldest of America's racial divisions – that between African-Americans and the rest – or between mainstream America and the latest wave of immigrants from south of the Rio Grande.* Instead, powerful

---

* "6.3% of all marriages were between spouses of different races in 2013, up from less than 1% in 1970. Some racial groups are more likely to intermarry than others. Of the 3.6 million adults who got married in 2013, 58% of American Indians, 28% of Asians, 19% of blacks and 7% of whites have a spouse whose race was different from their own." (Pew Research, 12 June 2015).

divisions of interest and self-definition often set these groups of Americans apart from each other, and create a space for a politics of ethnic animosity. Add to that the rapid demographic shifts now occurring in contemporary America – shifts that for the first time will leave white Americans as a minority population within the American mosaic by 2050 – and sprinkle on top economic insecurity and financial pressure; and the result is a political mixture almost perfectly designed for the return of white insecurity-based nativism, "know-nothingism" and intensified racism. The 2016 Trump presidential campaign exposed those tensions in a way that no other recent presidential campaign had ever done, but Donald Trump did not create these divisions. He simply gave them a voice and a legitimacy they had hitherto lacked.

Before Trump, the growing insecurity of white America had found expression elsewhere, as indeed it still does, through at least two other uniquely American phenomena, both of which will need to be fed into the final analytical mix. One route was and is through the whole issue of guns and gun rights in America. The other was and is through the recent political impact of white Evangelical Protestantism.

There is a very strong libertarian streak in conservative political culture in the United States, one that is largely absent from conservative political thought in other major industrial capitalisms. It is a libertarianism that prefers states' rights over federal ones, and individual rights over both; and it is a strand of conservative thought that is particularly resistant to any attempt (at either state or federal level) to restrict the right of the individual to bear arms. For guaranteed, as they are, the right to bear arms by the Second Amendment to the US constitution, contemporary Americans have chosen to bear those arms in phenomenal numbers. There are currently nearly 300 million firearms in private hands in the United States, and many of those firearms are particularly lethal ones. They include military-style assault weapons and semi-automatic assault rifles, as well as a plethora of smaller handguns that states often allow people to carry concealed into many public places (and even these days to carry openly in a growing set of public spaces). Not all Americans own or carry guns, of course. In fact, a majority of Americans do not; and indeed, the number of Americans with licensed firearms actually fell during the first Obama presidential term. But those who do own guns tend to own many of them, and they actually increased the total volume of gun sales during that same first term, inspired to do so by the nonsensical claim, from leading gun advocates, that the Obama Administration was set on eroding their Second Amendment rights.

For any attempt to lessen social tension by restricting access to the more lethal of the extensive weaponry currently available to private gun owners now generates a fierce political backlash – one that is currently orchestrated so well by the powerful gun lobby in Washington that no conservative politician (and only a few liberal ones) will propose even minor restrictions on gun use – and when they do, even those modest proposals fail. The vast majority of Americans (including the vast majority of gun owners) remain in favour of greater gun control; but the political class is immobilized on this issue, as on so many others, by the stridency of the minority who oppose reform. Which means that when American society faces real community tensions (as it does now), and when individual American families deal with increased levels of stress (as so many do now), the extra dimension of potential or real violence stalks their struggles. Americans kill each other – for personal and social reasons – on a scale and with a regularity unknown elsewhere in the advanced capitalist world: currently 30,000+ gun deaths a year (including the accidental killing of 214 children in 2016[132]), plus 80,000 gun-related injuries – the vast majority of which are the product of domestic disputes and petty crime, and not of terrorism either domestic or foreign.[133] The threat and reality of random violence and death is a dimension of the social problem on this side of the Atlantic that is still fortunately missing from the equivalent social problems in the UK; and it is not an American export that any society should voluntarily copy.

Then there is the small matter of religion. Although the American constitution is clear on the separation of church and state, and though several of the Founding Fathers were at most deists, the America that their constitution created was not a secular one. Nor did the formal separation of church and state enshrined in that constitution later prevent a generalized Christian religiosity being constructed around public institutions and ceremonies in the United States. In consequence, religion – and especially the varying forms of the Christian religion – still matters to many Americans in ways it once did to people in Western Europe, but now largely does not; and American churches have their own politics. For our purposes here, the important thing to note is the way in which, over the last four decades, the politics of many evangelical Protestant churches have changed, particularly in the American South and West. There, white evangelical Protestants have become a major force for social conservatism, standing out strongly against new forms of marriage, against abortion in all its forms, and against extensive provision of welfare services to the "undeserving poor". Not all of this is uniquely American, however. British readers of a certain age may well remember how unease with the erosion of traditional gender roles, and with new hedonistic cultures focused on the young, led many older and more conservative British voters to enthusiastically support Margaret Thatcher in the 1980s. Well, they and their concerns had their parallels in the United States in that same decade, in the increasing fusion of Protestant evangelicals with the socially conservative wing of the Republican Party. So that when we then move forward a generation, mix in a dash of libertarianism, put a black president in the White House, and see undocumented immigration grow and overseas military involvements bring individual acts of terror back home, the ultimate ultra-right-wing American cocktail comes clearly into place. It is one of "God-inspired" opposition to a whole swathe of liberal and progressive proposals from immigration reform and the Affordable Care Act to gay marriage and a woman's right to choose – opposition that replaced a progressive Democrat in the White House in 2016 with a narcissistic misogynist prone to bigotry. Which is why, when we are examining later how to create a progressive coalition for change in America, we will need to remember that America already has its conservative, Tea Party, equivalent – one that will be even more energized by any attempt on the Democratic Left to use public policy for socially progressive purposes.

Tea Party America is, however, still a minority voice in the contemporary United States. Tea Party Republicans are vocal, and they are mobilized. But they are also outnumbered by the current majority of Americans who actually favour the use of government policy for socially progressive ends.[134] That progressive support grows as we drop down the generations – it is weakest amongst the old, strongest among the young. And that should not entirely surprise us, because there is more in play in the social crisis of contemporary America than merely class, race, and gender – powerful as all those are, as determinants of life chances in the land of the free and the home of the brave.

147

There is also *age*. For as we began to see when touching on student debt, the heaviest of the burdens currently generated by a flawed American capitalism are now being borne by the millennial generation. It is millennials who now demonstrate an increased propensity to return to live with their parents after graduating from college, and (where they can) to depend on them financially well into their late-20s.[135] It is millennials who are struggling to find affordable accommodation as renters, and who feel increasingly shut out from the possibility of home-ownership. It is millennials who are struggling to break free of low and stagnant wages,[136] and who are in consequence pushing marriage, childbirth, and owner-occupancy back later and later into their 30s.[137] America may be exceptional in its gun culture and in its relationship to the Almighty, but it is entirely in lock-step with the United Kingdom in its depleted treatment of its young adults (regardless of their class or colour). There are still differences, of course – until recently, student loans were a bigger problem in the United States than in the United Kingdom, and the housing crisis is currently even deeper in the UK than in America[138] – but there is significant convergence on both those fronts and on others, as we shall now see as we turn to examine the social consequences of a similarly flawed capitalism on the other side of the Atlantic Ocean.

5

The Slow Disintegration of the UK's Postwar Settlement

"People are fed up. They are fed up with not being able to get somewhere to live, they are fed up with waiting for hospital appointments, they are fed up with zero-hour contracts, they are fed up with low pay, they are fed up with debt, they are fed up with not being able to get on with their lives because of a system that's rigged against them."

Jeremy Corbyn[1]

"My generation has not served its children well".

Will Hutton[2]

Modern economies can be very similar in their basic principles of organization and in their associated strengths and weaknesses, and still sustain very different kinds of societies. Economies have their logics, but societies also have their histories. The logics may be similar but the histories can be different – and in the US and UK cases they most definitely are. They are different in the ways in which the two societies were originally constructed and have developed over time. They are also different in the ways in which they now struggle to cope with the common set of economic problems released upon them by the shared nature of their flawed capitalisms. This overlap of the similar and the different is what allows so rich a cultural exchange between the two societies, with the similarities facilitating the exchange and the differences making the exchange perennially fascinating. Americans play baseball. The English play cricket. Nothing could be more different than that; and yet each sport carries the marks of a shared experience of imperialism. American baseball calls its end-of-season play-offs "The World Series", although only North American teams are permitted to participate.[3] The Japanese and the Cubans play baseball too – a legacy of previous decades of American dominance – but they are not invited. The English now regularly lose at cricket to teams from countries that only play the game because once they were British colonies. In the heyday of empire and as late as the early-1950s, the English always won at cricket, unless playing teams from the white dominions; but as this is being drafted, the national test team just lost a series of five-day games 4-0 to the Indians. Only an empire could sustain a game that lasted five days – the colonial masters had to find something to do while away their time – but only an empire long gone could regularly lose its defining game to former colonists of all colours, as is the English practice now.

Jeremy Paxman, when writing of "The English" in the 1990s, spoke of "living all his life in the England which emerged from the shadow of Hitler", and of having "to confess an admiration for the place as it seemed to be then, despite its small-mindedness, hypocrisy and prejudice".[4] We are of a similar age, he and I: and I too remember growing up in the 1950s in a society with very low levels of consumption – one that had only recently left war-time rationing behind, one that was just beginning to absorb the television age, and one that still took an annual weekly vacation to the local town on the seashore. It was a society in which most married women with children stayed home to rear them – washing on Mondays and ironing on Tuesdays, their clothes drying on a nation of outdoor clothes-lines whenever the British weather allowed. It was a society that was still predominantly white, and one that was profoundly insular. It was a society that was slow – and in the early 1950s reluctant indeed – to shed the habits and attitudes that had bound people together during the years of war, including those of deference to individuals of a higher social class; but those habits and attitudes did slowly begin to change, and for good reason. After all, the major domestic legacy of that war, as we saw earlier, was the creation of a universal welfare state that had not existed before or during the Second World War, and a guarantee of full employment for the soldiers returning from war that had been entirely absent during the Great Depression. It was that Keynesian-based welfarism which then slowly raised living standards for the wartime generation itself – changing attitudes as it did so – and from the 1960s sustained a new generation of better-educated, better-fed and better-resourced Britons who remain with us now as the ageing baby-boomers.

They, and in their turn their children, then lived through an ongoing set of interlinked but quiet economic and social revolutions. They experienced the unexpected economic upheavals of the 1970s, witnessed the Thatcher revolution that pulled the British state back from the direct ownership of core industries, and participated in the debt-based consumer explosion that eventually followed. They saw the economy move from one based on manufacturing to one based on services. They saw the rise and fall of UK trade union power, and the eventual re-entry into paid work of more-and-more married women with children. They saw successive waves of immigration, initially from Britain's former colonies, but more recently from an expanded European Union and a traumatized Middle East. And they saw the emergence – just before the unexpected financial crisis that started in September 2007 with the failure of the English equivalent of Bear Stearns, Northern Rock – of what we described in 2005 as "a gridlocked economy and society: gridlocked on interest rates because of the contradictory requirements of the manufacturing sector, the housing market and the trade deficit; and gridlocked – literally gridlocked – on its road system by the very volume of imported cars that low interest rates and soaring house values have enabled UK consumers to buy".[5]

Reviewing that set of changes in the early 1990s, when many of them were still only embryonic in form, it was possible to write of life-chances in the UK still being "unevenly divided ... between generations and within generations, between ethnic groups, genders and classes" with "the contemporary UK [being] run in the main by middle-aged white males"; and of social privilege being "transmitted between generations mainly by the inheritance of wealth and participation in privileged forms of education".[6] Yet even before New Labour took over in 1997 from a by-then largely discredited Thatcherite project, Will Hutton was able to describe "The State We're In" as "a 40:30:30 society, one in whose labour markets a privileged 40 per cent experienced rising incomes and high levels of job security, 30 per cent experienced far less security in both employment and wages, and a bottom 30 per cent were locked into various forms of social disadvantage".[7] New Labour inherited a society overwhelmingly divided by class – as well as by ethnicity and by gender – but it also inherited one in which the prosperous 70 per cent expected their rising living standards to continue, while remaining largely wedded to the continuation of the broad institutional structures set in place by the Attlee Government a generation before. Public support for the NHS, for example, remained either side of 2008 greater in the UK even than support for the monarchy – and that support (which had dipped briefly in the aftermath of the death of Princess Diana) continued to outstrip support for most major private civil institutions. UK society, as the financial crisis broke, was one with its own unique fusion of rising expectations and traditional identities. How else are we adequately to explain the decision to build the opening ceremony of the London Olympic Games in 2012 around a celebration of the British welfare state?

Both then and now, the general UK population expects things to get steadily better. They expect their social options to widen; and to a far greater degree than their American equivalents, they expect their politicians to deliver that economic growth and steady social reform. And if those politicians do not so deliver, they expect them to go. Indeed, the Conservatives outstayed their welcome so badly by 1997 as to fall to the largest electoral defeat in their party's history since 1846; and the party that defeated them, New Labour, met a similar fate just 13 years later, dropping from an overwhelming majority to opposition status in just three election cycles. The collapse, over seven decades, of two major political projects – one Keynesian in the 1970s, one neoliberal three decades later – left key sections of UK society by June 2016 alienated from both political parties to such a degree that, as the United States would demonstrate on an even grander scale five months later, for a majority of the electorate any change was thought preferable to a continuation of the status quo. Why that political volatility should have come to affect even old stale Britain is the underlying question we shall explore now as we trace the stage-by-stage disintegration of the UK's postwar settlement.

Families just managing

Americans and the British tend to use the term "middle class" rather differently. In the United States these days, it is conventionally used in a catch-all way – particularly by politicians on the stump – to encompass everyone not on welfare or part of the super-rich. There is a tighter American definition, of course: one that we discussed at the beginning of Chapter 4. In the UK, how-ever, the term has a more precise popular as well as academic meaning, because there both the culture and the academy are still comfortable using the term "working class" in ways that contemporary Americans apparently are not. (Indeed, when UK social attitudes were last surveyed in 2015, a full 60 per cent of those polled declared themselves to be "working class", even though in the UK now only 25 per cent of workers are in manual occupa-tions).[8] The official statistics in the UK used to split the population into five/ six categories by income (A, B, C1, C2, D, E) with the lower-middle class as category C1 and the upper-middle class as B. That has changed lately – the new schema splits the population into eight categories, in recognition of the decline of manual work and the proliferation of service employment* – but still the term "middle class" is generally applied to just a limited set of people. It is used to encompass people in managerial, professional and semi-professional positions, and shades away at the bottom into lower adminis-trative and service positions (into a white-collar working class) and at the top into very senior managers and professionals (the UK's famous Establish-ment).[9] There are clear US parallels here, as well as clear US differences; underscoring the fact that the bigger differentiation between the US and UK experience of middle-classness lies less in the labelling itself than in the label's structural underpinnings. For to a far greater degree than in the US, in the UK it still makes sense to think of there being *two* middle classes, not simply *one*: a middle class of managers and small entrepreneurs in the private sector, and a middle class of public sector employees with university

---

* The old official schema, in use in the UK census from 1921, was: Class A, professional occupations; Class B, intermediate occupations; Class C, skilled occupations; Class D, partly skilled occupations; Class E, unskilled occupations. The new one, first used in the 2001 census, is: 1, higher managerial and professional occupations; 2, lower managerial and professional occupations; 3, intermediate occupations (clerical, sales, service); 4. Small employers and own account workers; 5, lower supervisory and technical occupations; 6. Semi-routine occupations; 7, routine occupations; 8, never worked or long-term unem-ployed. The 8 tend to be grouped into three; higher, intermediate, and lower. The BBC recently came up with yet another classificatory system, this time with seven categories: elite, established middle class, technical middle class, new affluent workers, traditional working class, emergent service workers and a precariat (or precarious proletariat). (BBC, 3 April 2013).

education behind them – teachers, doctors and nurses, social workers, civil servants, and health-care administrators. The two differ by the sectors in which they work – the private or the public – but currently they are united by the fact that they are both being squeezed.

The most recent evidence for this has come from a string of reports from the Resolution Foundation focused on the lower-middle class and their closest working-class equivalents: particularly their 2011[10] and 2013[11] reports. The consistent message coming from what are now a string of annual reports from the Foundation on low- and middle-income families* is that the majority of such families were and are just getting by – just managing. Indeed JAMs ("just about managing families") entered the political lexicon in 2016, as the group most in need of help from the new Conservative Government led by Theresa May. Theresa May recognized that herself when, in her first public statement as prime minister, she said this to what she termed "ordinary families":"You have a job but you don't always have job security. You have your own home, but you worry about paying a mortgage. You can just about manage but you worry about the cost of living and getting your kids into a good school. If you're one of those families, if you're just managing, I want to address you directly".[12]

As early as 2011, the Resolution Foundation found "worrying signs for people on low-to-middle incomes" as "the highest earners take more-and-more of the proceeds of limited growth and so-called 'middle-skilled' jobs are replaced by advancing technology". Echoing the findings of Tüzemen and Willis cited in the previous chapter, their reports point to causal forces in play here that include, among other things, "the rise of mass automation and the digitalization of production, twinned with greater globalization", with "harsh consequences for millions of workers, particularly those in mid-level jobs in administration and manufacturing, who have seen their roles displaced". The next change, they think, will be "the levelling-off of the growth in female

---

* "We define low to middle income households as comprising those in the bottom half of the income distribution who are above the bottom ten per cent and who receive less than one-fifth of their income from means-tested benefits. This covers around six million working households and ten million adults. Despite five-in-six of these families having at least one member in full-time work, nearly four-fifths of these individuals earn less than £21,000 (the median gross wage)." (David Finch, "Hanging On: The Stresses and Strains of Britain's 'Just Managing' Families". London: Resolution Foundation, September 2016, p. 2.)

participation in the labour market, not least as the punitive cost of childcare takes its toll": not to mention "recent cuts to the system of tax credits and benefits" that were "bringing to a screeching halt the growing role of the state in lifting household incomes".[13]

The Foundation's chief economist in 2011 tried to capture the impact of these three daunting headwinds – globalization, falling labour market participation rates, and capped welfare spending – through the experience of one household: one positioned, as he put it, at "the top end of the 11 million adults living on low-to-middle incomes". The experience of that household is worth recording here in detail:

> Both work full-time, Karen for a children's centre and Darren for a software company, each earning a bit less than the average wage, making for a decent household income. The proud parents of four children ... they nurture high hopes for their future. But scratch the surface, and there is palpable frustration. Life has not panned out how they thought it would: in their mid-30s, they still can't afford to buy their own home, the cost of running a family is escalating, the constant grind of financial insecurity takes its toll, and – underneath all this – is their entrenched belief that their living standards are flatlining, and will continue to do so. 'My mum and dad's generation saw their wages go up ahead of prices, with us it's the other way round,' says Darren.

As Giles Kelly then reported, Karen and Darren were "not alone – indeed in many ways theirs is an ordinary tale. Millions of people ... coming to terms with the sense that their living standards are falling short".[14] A later Resolution Foundation report (this one from 2016) put it this way: according to their data "a 28-year-old couple with a baby, with one parent on low pay, were £760 worse off in 2016 compared with 2008. When the couple are older, aged 35, with two children and both working full time on a medium and low wage, they are still £530 poorer". The report also found that these "just managing families" were "more than twice as likely to rent privately rather than own their own home" and were now spending "a quarter of their income on housing costs alone", cushioned by "less than a month's income worth of savings".[15]

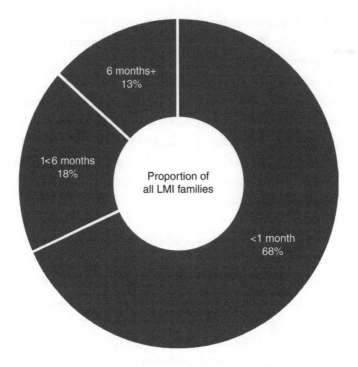

Figure 5.1 Number of months' net income held in savings/financial assets by low- to middle-income families in the UK
(Source: David Finch, "Hanging On". London: Resolution Foundation, September 2016).

Moreover, what Giles Kelly did not report in 2011, but others later did, was the degree to which, for families like Karen and Darren's, family living standards were being sustained in the wake of the 2008 crisis and subsequent recession (if they were being sustained at all) only by the acquisition by the adults within those families of alarmingly large quantities of personal debt. And not just mortgage debt – getting a house (as the Kelly example indicates) is less and less an option for more-and-more middle-class members – no, as we first mentioned in the Introduction, what is accumulating here is predominantly credit card debt and student debt. Accumulating so quickly and in such volume that by 2016, according to NEF's recent report,[16] it will take the average Briton until they were 69 to be free of all debts. As the report said, "average personal debt has grown by a fifth since the financial crisis: not including mortgages it is now £9,000 per household, with 1 in 10 indebted household's consumer debts exceeding 60 per cent of their incomes". Recent TUC data is similarly alarming: consumer credit, which had peaked in the UK at £230 billion before the financial crisis, was back to £212 billion by the end of 2015; and total unsecured debt for UK households (including credit cards, payday loans, car loans and student loans – but not mortgages) that had peaked pre-crisis at £364 billion, was up £48 billion between 2012 and 2015, to total £353 billion again.

Behind these daunting total figures stand two particularly disturbing trends. The first is a rise in households that are *over-indebted* (that is, have debt repayments that consume more than 25 per cent of their gross income). That figure was up 28 per cent between 2012 and 2014. The TUC estimated for 2014 that "3.2 million households (one in every eight in the UK) were paying out more than one quarter of their gross incomes to their unsecured creditors" and that "half of those households were extremely over-indebted: required to pay out more than 40 per cent of their gross income"[17] in this fashion. The second is this: that the latest driver of rising debt among these hard-pressed middle-class families is not the purchase of immediately-consumable goods and services. It is *student loans* – a relatively new phenomenon in the UK but one that is now rising fast. Student loans in the UK still attract a lower rate of interest than do other unsecured loans, and are only paid back after certain earning thresholds are reached: but even so, student loan debt in the UK rose in 2015 by 17 per cent, to £86.2 billion, as the first cohort of students to pay higher fees graduated, and crossed the £100 billion threshold for the first time in March 2017.[18] Current estimates suggest that those graduates will leave university with an average of £44,000 of debt/head – compared with an average of only £16,200/head for those graduating five years earlier.[19] If true, that makes their debt levels "higher, on average, than their peers in any other English-speaking country, *including the US*".[20] If true, it also means that perhaps 70 per cent of them will "never pay off the debt... instead they will have to make repayments for 30 years before then having the unpaid loan written off".[21]

What figures of this kind also suggest is that it is now more difficult for most middle-class families to climb up the social ladder at the top than it is to slide down that ladder at the bottom: more difficult, that is, to go from rags to riches than it is to go from modest affluence to genuine poverty. This was not true for the baby-boomer generation. Then, the proliferation of new manage-rial jobs in both the public and the private sector that had to be filled for the first time allowed the brightest of working-class boys (and it was almost exclusively boys) to move – via grammar school normally, rather than via uni-versity – into the bottom ranks of the middle class, thereafter to rise by the quality of their managerial performance. But those days have largely gone, as both the data on income and wealth distribution in the contemporary UK, and on the current scale of social mobility, make abundantly clear. It is not simply that this first generation of postwar private- and public-sector man-agers had sufficient children to fill its vacancies as its members began to retire. It is also that the gaps in income that now need to be bridged as indi-viduals seek to climb have – in the UK as in the US – recently become ever wider: and for much the same reasons in both cases. This, for example, is Will Hutton on prevailing trends in the distribution of income in the UK:[22]

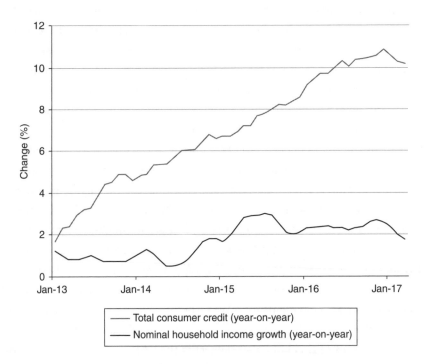

Figure 5.2 Consumer debt growing faster than incomes
(Source: Frank Van Lerven, "Northern Rock Ten Years On". London: New Economics Foundation, 15 September 2017).

For twenty years, the great British inequality machine has hurtled on, driven largely by the burgeoning incomes of the top 0.1 per cent – almost all of whom are directors, bankers or work in business services and real estate – who captured the lion's share of any gains in real productivity. In 1995, they took 3.2 per cent of all income; by 2009 that had more than doubled to 6.5 per cent, falling back to 4.8 per cent in 2011 as bonuses fell during the recession. The other top 0.9 per cent were not slouches: together with the 0.1 per cent, the top 1.0 per cent saw its share rise from 10.8 per cent to 15.4 per cent over the same period, then fall back to 12.9 per cent, impacted by the same cyclical effect on bonuses as the top 0.1 per cent. But 70 per cent of the rise in the income share of the top 1 per cent was driven by the top 0.1 per cent.

The pattern of income inequality in the postwar UK is not quite the same as that in the US. Income inequality increased sharply in the UK through the Thatcherite 1980s, but stabilized through the 1990s. "The Gini coefficient, a scale on which zero is absolute equality and one is pure inequality, rose from 0.25 in 1979 to 0.34 in 1991".[23] What has happened to income inequality since then is a matter of dispute – recent academic research suggesting a sharpening of inequality again, the latest ONS figures suggesting the reverse. Either way, income inequality in the UK remains significantly higher now than it was in the 1970s, and higher than is common today in other advanced economies in Europe.[24] As the chair of the government's Social Mobility Commission reported in June 2017, since the financial crisis, "the gap between the highest and the lowest paid [has] increased dramatically. In 1998, on average the highest earners were paid 47 times that of the lowest. By 2015 the equivalent gap was 128 times more".[25] What we are currently witnessing, in relation to income inequality at least, is possibly a degree of "re-convergence" with the United States. Certainly in 2011, the High Pay Commission in London estimated that "if current trends continue, by 2025 the top 0.1 per cent of [UK] earners will take home 10 per cent of the national income and by 2030 we will have gone back to levels of inequality not seen since Victorian Britain". A top executive in a FTSE 100 company "is currently paid 145 times the average wage. If we return to trends seen before the crisis", the Commission reported, "by 2020 that differential will be 214 times".[26] And with income inequality rising on this scale and in this manner, wealth inequality inevitably rises also. In fact, the Institute for Fiscal Studies recently showed the UK to be *more* unequal a country when measured by wealth even than when measured by income: a Gini coefficient for wealth inequality in 2015 in the UK of 0.65.[27]

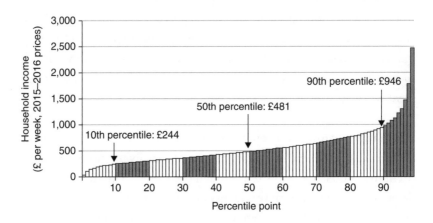

Figure 5.3 Weekly net household income at each percentile point, 2015–16 (UK) (Source: IFS and Rowntree Foundation, *Living Standards, Poverty and Inequality in the UK, 2017*).

In such a climate, it is hardly to be wondered at that the wage-premium accruing to core middle-class jobs (all uniformly "graduate-only ... examples include academics, natural scientists, mechanical engineers, accountants, and teachers") should now be falling.* "A teacher, for example, earned 24 per cent more than the average in 1975, but only 6 per cent more in 2013".[28] Nor is it surprising that the UK now records a lower rate of upward social mobility

---

* "Time and again, successive governments, both left and right leaning, have bandied about a £400,000 average lifetime graduate premium; but as the latest research has highlighted, the average graduate premium has been reduced to around £100,000. This paper argues that this estimate is still too high, but even if you accept [it] spread over 45 years it only gives an annual premium of just £2,222 per year, before Income Tax and National Insurance. That is simply not enough to cover the interest accruing on the average loan." (Angus Hanton, in Stephen Kemp-King, "The Graduate Premium". London: Intergenerational Foundation, August 2016).

(defined as people ending up in a different occupational or social class, or a different point on the income scale, to their parents) than do a string of other major industrial economies with more equal income distributions. For all the claims that the Thatcherites made about freeing up the entrepreneurial spirit by removing the dead hand of government, we now see that "those born in the 1980s – the Thatcher generation* – are the first to start with lower incomes than their parents".[29] As the government's Social Mobility Commission put it, in November 2016:

> Britain has a deep social mobility problem which is getting worse for an entire generation of young people ... Our country has reached an inflection point. The rungs on the social mobility ladder are growing further apart. It is becoming harder for this generation of struggling families to move up ... People born in the 1960s, 1970s and early 1980s have lower incomes than their predecessors did at their age. The twentieth century expectation that each generation would be better off than the one preceding it is no longer being met.[30]

The Institute for Fiscal Studies summed up the current condition of the UK middle class in this way:

> In key respects, middle-income families with children now more closely resemble poor families than in the past. Half are now renters rather than owner-occupiers and, while poorer families have become less reliant on benefits as employment has risen, middle-income households with children now get 30 per cent of their income from benefits and tax cuts, up from 22 per cent twenty years ago.[31]

---

* "... the expectation that each generation would be better off than the previous one is no longer being met. Individuals born after 1911 had higher incomes than the previous generation until the 1980s. Those born between 1981 to 2000 are the first cohort to show signs of falling behind their predecessor generation by the age of 30." (Social Mobility Commission, "Time for Change". London, OGL, June 2017, p. 14).

The persistence of poverty

If you drop out of the middle class in the contemporary UK, where do you end up? You end up in the growing ranks of the British poor; and sadly, there are currently plenty of such ranks for you to join.

As we saw earlier, official America only recognized the persistence of poverty, and began to wage a war upon it, in the 1960s. By contrast in the UK, a sensitivity to the problems of the poor, and to the extent of poverty in particularly the emerging industrial and commercial cities of a by-then imperial Britain, stretches back in modern times to at least the late-Victorian period; at which point (and forever thereafter) poverty-resolution settled in (generation after generation) as a major target and motivating force for British radicals of many political persuasions. But there is a sense too that in the UK, as in the US, this long-recognized poverty was also "rediscovered" in the 1960s: in that as general living standards in Britain began incrementally to rise as the baby-boomers came to their maturity, it became increasingly obvious to their political leaders that certain groups of British voters were being left behind. The poverty of those groups – the impaired nature of their living standards relative, that is, to those around them – became too visible for politicians easily to ignore; and so it was from the 1960s that official UK, like the EU more generally later, began to define poverty not against an absolute minimum standard of living (fixed by a money amount and varied only by family size) but as any standard of living that was significantly lower than that normal in UK society as a whole. In that way, poverty in the UK came to be measured as an income level of less than 60 per cent of median income – it became a moving target, that is, rising as incomes rose – and understood in that fashion, became also an unavoidable reality for New Labour as the Blair-led government came to power in 1997.

To its credit, New Labour entered office determined to tackle the varying kinds of poverty that had built up in the Thatcher years, an accumulation that had helped ultimately to discredit her acute form of deregulated capitalism.* New Labour entered office convinced that the main source of poverty

---

* "In just two decades of predominantly Conservative rule, the proportion of the population with access to less than half the average income had actually tripled." (David Coates, *Prolonged Labour.* Cambridge: Polity, 2005, p. 20).

was not income inequality *per se*, but the exclusion of the poor from mainstream sources of income. Leading Labour politicians were not foolish, of
course. They recognized that the sources of poverty compounded each other
over time, to leave in many UK towns and cities certain areas of acute cumulative social deprivation; and so initially created a Social Exclusion Unit to
plan what they called "joined up" policies to bring extra resources to the
communities in greatest need.[32] But over time, New Labour came to put the
weight of its anti-poverty initiatives elsewhere: not into community regeneration of the Social Exclusion type, but into welfare-to-work programmes
modelled on those developed by successive American administrations from
the Nixon years on; into "stealth socialism",[33] as Gordon Brown was want to
term it, tax changes and welfare spending to guarantee improving minimum
living standards for both the old and the low paid; and – most of all – into
a string of initiatives to break the cycle of deprivation generation-by-
generation, through policies to halve the rate of child poverty by 2010, and
to end it entirely by 2020. This last was particularly important, given that
"in 1998 the UK was bottom of the European League, with the highest child
poverty rate in the EU".[34]

Prior to the 2008 financial crisis and its subsequent recession, New
Labour made significant progress on at least some of these anti-poverty
fronts. In its first decade in office, it moved a quarter-million welfare recipients from welfare to work.[35] It raised living standards among the elderly poor,
taking the bulk of British pensioners *out* of poverty entirely for the first time
in UK history; and it significantly lowered the scale of poverty amongst children. Between 1997 and 2010 "relative child poverty fell from 26.7 per cent
to 19.7 per cent, or by some 800,000 children".[36] That was to be welcomed, of
course, but even before the financial crisis broke, the tenacity of poverty in
the UK was already creating a significant New Labour undershoot. There
were 1.5 million poor children living in households with a full-time working
adult in 1998; and that number had not altered a decade later; and as Richard
Dickens put it at the time, "poverty among children would have to fall another
900,000 children in just one year in order to achieve the ... target of halving
child poverty over ten years".[37] In the event, that simply proved impossible,
leaving the Institute for Fiscal Studies reporting that child poverty, pensioner
poverty, and income inequality were all *up* and rising even before the financial

crisis then accentuated them all.[38] The ultimate tragedy for New Labour's anti-poverty ambitions was that the financial crisis of 2008 not only wiped away in one year all the gains of the previous eleven on employment, fuel poverty, and the number of children living in poverty homes.[39] It also eventually triggered the replacement of New Labour in power by a Coalition Government whose deliberately adopted austerity policies combined to eradicate the rest of the modest anti-poverty gains that had been made since 1997.

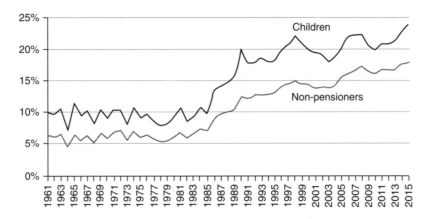

Figure 5.4 Relative poverty rates (after housing costs) among individuals in working households since 1961 (GB)
(Source: IFS and Rowntree Foundation, *Living Standards, Poverty and Inequality in the UK, 2017*).

The resulting scale of contemporary UK poverty is both striking and disturbing. "The proportion of the population living in poverty, after taking account of housing costs, has been about a fifth for more than a decade".[40] According to the Resolution Foundation's latest figures, 13.5 million people in the UK are currently living in poverty: 21 per cent of the entire UK population, including 7.9 million working-age adults,* 3.9 million children and 1.6 million pensioners. But quite who is caught up in poverty is actually changing: as the report notes, "in past decades, old age was virtually synonymous with poverty" but "this is no longer true". Over the last quarter century,

---

* The equivalent Joseph Rowntree Foundation figure is 7.4 million.

"income poverty amount pensioners [has] plummeted from around 40 per cent to 13 per cent" while simultaneously "child poverty rates rose and fell twice and remain high at 29 per cent". Poverty among working-age adults without dependent children, by contrast, "has slowly but steadily risen from around 14 per cent to around 20 per cent", to leave the UK "firmly in the middle of the European league table on material deprivation": higher in this regard than "Spain, the Czech Republic, France and Germany among others". The CEO of the Joseph Rowntree Foundation put it this way in 2016:[41] "There are signs of the changing nature of poverty: there are more people in working families in poverty compared with five or ten years earlier, and fewer people in poverty in workless ones. Progress on both pensioner poverty and child poverty has stalled, with no change in the last five years."

UK poverty currently comes in many forms, and brings many ills with it to the individuals and families it strikes.[42] It brings *food poverty*. One in eight workers in the UK are currently skipping meals to make ends meet, according to the TUC.[43] It brings *fuel poverty*. At the height of the recession in 2011, heating fuel poverty affected a quarter of UK's households, up from a fifth in 2010 as bills soared and pay remained unchanged.[44] There were still 2.3 million households who were fuel poor in 2014.[45*] It brings *homelessness and housing insecurity*. "The number of people sleeping rough in England has risen for the sixth year in a row, according to the latest official figures. An estimated 4,134 people bedded down outside in 2016 ... an increase of 16 per cent on the previous year's figure ... and more than double the 2010 figure".[46] It brings depleted access to resources by the very young – poverty currently experienced by one child in every four in Britain – children who are entirely innocent of any responsibility for their own plight. And it brings actual *destitution*. Currently, "more than one million people in the UK are so poor that they cannot afford to eat properly, keep clean, or stay warm and dry ... and are left dependent on charities for essentials such as food, clothes, shelter and toiletries".[47] Young men, and recent migrants, are particularly at risk of destitution of this kind.

---

* Poverty is not just a matter of low income. It is also a matter of living costs. The IFS found, for example, that between 2008 and 2014 the cost of energy rose by 67 per cent, food by 32 per cent, and the overall retail price index by only 22 per cent. But the poorest spend a bigger proportion of their meagre income on fuel and food than do the rich: 8 per cent on energy and 20 per cent on food, as against 4 per cent and 11 per cent respectively by the rich. (*The Guardian*, 5 November 2014).

With numbers like this, it is clear that poverty in Britain is currently so ubiquitous that you have to stay indoors to avoid it. It is a poverty found among
families in suburbs and small towns far from London. It is a poverty found too
in inner-city areas in each major city and urban area; and there, poverty is
particularly prevalent among ethnic minority communities and among
recent immigrants from the European Union and the Middle East. Broadly
speaking, that is, poverty in the UK is predominantly white in the north and
the suburbs, and predominantly non-white in the cities and the South.

UK poverty is not distinctly rural, as it is in parts of the United States,
because there is very little rural Britain left in which to be poor. But urban
Britain is blighted by it, and its sources there – as in the US – take at least
three forms. There is poverty produced by *involuntary unemployment*, although
that currently is on the wane. There is poverty caused by *low wages* – and that
is *not* on the wane. On the contrary, and as we first saw in Chapter 3, there
are currently more than 5 million people in Britain working full-time for less
than a living wage, and at least a further three-quarters of a million exposed
to zero-hours contracts with all their attendant evils (the latest data suggests
the existence of 1.7 million such contracts, suggesting that most of those on
them – disproportionately young and female workers – survive by working
two such jobs simultaneously).[48] Working full-time and still being poor is
more common now than once it was: in the early 2000s, "about 40 per cent of
absolutely poor people lived in 'working' households, which included people
in some sort of employment. Today, over half the poor do"[49]– 55 per cent in
2014–15, some 7.4 million people living in poverty in households in which
at least one adult was working. In total, 3.8 million workers, "200,000 higher
than a year earlier and one million more than a decade earlier".[50]

And then in the UK, as in the US, there is poverty caused by *welfare dependency* – particularly poverty caused by *disability*. Latest findings from the New
Policy Institute suggest that "28 per cent of those in poverty in the UK are
disabled (3.9 million people) while a further 20 per cent of people in poverty
(2.7 million) live in a household with a disabled person".[51] Doing the sums:
that means that "nearly half of the poverty in the UK is ... directly associated
with disability". That said, however, it is also true for the UK, as for the US,
that the rate of poverty in the other categories would be much higher if welfare provision were somehow to be taken away. Certainly "the lowest paid

15 per cent of the workforce is the only part of the British labour market to have seen a pay rise, in real terms, over the past decade because of the impact of the rising minimum wage".[52] The current best estimate is that welfare programmes such as housing benefits and earned income tax credits keep a further tranche of British citizens just out of the poverty zone, parking them just above the 60 per cent threshold. The cumulative result is something the TUC refers to as "rubber band" poverty: "recurrent poverty, lots of people who bounce between being and not quite being poor".[53] And in truth it is a striking feature of UK politics since the financial crisis that this third source of poverty (welfare dependency) has generated more-and-more "rubber band" hardship – affecting perhaps one Briton in three – because of austerity policies designed to cap, and ideally reduce, the overall welfare budget. Indeed, so significant is that attempt that we shall discuss it more fully in Chapter 7. All we need to note now is its consequence – the way in which "a mix of continuing cuts to social security and public services, squeezed wages and rising living costs mean that 2017 is set to be another tumultuous year for many ... and to be particularly tough for Britain's poorest children".[54]

Those children will pay the greatest cost, of course, for the persistence of poverty in the UK; but poverty is not costless even to those who avoid it. On the contrary, and on the government's own figures, poverty in Britain cost £78 billion in 2016 – mainly in the form of healthcare costs, education, policing and depleted tax revenues[55] – and there is nothing to suggest that that cost will be any less in years to come. On the contrary, if the prognosis made by Stewart Lansley and Joanna Mack is correct – in their remarkable study of the rise of mass poverty, *Breadline Britain* – without a fundamental redesign of the social underpinnings of the UK economy, things can only get worse. They wrote this:

> Since the late 1970s, Britain has built a high propensity to poverty into its economic and political system, one linked, in essence, to the increasingly unequal division of power, opportunities and rewards. Not only are increasing numbers living in deprivation poverty, but a growing proportion of the population is at risk, facing a range of deprivations that increase their chances of falling below the living standard defined as the minimum necessary in Britain today. Over the last thirty

years, the precise nature of the deprivations that the poor face has changed. But while the poor of today do, in some respects, have more possessions than they had in the past, they share with the poor of previous times a fundamental inability to fully participate in the society in which they live. Despite rises in overall prosperity over time, far greater numbers have become unable to meet the requirements for living in contemporary society.[56]

Gender inequality and work–life balance

In the UK, as in the US, the burden of that poverty falls more heavily on women than on men because, like American women, British women continue to have less access than do the men with whom they live to the full range of resources and life-chances available in a modern economy. Both societies are still heavily scarred by sexist attitudes and by patriarchal practices,* and in that sense are very similar; but they do differ in the degree to which public policy has recently been developed to address – at least in some modest fashion – the worst excesses of male dominance. On issues of poverty, the UK looks very American. On issues of gender, it looks rather less American than it does northern European.

Gender issues did not figure centrally on the UK's political agenda until relatively recently. The UK led the way on abortion reform in the 1960s, and passed both an Equal Pay Act and a Sex Discrimination Act under Labour Governments led by Harold Wilson in the 1970s. But the postwar welfare state created and sustained by "Old" Labour governments, and by pre-Thatcherite Conservative ones, had been constructed on the premise of the "male breadwinner model" – and that premise held good for at least a generation, until it was undermined by the steady return to paid work of married women with children, the rise of the two-income family, and the entry of

---

* In 2013, for example, official crime figures showed that nearly five million women (or 30 per cent of the adult female population in the UK) have experienced some form of domestic abuse since age 16, and that in 2013 alone there were 406,000 victims of sexual assault and nearly one million victims of stalkers, two-thirds of those victims being women. (Source: *The Guardian*, 13 February 2014).

women into secondary and then higher education in increasing numbers. Margaret Thatcher may well have been the UK's first female prime minister, but there was no "gender revolution" on her watch. On the contrary, old gender assumptions prevailed throughout the 1980s as the limits of the male breadwinner model began to manifest themselves, and as the special needs of women as mothers continued to be met primarily by the direct payment to women having and raising children of a cash payment – a "family allowance" as it was called – for each child of school age.

But as New Labour entered office in 1997, things were beginning to change. The new government inherited an economy in which more and more women carried the double-burden of paid and unpaid work.* It also inherited a society in which the vast majority of lone-parent families were headed by women, and one in which women – either married or living alone – were significantly "under-pensioned" relative to men.[57] A greater percentage of women worked outside the home, and for pay, than ever before; but they did so, in the main, from within family structures in which the distribution of domestic roles still left them with the bulk of responsibility for child rearing and for the care of the old. The rules governing paid work in most privately-owned businesses, the length of the male working day in those businesses, and even the structure of the school calendar in the UK of the 1990s – all remained largely insensitive to the cross pressures they inevitably created for women attempting to mix unpaid work inside the home with paid work outside it; so obliging large numbers of those women to settle for low-paid and part-time employment of an inherently unsatisfactory kind. These cross-pressures of home and work then fell unevenly on women of different class and ethnic backgrounds. Traditional work roles were most heavily entrenched in Asian ethnic communities. Poverty and job insecurity were greatest among working-class women. Access to public health and education were easiest for women (and children) in the middle class, and so on; and in consequence New Labour policies were bound to impact different categories of women in different ways.

But New Labour did at least try to address gender issues linked to the balancing of work and life. New Labour's Chancellor of the Exchequer for its first

---

* In 2016, the Office of National Statistics calculated the value of unpaid work performed in the home at more than £1 trillion. It calculated the value of the official economy (the one based on wages) at £1.8 trillion.

decade in power, Gordon Brown, was sufficiently sensitive to traditional feminist concerns, and sufficiently aware of the gendered nature of the UK labour market, to give high initial priority to the creation and funding of a national system of childcare. As he told the House of Commons in his first budget speech: "from this budget forwards, childcare will no longer be seen as an afterthought or a fringe element of social policies but from now on – as it should be – an integral part of our economic policy".[58] That first budget planned for 50,000 young people eventually to train as childcare assistants, as part of its "New Deal" for the young unemployed. It also allowed families receiving family credit, housing benefit or council tax benefits to have the first £100 of their weekly childcare costs disregarded in the calculation of their in-work benefits; and that was just a beginning. Each subsequent budget and pre-budget statement built on that "first step" and did so in a steady, incremental and consistent fashion.

In budget after budget, the aim of policy was the same – "to enable parents and carers to balance work and family responsibilities". And the response was equally consistent: "extra help for childcare" in the form of funds for childcare places and changes in the tax code to give the poor and low-paid easier access to them. Indeed, over time the Treasury became ever more inventive of ways in which public spending and welfare institutions could ease the cross-pressures experienced by parents in the UK's increasingly ubiquitous two-income families. Tax relief on expenditure for childcare was just the beginning. Public funding of wraparound schooling* followed, as did the 2000 Work-Life Balance Challenge Fund and the later consultation document on "Work and Families, Choice and Flexibility". From that consultation exercise came a Treasury commitment to the financing of a fairer, and less gendered, balance at the point of birth itself: increasing the level and duration of maternity pay and the length of maternity leave – and introducing two weeks paid paternity leave and 26 weeks paid adoption leave (both at the same level as maternity pay).

Nor, given the disproportionate way in which poverty impacts on women in the contemporary UK, should we forget that from the very outset the New

---

* "Wraparound" schooling: the school buildings open and staffed before and after the conventional school day, to enable working parents to drop children at school early, and collect them late.

Labour government was highly sensitive to the particular difficulties experienced by families on low incomes; and was prepared directly to address issues of low pay through the introduction of a national minimum wage and the resetting of the tax code to guarantee an improved (and steadily rising) minimum family income. Twice during New Labour's first two terms, the Treasury totally reset the tax system in an attempt to lift low-paid full-time working families with children out of poverty. Gordon Brown did so first through a significant increase in child allowances and the introduction of a new working-families tax credit, which from October 1999 guaranteed to any family in which at least one person was working full-time a minimum income of £180 a month and a freedom from income tax until that income reached £220 a month. Then in 2002, he extended the working families tax credit to take in childless couples on low pay, and introduced a new unified child tax credit from April 2003, to be paid on top of universal child benefit, to integrate all means-tested income-related support for children into one payment: and as such into a "single, seamless system of income-related support for families with children". Significantly, the Chancellor told the House in 2002 that all this support was "to be paid to the main carer – normally the mother".[59]

Yet for all this effort, gender differences on pay in the United Kingdom proved largely impervious to reform. There was slight improvement: "the gender pay gap was 20.7 per cent in 1997, it narrowed to 20.1 per cent in 2002, and ... to 17.1 per cent in 2005".[60] But even today, more than a decade later, female weekly pay in the UK is still lower than that for men: "£325 per week compared to £470 for men. This gap has been narrowing, and partly reflects that women are more likely to work part-time than men".[61] In 1997, 85 per cent of all part-time jobs were filled by women. That figure is now down to 74 per cent, as more men find themselves restricted to part-time employment; but it remains the case in the UK, as in the US, that part-time work is still overwhelmingly carried out by women. And it is carried out by women primarily because that is the way in which working women with children balance their ongoing unpaid domestic responsibilities with the need to bring in a second income to maintain or improve family standards of living. And on the importance of this second influx of income, the data is very clear: that "women have been the main drivers of the rise in living standards in the UK over the last 40 years for low- and middle-income families". In fact, in 2009, the Institute for Fiscal Studies estimated that "looking at just the increase in employment and ignoring the growth in tax benefits and credits, 78 per cent of the growth in these households came from women, while income from men's work [had] barely increased in this cohort since 1968".[62]

The tenacity of the gender pay-gap is evident in the latest report available to us on women, work and wages in the UK – the one compiled for the New Policy Institute. Among the report's key findings are the following:

- There were 14.6 million working women in the UK in 2015, concentrated in four main sectors: health and social work (3.2 million); education (2.3 million); white collar services (2 million); and wholesale and retail (just under 2 million). There has recently been strong employment growth in the relatively higher-paying sectors (the first two) and weaker growth in the lower-paying ones.
- There were 14 million working-age parents in Britain, 12 million of whom live with a partner. Among the 2.2 million single parents, over 90 per cent were women.
- The median female employee has an hourly pay rate of 80 per cent of the male hourly pay rate. The pay gap is narrowest towards the bottom of the income distribution, and tends to widen as pay increases.
- Women are more likely to be low-paid than men if they work full-time. There were about 5.1 million low-paid workers in the UK in 2015, of which 62 per cent (3.2 million) were women.
- On average in 2014, 270,000 men and 350,000 women reported being on zero-hours contracts[63]

The tenacity of this gender pay-gap in the contemporary UK has a series of important consequences. Its tenacity is such that, at the present rate of reform, it will still take over 80 years to bring average wages for men and women into harmony; and the width of the gap means that the real cost of having children falls directly onto the shoulders of working women. There is now no significant gender pay-gap on full-time work by men and women in their 20s, but when the children start to arrive, the gap reappears with a vengeance. "The pay gap between men and women widens to 33 per cent 12 years after a woman has her first child, says the IFS";[64] and "women who become mothers before 33 earn 15 per cent less than their peers who have not had children".[65] For women in low-paid jobs, the arrival of the second child seems particularly burdensome in financial terms, obliging them to reduce their hours considerably or give up paid work altogether for lack of affordable child care;[66] in the process helping to open up a gender pay gap that "is particularly acute for women over 40 – and that is because of the lack of quality part-time working and lack of effective shared parental-leave policies".[67] The TUC quite properly refers to this as a "motherhood pay penalty".[68] All this before the other problem arrives – the one that runs deep in UK industry and is so hard to stop – namely the sense that many pregnant women and working mothers have, that they are discriminated against at work as soon as they begin to have children.[69]

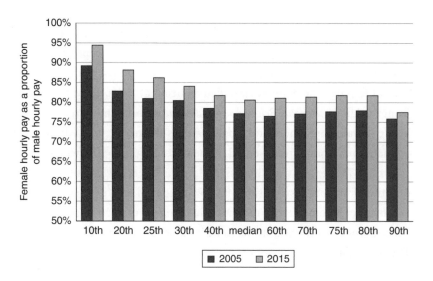

Figure 5.5 Female hourly earnings as a proportion of male hourly earnings across the distribution (UK)
(Source: New Policy Institute, "Women, Work and Wages in the UK", October 2016, p. 15).

The breaks that women with children take to have those children, the part-time work into which so many of them settle as their children grow, and the loss of promotion into more senior positions that still affects women

– parenting or childless, it seems still to make no difference – then leaves women much more vulnerable than their men to poverty in old age. Women live longer than men, and still find themselves in the UK less well-resourced than their men to cope with the long years of retirement that stretch before them. New Labour did at least introduce a "carers' benefit" to allow women working unpaid at home, rearing children or tending infirm relatives, to count those years for the state pension – but in the United Kingdom the state pension had been allowed to wither on the vine during the Thatcher years, and although more generous now, is still far less so than its US equivalent (Social Security). Rely on the state pension alone for income in the UK, and you will be poor: and more women than men in the UK still ultimately find themselves in that condition. Claire Annesley's 2011 UK report for the European Commission was particularly damning on this gender-structured vulnerability:

> There are two groups of women who are particularly at risk of poverty or social exclusion: women in retirement with 27.1 per cent of retired women deemed at risk of poverty ... and single-parents, with 56.1 per cent of female lone parents classified as being at risk of poverty. Data from the UK *Households Below Average Income* report demonstrates that single female pensioners and single parents (91 per cent of whom are women) are strongly represented in the bottom quintile of income distribution. 29 per cent of single female pensioners are in the bottom quintile of income distribution and 34 per cent of single parents are. If we consider income distribution after housing costs, then 41 per cent of single parents are in the bottom quintile of income distribution, but only 16 per cent of female pensioners.[70]

The rights of women at work, and the ability of the families they sustain to effect an easier work–life balance, definitely improved under New Labour, and at least some of the initiatives begun then – not least free nursery education – were continued and extended by the Coalition Government that followed. But progress overall stalled after the financial crisis, and did so for two major reasons. It did so because of new policies introduced by the new government to deal with the fallout from that crisis – politics seeking a route to economic recovery by cutting government spending. And it did so because of policies that the new government failed to introduce – policies designed to alleviate the childcare crisis that is now so crippling a feature of the lives of families with young children and two working adults.

The effects of austerity first: they have hit women in Britain the hardest. That is partly because the austerity strategy adopted by the incoming Coalition Government involved major cuts in public services, and it is women who disproportionately staff those services and depend upon them. It is also because the associated establishment of strict caps on welfare spending has intensified the problem of poverty in the United Kingdom, and women have been disproportionately exposed to the consequences of that strictness. Of the cull of eventually 710,000 public employees planned by the new government in 2010, 65 per cent were cuts to jobs occupied by women; and as those plans began to bite, unemployment among working women then predictably began to soar: it reached a 25-year high of 7.5 per cent in 2012. And by then, in two successive austerity budgets, the government had announced a series of cuts in welfare payments designed to save £8 billion: "either by scrapping existing benefits (e.g. Health in Pregnancy grant), reducing eligibility (e.g. Sure Start maternity grant, Child Benefit), reducing the value of benefits ... or capping the amount that could be claimed". "Independent evidence" then showed "that these measures ... disproportionately impacted on women"[71] – to such a degree indeed that the Fawcett Society immediately challenged them, taking the Government to court for failing to carry out an "equality impact assessment" as required by law. The three-year freeze on benefits and tax credits announced in 2013, for example, directly affected at least 4.6 million women in the UK who receive child tax credit, and hit low-paid pregnant women particularly hard (a woman earning £12,000 stood to lose £1,300 during her pregnancy and the baby's first year of life via cuts to maternity pay, pregnancy support and tax credits).[72] Little wonder then that critics of the Coalition Government's austerity programme should have pointed to the contradiction between its claims about being uniquely "pro-family" and the reality on the ground: the reality of using women as the "shock absorbers"[73] of policies focused overwhelmingly on the reduction of public debt.

And if that was not bad enough, there was also this – the deepening crisis of childcare for British families increasingly squeezed between stagnant wages and rising costs. It is not that public policy here is missing, as it largely is in the United States. It is rather that the public policy in place remains visibly inadequate. UK governments of all stripes have helped to finance childcare and early childhood education in at least three ways since 1997: by vouchers to spend on registered childcare; by subsidies (in the form of tax credits) to middle-and low-income families with dependent children; and by free places in preschool education regardless of parental income or work status – subsidized by public funds. The Coalition Government continued these New Labour initiatives. So now is the current Conservative Government. But the subsidies are still too small, and the costs of childcare still too high, for families of limited means. With childcare costs rising more rapidly than wages year-on-year and averaging over £5,000 per year per child in 2013,[74] and with the costs of full-time holiday care averaging out now at over £120/week/child,[75] more-and-more middle-income families are finding that the cost of childcare is pushing them back towards a poverty life-style,[76] and many low-paid families are finding that it is less expensive for the mother (it is invariably the mother) to leave paid employment entirely to provide the childcare herself. Children are expensive – the minimum cost of raising a child to adulthood in the UK is currently said to be at least £83,000*[77] – and the state cannot be expected to pick up all of that. But even so, there is clearly something profoundly wrong with a system that, as Martin Sandbu put it, "manages to combine an extraordinarily inefficient combination of a very high rate of public spending on families with an extortionate price level for professional childcare even after public subsidies are included". Recent OECD figures suggest that the net-cost of childcare in the UK, as a proportion of average wages, is currently higher than in any other member country, and that includes countries in Scandinavia that insist on higher qualifications and salaries for professional childcarers.[78] Earlier OECD figures suggest that "after accounting for childcare, over two-thirds of the [UK] family's second income is effectively taxed away: a rate that is well above the OECD average (68 per cent in the UK versus 52 per cent on average)".[79] These findings were entirely at one with those in the highly critical final report from the Commission on Living Standards sponsored by the Resolution Foundation. "For women with children", the report concluded:

---

* The equivalent US figure, from the US Department of Agriculture, is currently $245,340.

... the UK's underperformance stems from a toxic mixture of unusually high childcare costs, a lack of high quality part-time work and a poorly designed tax and benefit system. Together these factors mean that work simply *does not* pay for many women in modern Britain. A full-time second earner with two small children in a typical middle-income household on a salary of £19,950 keeps just £1,060 a year after childcare costs, taxes, and lost benefits – just £20 a week.[80]

The housing crisis of the young

The focus of this chapter thus far has been on income flows and their inadequacies; but the other side of the financial pressures now operating on so many British families is that of rising costs – particularly the rising costs of housing. Indeed, the financing and expense of housing bears a huge responsibility on both sides of the Atlantic for the current pressures to which we are all subject, playing as it did such a catalytic role in both the emergence of a credit crisis in 2007/8 and the subsequent prolongation of the global recession that followed.* Many people in the UK struggle today to make ends meet in no small measure because house prices initially fell in that recession, trapping many in negative equity and exposing some to foreclosure; only subsequently to rise sharply again, denying many first-time buyers the chance to purchase their home. And as property ownership stalled in the wake of the 2007/8 financial crisis, the pressure on the rental sector in the UK increased; putting up rents in the private sector at the very moment at which the supply of social housing was sinking to a postwar low. People need to live somewhere – housing, like food, is basic to life – but that "somewhere" has become increasingly problematic for many people in the UK of late, in the process exacerbating already existing tensions between the rich and the poor, and between the young and the old.

---

* Although not just housing – also the costs of gas, electricity, water, television and phones. Since 2006, these bills – that have to be paid – have risen far faster in the UK than average wages: the average gas bill by 76 per cent, electricity 72 per cent and water 41 per cent (figures not adjusted for inflation). This from research by Santander, reported in *The Guardian*, 1 July 2017.

Postwar Britain began life short of housing, with much of its urban housing stock destroyed or depleted by war. Building houses – first council houses
provided by the local authority for rent, and then private homes bought
by flexible-rate mortgages – became a high political priority first for the
Labour Government elected in 1945 and then for Conservative Governments
returned to power three times in the 1950s. The Attlee Government oversaw
the building of more than a million homes – 80 per cent of them council
houses – and by the 1960s private builders were expanding the housing stock
by over 350,000 units a year. Council house building peaked in the 1970s,
but thereafter the stock of social housing was steadily depleted as Margaret
Thatcher's government gave council house tenants the right to buy the
houses they occupied (at hugely subsidized prices) while denying local
authorities the funds to replace the social housing that was lost. The parallel
Thatcherite deregulation of the UK banking sector after 1979 then opened
the way to heavy bank participation in the mortgage market, triggering first
an increase in credit flows for house purchase – domestic mortgage lending
increased from 40 per cent of GDP in 1990 to a remarkable 60 per cent by
2008[81] – and then eventually the erosion of underwriting terms and conditions. As we have noted already, the subprime lending that brought the US
housing market down in 2008 was prefigured by similar practices in the UK,
culminating in the collapse of Northern Rock in September 2007 and the first
run on a bank seen in the UK since the Barings crisis more than a century earlier. And even before that crash occurred, and in spite of New Labour's best
intentions to stimulate a flow of affordable housing,[82] the flow of funds available for house purchase in housing markets with limited and only slowly
growing supply had already triggered a remarkable price explosion there:
"house prices increased on average by 25 per cent in 2002, 22 per cent in 2003,
and by a remarkable £1,100 a *week* in the first half of 2004";[83] to leave the average price of a home, as the Halifax Building Society reported in 2004, already
beyond the reach of a nurse in 496 of the UK's 634 towns and cities, beyond
the reach of a policeman in 400 of them, of a teacher in 390 and of a firefighter
in 251.[84] The very people, that is, whose services were vital to the quality of
urban life in Britain were being increasingly priced out of the communities
they were called upon to serve, even before the 2008 financial crisis then
qualitatively altered the nature of the housing game.

The housing crisis which broke in the UK in September 2007, and the financial crisis that followed a year later, initially hit hardest those who had brought houses at the peak of the price boom.[85] As house prices fell, many were left with negative equity, and a significant number (40,000 in 2008, 48,900 in 2009, 28,900 in 2013 and still 21,000 in 2014) had their houses foreclosed under them. The collapse in house prices left "almost a quarter million UK mortgages in arrears in 2010, and over 116,000 still there in 2014, at a moment at which one UK mortgage in every seven was over four-and-a-half times bigger than the income sustaining it, in a housing market in which average house prices were by then nine times higher than incomes (and in more desirable areas were up to 20 times higher)".[86] But as house prices began to recover in 2014 and 2015, the burden of housing finance incrementally switched from the over-committed to the under-resourced: hitting particularly hard first-time buyers facing both rapidly rising property prices and tougher underwriting standards. In consequence, the scale of home ownership among the young rapidly dipped in volume and slipped back in age, with one recent study suggesting these four things: "that it will now take low- and middle-income families a staggering 24 years to accumulate the deposit for a mortgage – the equivalent figure in the 1990s was just three years; that currently 48 per cent of first-time buyers in the UK find that they need help from more senior members of their family to generate that deposit; that only solid middle-class families can provide that help; and that right now, the typical 30 year-old is 30 per cent less likely to own a home than was the case 15 years ago".[87] Indeed, as James Pickford has recently reported, it is a measure of just how difficult it is in the UK for young adults to finance their own first mortgage that:

> the Bank of Mum and Dad has unofficially become Britain's ninth-biggest 'mortgage lender' with loans and gifts from family or friends increasing 30 per cent this year to £6.5bn as house prices keep rising. The scale of lending from the 'Bomad' which now helps fund 26 per cent of all UK property transactions, puts it on a par with Yorkshire Building Society, the ninth-biggest residential lender in Britain, according to new research. For those under the age of 35, the proportion seeking help from parents, friends and family for property purchases stands at 62 per cent.[88]

House prices in the UK rose 4.5 per cent in 2015, with prices in London surging 12.2 per cent in the year. The pattern in 2016 was similar, with prices rising at about 6 per cent overall, leaving "the typical price tag on a first-time property – one with up to two bedrooms – now at a record high of £194,881".[89] This is a classic case of price inflation caused by inadequate supply and rising demand: making house prices per square foot in London, for example, where that demand is so high, second only to Monaco in the global rankings of expensive cities.[90] When *The Guardian* analysed 19 million sales over 20 years using Land Registry records, they found that "a homeowner earning the median salary for their region in 1995 would have had to spend between 3.2 and 4.4 times their salary on a house, depending on where they lived". But by 2012–13 "the median house price had risen to between 6.1 times and 12.2 times median regional incomes".[91] Total mortgage debt reached the £1 trillion mark in July 2015,[92] when more than one million UK householders had mortgage debt that was over 4.5 times their income;[93] and yet home ownership was by then falling steeply – down from its April 2003 peak of 71 per cent of households to now just 64 per cent.[94]

Figure 5.6 UK house price index, 1945–2016
(Source: Intergenerational Commission, "The Generation of Wealth". London: Resolution Foundation, June 2017, p. 51).

First-time buyers were again particularly badly hit by these rising prices. Even though it is widely recognized that home ownership is more cost-efficient than renting over the course of an adult lifetime – by at least £200,000 according to the Barclay data[95] – first-time buyers moving into the housing market in the UK in 2016/17 faced house prices that had increased for them by 48 times since 1968, "far outpacing incomes which have only grown 29 times".[96] Indeed, housing groups are now warning of the emergence of a "priced-out" generation, as the "proportion of 25–34 year-olds who were owner occupiers ... dropped from 59 per cent to 36 per cent over the last ten years".[97] And because so many younger people who might otherwise have been buying houses remained in the rental sector instead, rents have risen in consequence, with that rise again hitting most heavily the under-resourced – this time, the young poor. Ironically, "over the last five years, huge numbers of potential first time buyers have effectively ended up spending on exorbitant rents more than enough for a first deposit several times over";[98] and in the process, have likely been turned as a generation into permanent renters of their housing rather than its owners. And even staying in the rental sector is not that easy in contemporary Britain: where the Royal Institute of Chartered Surveyors now anticipates a 1.8 million shortfall in the number of required rental units;[99] where the average monthly rent for a home in England and Wales has already reached £846;[100] and where rents are expected to rise sharply over the next five years – maybe by as much as 25 per cent in the over-heated London housing market.[101] That prospect is quite literally terrifying, given that currently in the UK, "almost 20 per cent of in-work renters rely on housing benefit to pay their rent – half a million more people than in 2010 – and tenant evictions in 2015 were at a six-year high, the product of rising rents on the one side and of cuts in housing benefits in the other".[102] Terrifying too for the very young, if the minority Conservative Government ever fully-implement the Cameron-Osborne plan to remove housing benefit entirely from 18–21-year-olds.[103]

If that was not bad enough, there is also this: the way in which non-market housing – social housing – has been allowed to erode in the United Kingdom. It was not always so. "By 1981, non-commodity (non-market) housing, built during the twentieth century by councils, new town corporations and housing associations, accommodated a third of all households, and much higher proportions in many cities".[104] But that was before Margaret Thatcher's right-to-buy policy of the 1980s, or George Osborne's equivalent policies between 2013 and 2016, both of which have helped bring that proportion down to between 15 and 20 per cent, and falling. A remarkable 40 per cent of the properties bought under the Osborne "help to buy" scheme were purchased by landlords treating the housing as an investment asset – capturing the housing benefits via the rents they charged, and evicting those still unable to pay. This was a genuine tragedy, when there are still 1.8 million people in the UK on waiting lists for social housing, and a further 5 million in receipt of housing benefit – half a million more than in 2010 – the total cost of which to the Treasury is now running at £27 billion a year. That is more than the government spends on policing and the purchase of military equipment. In fact, it reflects a complete reversal of housing policy priorities in the space of one generation: "in 1975 more than 80 per cent of public expenditure on housing went on supply-side capital funding (building homes and their upkeep), with rent support and rebates low". Today "85 per cent of spending [is] routed through demand-side revenue funding in the form of housing benefit [and] 40–50 per cent of the annual ... cost of housing benefit goes to private landlords".[105] The policy is crazy, and its impact is negative way beyond the housing sector alone. To quote the Resolution Foundation:

> Housing costs have functioned as a headwind, dragging on incomes over time. When we include housing costs in our wider consideration of living standards, we find over half of households across the working age population have seen falling or flat living standards since 2002. While low and middle income households have been hit the hardest, all parts of the country have seen improvements in their living standards impeded by our failure as a country to deliver affordable housing.[106]

You know that a housing system is in crisis when "the number of householders who own their houses outright outstrips the number of people buying with mortgages",[107] as was the case in the UK in 2013–14. You know that a housing system is in crisis when "under-35s face becoming permanent renters ... with nine out of ten Britons on modest incomes under the age of 35 ... frozen out of home ownership within a decade",[108] as was the case in 2015. You know that even the rented sector is in crisis when research by the housing charity, Shelter finds "that one in three low earners have borrowed money to pay their rent, either from family and friends or through credit cards and payday loans", that "a full 70 per cent of low earners are either struggling or falling behind with rent payments, barely managing to keep a roof over their heads",[109] and that "more than a million households living in private rented accommodation are at risk of becoming homeless by 2020 because of rising rents, benefit freezes and a shortage of social housing".[110] And you know that a housing system is in crisis when rates of overcrowding begin to rise, and when large numbers of young adults begin to share housing or to return to the housing of their parents.* "The London borough of Newham had a 25 per cent rate of overcrowding in 2013";[111] and in 2015 a well-publicized crisis in the availability of student rentals combined with a less-publicized one for young professionals to leave England with as many as 3.5 million households containing "a concealed adult or couple". "If homeownership rates among 25–34 year-olds in 2016 were the same as in 2001 ... an additional 1.8 million people in this age bracket would be home owners in England".[112] But the rate is not the same. Instead, "there has been a major expansion of young people in the private rental sector"[113] – the proportion more than doubling (from 21.4 per cent to 48.2 per cent) between 2003/4 and 2013/14. Angus Armstrong, surveying all this for the NIER in 2016 put it this way:

> There is mounting evidence that we are failing to deliver decent housing, especially for the younger generation. First, more and more houses are being bought for investment purposes which raises the cost of housing. Second, older generations appear to be 'under-occupying' and even hoarding homes while younger generations are struggling to move into homes. Third, the number of new homes continues to fall below the number of new families ... Ownership can adversely affect other citizens through intergenerational fairness. The 50 per cent rise in house prices

---

* "The number of people forced into homelessness is expected to more than double to half a million by 2041 unless the government takes immediate action, a homelessness charity has warned ... the number of people will reach 575,000, up from 236,000 in 2016. The forecast comes as the number of homeless households has jumped by a third in the past five years. The majority of those affected are 'sofa surfers,' with 68,300 people sleeping on other people's couches." (*The Guardian*, 10 August 2017).

over the past decade benefits the existing owners at the cost of those wanting to become owners. The younger generation, perhaps simply not old enough to own in 2004, now have to save 50 per cent more, or £93,000, from after-tax income just to afford an average UK home.[114]

The corroding foundations

When Larry Elliott, the respected *Guardian* journalist, took a rail journey from one end of the UK to the other in 2014, the better to gauge how the country was fairing in the wake of the recession, he reported back on five big themes that he had discovered:

> Theme number one is that modern Britain can be divided into a comfortably off third at the top; a middle third one pay cheque away from financial trouble; and a third at the bottom struggling – and often failing – to make ends meet … Theme number 2 is that the recession accelerated a structural shift in the labour market … poverty is no longer something that happens to the unemployed. It is something that happens to those moving in and out of low-paid jobs and even those in full employment … The third theme is how tough life is for the young … the paradox … is that the young have been the real victims of the crash and its aftermath, but they are much less likely to vote for UKIP than elderly people, who have done much better … Theme number four is the impact of benefit changes … the current system is that if you have a pulse you can work. The fifth theme is the patchy nature of the recovery … with some parts doing fine while people at the bottom rely on food banks.[115]

As now should be obvious from all that Larry Elliott discovered, and from all that has been gathered in this chapter, there is a lot of economic stress around in contemporary Britain; and with it a lot of wear and tear on people's ambitions, their relationships and their confidence in the future. The consequences of the Brexit vote are currently adding to that lack of confidence, leaving even the UK political class unsure of the best way forward; and yet the political class in Britain find themselves in this new age of uncertainty only because their own programmes had systematically failed down the years to address that stress adequately, or to connect in a direct way to their electorate's personal ambitions and private relationships. The UK political class is now having to find a way for the United Kingdom to extricate itself from the European Union because the differential experience of that stress by different groups within the UK electorate had an equally differentiated impact in the referendum vote. In the most general sense, it would appear that the alienation of northern- and midland-workers from their traditional Labour Party roots – and their unease with an influx of Eastern European (and then Middle Eastern immigrants) when their own economic circumstances were so precarious – helped tip the balance of voting in favour of the "Leave" campaign; while the alienation of more-and-more young Britons from conventional politics left many of them omitting to vote at all. All the pre-referendum opinion polls suggested a close relationship between voting and age – the young wanting to stay in the EU, the old wanting to leave – and the UK is leaving the European Union now because the old voted in overwhelming numbers and the young did not.

Which points to the existence of at least three overlapping, and to a degree, conflicting sets of losers in contemporary Britain: a traditional working class (both an old one based in the north and a more modern one located further south), a new ethnic minority population, and a generation of young workers and professionals unable easily to replicate the living standards of their parents. Ethnic and generational tension is nothing new in Britain, of course. Nor is the North–South divide. That goes back at least as far as the original Industrial Revolution, which was almost exclusively centred in the northern quadrant of the United Kingdom, the one bounded by Belfast and Liverpool to its west, Manchester and Sheffield to its South, Newcastle and Sunderland to its East, and Glasgow to its north. That divide has never gone away. It remains as strong now as ever – a divide of wealth, income, social capital and even dialect – that is now ever more deeply embedded, as "many regions have fallen further and further behind London and the South East", to produce what the Social Mobility Commission recently called "a new geography of disadvantage, with many towns and rural areas – not just in the north – being left behind the affluent south-east".[116] Moreover, as an imperial power, down the years Britain drew many of its imperial subjects to the "mother country", there to meet on a daily basis the culture of white superiority that justified imperialism in the first place; and when an imperial power, Britain remained a society (and a polity) run by old men to whom the young were expected both to defer and to obey. No, what has brought fresh flame to these older established fires is the manner in which each now is linked to a weakening of the set of social forces and political relationships that first created, and then sustained, the postwar UK social settlement. At the heart of the UK's malaise is the disintegration of "labourism" as a political project and of the Labour Party as the vehicle for the realization of working-class aspirations.[117]

The rot started with the Thatcherite destruction of the UK's trade union base – a project to which (as we first noted in Chapter 3) the "Iron Lady" was entirely committed, and at which she was entirely successful. The rot was compounded by New Labour's capitulation to that anti-trade union stance: its erosion of its links to the trade union movement when in opposition in the 1980s, and its refusal to reconstitute and strengthen those traditional links when in power.[118] As we saw earlier, when Margaret Thatcher fell from office in 1991, the Chancellor of the Exchequer, singing her praises, told the House of Commons that her great legacy was that of making the idea of the market central to British political discourse; and he was right. She effected a great moving right show. She made privatization preferable to nationalization, deregulation preferable to regulation, and individual wage negotiation preferable to collective bargaining; and she did so in such an effective manner that – as again we noted earlier – the Labour Party fought its way back to power only by accepting these new sets of understandings in full.

Deregulated, privatized British industry then increasingly located its production facilities abroad, relying less and less on the energy sources mined in the English north, or on the labour forces solidly rooted there in now-declining Victorian-style industries (iron and steel, shipbuilding and heavy engineering). Even employment in the more "modern" industries located in the English Midlands – the car industry in particular, but also consumer goods production for the new and more affluent UK home – also increasingly fell victim to cheaper and more efficient competition from abroad – so that (as we discussed more fully in Chapter 3) the UK increasingly survived as an industrial power in the post-Thatcher years only by acting as a "screwdriver economy" for Western Europe – a source of cheaper and less protected labour than that in continental Europe, and as such a poorer market for manufactured products but a cheaper place to put ("screw") them together. Even that role is now jeopardized by Brexit; and it is because the vote in the referendum, when it came, was a huge howl of protest by an abandoned northern and midlands-based working class against the shift of prosperity south into London and the Home Counties.* If New Labour had spent its years in power correcting that imbalance, and retooling UK industry for the new competition, it would likely still be in government and the UK still in the EU. But it did not, and inevitable consequences followed.

John Lanchester recently labelled these "Brexit Blues", and summed up the UK's contemporary reality in the immediate wake of the 2016 vote this way:

> What strikes you as you travel to different parts of the country ... is that the primary reality of modern Britain is not much class as geography. Geography is destiny, and for much of the country, not a happy destiny. To be born in many places in Britain is to suffer an irreversible lifelong defeat – a truncation of opportunity, of education, of access to power, of life expectancy. The people who grow up in these places come from a cultural background which equips them for reasonably well-paid manual labour, un- and semi-skilled. Children left school as soon as they could and went to work in the same industries that had employed their parents. The academically able kids used to go to grammar school and be educated into the middle class. All that has now gone, the jobs and the grammar schools, and the vista instead is a landscape where there is often work – there are pockets of unemployment, but in general there is no shortage of jobs ... but it's unsatisfying, insecure and low paid. The new work doesn't do what the old work did: it doesn't offer a sense of identity or community or self-worth [And] what, over the last few decades, has been the political 'offer' to these people? In truth, nothing much.[119]

---

* Even before the 2008 recession, when "average disposable household income was £19,038 in London and £16,792 in the south-east, the ONS said, compared to £12,543 in the north-east." (*The Guardian*, 1 April 2010).

That the sense of abandonment should have been so focused on the question of immigration was partly an accident of timing – the product of an unexpected refugee tsunami sweeping out of the Middle East into the European Union's open borders as the horror of the Syrian civil war escalated. But that the focus should have been so negative – that there were so many votes against immigration in the June 2016 referendum and so few for it – speaks to the existence of a deeper and a more engrained antipathy to immigration in the United Kingdom. The first wave of immigration in modern times in the UK was a mid-nineteenth century Irish one, into the northern factories of Victorian England at the height of their competitive success: and that wave was certainly met with anti-Irish riots. Likewise, the Jewish influx into the UK's major cities after the Russian pograms of the 1890s was met a generation later with fascist marches as the Depression deepened in the 1930s (the last anti-Jewish riot in the UK took place in Manchester in 1947, triggered by the killing of British soldiers in Palestine).[120] Like-wise too, there was local resistance to the arrival in the UK after 1948 of immigrants from both the Caribbean and South Asia drawn by the shortage of labour in full-employment Britain. The fact that those immigrants did the grunt work – the shift work, the long hours – that kept fundamentally uncompetitive UK industries like textiles alive economically for another two or more decades, did not ease tensions between the new immigrants and the old workers. Rather, it exacerbated them, as they competed for employment, and as they shared depleted levels of social capital (run down housing, poor schools, limited health services and so on). There were race riots in Nottingham in 1958. London dockworkers marched in support of Enoch Powell after his "rivers of blood" speech in 1968, and there were major riots again – this time, of protest by the black as well as by the white urban poor – in 1981 and 2011. Race relations are not the daily tinderbox in the UK that they are in the US, but the tensions are there nonetheless, just under the surface, available to be galvanized by the extreme Right when circumstances serve. And they served in June 2016 in a way that even the most extreme of the "Leave" campaigners – UKIP's Nigel Farage (Donald Trump's main UK ally in 2016) – failed to anticipate. They served very well then,[121] to our long-term grief and cost.

Racial tensions might ease again in the UK if and as immigration slows; but the plight of the millennial generation there is likely to be less easy to ameliorate. The signs of stress among the millennials are everywhere. The newspaper headlines tell it all. These are from *The Guardian*: "Growing numbers of would-be-first time buyers are moving back in their parents ... 28 per cent in 2015 compared with 24 per cent in 2012".[122] "Almost half of students who are among the first cohort to graduate after paying the £9,000 tuition fees have moved back in with their parents after leaving university".[123] "Average alcohol consumption has fallen in many nations, but it has gone up in the UK ... binge drinking [is turning] our towns and cities into ugly and threatening places at night".[124*] And this from the Compass report, "Something's Not Right: Insecurity and an Anxious Nation": "In Britain last year, 50 million prescriptions were issued for antidepressants and more young men died from suicide than from any other cause".[125] None of this ought to be acceptable in a successful society – the young should not need to use alcohol and drugs on this life-threatening scale to soften the reality they know and the reality that lies before them. It should not be acceptable to them, nor should it be acceptable to the rest of us. For the millennial generation are our collective future, and in truth they are already the core of the labour force of our present. But neither the present they experience, nor the likely future they face, is adequate either to their needs or to their desserts. If this chapter tells us anything, it is that both are flawed, and that both need to be fundamentally changed.

---

* And not just among the young. The United States is not the only country struggling with a dramatic rise in alcohol-related escalating health costs and increased deaths. Senior UK doctors are currently warning that, without a dramatic rise in minimum alcohol pricing, "almost 63,000 people in England will die over the next five years from liver problems related to heavy drinking, and that alcohol abuse will cost the NHS £16.74bn to treat." (*The Guardian*, 23 July 2017).

PART III

Inadequate Politics

6

The Continuing Cost of Empire

"Every gun that is made, every warship launched, every rocket fired, signifies, in the final sense, a theft from those who hunger and are not fed, those who are cold and are not clothed."

Dwight D. Eisenhower[1]

"My Lord, you can do anything you like with bayonets, except sit on them."

Talleyrand[2]

You might be forgiven for thinking that, with this degree of economic difficulty and social distress all around them, the full attention of the political class in both the United States and the United Kingdom would be focused on these two features of life alone. But, of course, the full attention of those who govern us is not so singularly focused, because in each case those in power in Washington, DC and in London do more than govern internally. They also move around the world stage as important and intrusive players. They each supervise economies, one major export of which are armaments sold to governments and individuals abroad;* and they each rely on societies, part of whose stability is underwritten by both the legacies and the contemporary practice of empire. There is an external dimension to the flaws of contemporary capitalism in both the UK and the US. We therefore need both to understand the linkage between external role and internal weakness in each case, and to see that – in consequence – going beyond the internal flaws

---

* The US is currently the world's greatest seller of arms, and the UK is second, with two-thirds of all UK arms sales since 2010 going to the Middle East (Source: *The Independent*, 16 December 2016).

of each economy and society will require, as one element of reform, a major resetting of those external roles.

The most immediate costs of empire are most visible in the empire which is most immediate: namely the American one. The British empire is now very much a thing of the past, and the British like to think of themselves as fully post-imperial. But to the degree that they do, they partially delude themselves: because the economy and the society of the contemporary UK continues to be shaped by the legacies of an empire now gone. Those longer and more subtle costs of empire await America down the line; which is why here it makes sense to focus on the immediate costs of empire through American data and the longer consequences of empire through British data. America and its empire, first then; the legacies of the British empire, second; and the ongoing need to break fundamentally with imperial practices and mindsets, third.

The immediate costs of the American empire

There is no controversy at all these days about the existence in the past of something called "the British Empire". There is not even much controversy about why that empire was lost. But there is an enormous debate about whether America, in picking up the role of global leadership from the British in the last years of the Second World War, did or did not also in the process pick up the trappings of empire; and in that debate, one very strong voice is that of denial. Donald Rumsfeld, of all people, once famously told the Iraqis that "we're not imperialistic. We never have been".[3] Bizarre as that claim may seem to many people outside the United States, it does make a certain kind of sense when we recall that the United States tells its own history as one of rebellion against imperial rule, and when we note that, once independent, the United States certainly avoided – although it was at times tempted to indulge in – the acquisition of extensive colonial holdings outside the continental United States itself (it took great chunks of the Mexican empire in the 1840s, of course, and even bought Alaska from the Russian empire a generation later). Puerta Rico, Guam and Samoa can certainly be thought of as US colonies, but they are not extensive; and the one that was – the Philippines – the

US lost briefly to Japan in 1941 and then permanently to independence in 1946. But empires come in a variety of forms; and in the modern era are as much based on economic dominance and military hegemony as they are on territorial holdings. Understood in those terms at least, the United States definitely possesses an empire, and it is one that is currently generating its own version of the standard costs and benefits of imperial rule experienced by other empires before it.

THE IMMEDIATE COST OF US MILITARY SPENDING

The costs of this modern form of empire are – at their most obvious – those of military expenditure, which in the case of the United States post 9/11, have been and remain truly enormous. In the fiscal year 2017, the Pentagon had a budget of $617 billion. That budget laid claim to 3.3 per cent of US GDP (down from its recent peak of 4.8 per cent in 2010–11),[4] made up nearly 40 per cent of military spending in the world as a whole, and in 2010 was bigger on its own than the equivalent budgets of the next 17 largest military spenders combined, many of whom also happened to be US allies. But the Pentagon budget, although enormous, is not the sum of it. As we first noted in Chapter 2, sixteen different intelligence agencies, and a swathe of federal depart-ments (most notably the Department of Homeland Security) also spend money as part of the US national security effort; and a number of others spend money now because of the current legacies of national security efforts in the past – legacies of debt to the Treasury, and of damaged soldiers to the Veterans Administration. When you also factor in the cost of two ongoing Middle Eastern wars ($8 trillion expended, with more on the way) and the cost of the US's clandestine services and overseas covert operations (over $50 billion in 2013, for example), it is at least possible that the actual cost of sustaining the United States as a global military power doubles the official Pentagon budget, absorbing as it does so almost half of total federal expendi-tures in the United States and taking up perhaps 10 per cent of US GDP. William Hartung, recently calculating the overall cost of "national security" for *TomDispatch*, put that number at $1.09 trillion for 2017;[5] and the *War Resisters League* put the total cost of the US military for 2017, even higher (and even before the Trump budget was factored in) at $3,000 billion![6] Those numbers may be a tad on the inflated-side for most people's tastes, but there is no getting away from the fact that the amount of money spent by and in the United States on military matters these days is truly vast.

It is not just, however, that these costs are high now. It is also that they were even higher in the immediate past, before the drawdown of troops in Iraq: and that then and now, they are not new. On the contrary, in a real sense the United States has been at war regularly since 1941: sometimes locked into a Cold War of defence and attrition, and sometimes into a more conventional kind of war with full-scale military deployment and boots on the ground. US ground troops were deployed in significant numbers in Korea between 1950 and 1953, in Vietnam between 1964 and 1975, in Afghanistan after September 2001, and in Iraq from March 2003. Mix in to that set of formal large-scale deployments a string of smaller and briefer military engagements – from Lebanon in 1958 to Kosovo in 1998 – and the sense of permanence grows; and exists even before we bring into the calculation the range and scale of covert operations undertaken down the years by the CIA and now formally under the command of the US military's SOCOM (Special Operations Command). In relation to this, as we noted in *America in the Shadow of Empires*:

> Since at least the days of the failed raid to rescue American hostages from Iran in 1980, the US military has trained and used special operations forces in an increasing number of countries. During Barack Obama's first term as president, black-op teams operated for certain in at least 75 countries (and possibly as many as 120), up from the 60 into which such units were deployed under George W. Bush. SOCOM ... now has some 60,000 personnel and a budget of at least $6.3 billion; and CIA operations, though never publicly recorded, have now clearly expanded to include the maintenance of secret prisons, rendition and torture.[7]

America now possesses a land army (of some 1.2 million active-duty personnel, with a further 800,000 in the reserves). It deploys a naval capacity on each ocean built around 10 Nimitz-class nuclear-powered aircraft-carriers (no other country does that: Russia and China, for example, each have just one aircraft carrier); and it retains a set of intercontinental nuclear missiles siloed in the centre of the United States and ready for immediate deployment if required. No other major capitalist nation has a military capacity of this scale and kind. The French and the British retain many of the trappings of empire, including spheres of influence in some of their former colonies, and a limited nuclear capacity; but each currently possesses only a shadow of the military potential they enjoyed at the height of their imperial greatness – and Germany and Japan, stripped of empire by military defeat in 1945, have built up considerable military capacities, but ones which they choose to use purely for immediate defensive purposes. Only the United States in the modern era combines global economic leadership with global military deployment; and that military deployment now comes at such a cost that it potentially threatens the American economy's capacity to lead.

Not that the current generation of political leaders, on either side of the aisle, necessarily see it that way. They do not. On the contrary, they think that US military spending is a price worth paying; because they believe, as Barack Obama explained when receiving the Nobel Peace Prize, that the US military role abroad is a vital prerequisite for global prosperity, and that the sustenance of rising global prosperity is a vital long-term US economic interest. The United States voluntarily chooses to bear "this burden", the new President told the assembled notables in Oslo in 2009, "not because we seek to impose our will ... [but] because we seek a better future for our children and grandchildren, and we believe our lives will be better if others' children and grandchildren can live in freedom and prosperity". His first Secretary of State put it similarly – that the United States prides itself on being "the indispensable nation": "when America is absent", she said, "especially from unstable environments, there are consequences. Extremism takes root; our interests suffer; and our security at home is threatened".[8] Armed with self-confidence of this kind, indeed, the United States may not seize and retain whole countries – by the time America became a global power, the non-industrialized world had been largely carved up by other industrialized powers – but it does take and retain land for a global network of American military *bases* (at the height of the Iraq War, nearly 1,000 in total), and it does deploy drone-strikes across national boundaries whenever its intelligence sources locate a target of interest. The United States allows no such intrusion into its own airspace, of course – double-standards being central to imperial rule whenever it occurs – but the US military regularly invades the airspace of others, just as in the past it calmly invaded sovereign nations whenever its government, and its government alone, decided that full-scale military deployment was necessary.* Not that those invasions have been wonderfully successful, however: the current post-Second World War tally is a draw in Korea, a defeat in Vietnam, and a first excursion into the Middle East in 1991 that a decade later brought a second war from which the United States has so far found no credible route of retreat. This, plus a record of covert operations in other countries' territory – proxy wars – that came with some remarkable and unanticipated blowback: secret wars that, for example, "included covert support for the mujahidin in Afghanistan against the Soviets in the 1980s, support that came back to haunt us in a very big way in September 2001".[9]

THE OPPORTUNITY COSTS OF MILITARY SPENDING

The most obvious and terrible costs of all this global military spending and deployment are not opportunity ones, in the way in which economists treat these things. The most obvious and terrible costs are human ones: costs to the soldiers, sailors, and airmen that the US military sends into harm's way, and costs to the civilians caught up in the wars that such spending and deployment sustains. Since the attack on the US homeland on 9/11, which on the day took almost 3,000 lives, the United States has fought prolonged ground wars first in Afghanistan (where bin Laden was based) and in Iraq (where he was not). To date, nearly 7,000 US soldiers have been killed in action in those two theatres of war, and at least 32,000 have returned to the US seriously physically damaged. The mental damage to returning veterans has been even greater and more ubiquitous. To date, more than 500,000 veterans with service in either Afghanistan or Iraq (and often in both) – one in three of the men and women deployed – have returned home with some form of post-traumatic stress disorder, depression or traumatic brain injury; and that number holds true even before we supplement it with the scale of post-deployment domestic violence, separation and divorce triggered by the traumas of war. The burden on the civilians in each war zone was likely heavier still, although less carefully-calculated. The number of Iraqi civilian deaths

---

* The US dropped 26,171 bombs on 7 Muslim-majority countries in 2016 (Source: Alternet.org, 10 January 2017).

during the American occupation totalled anywhere between 110,000 and 1.2 million, depending on the source used. The number of Afghan civilian deaths is not even known. The number of internally displaced Iraqis was probably 1.25 million out of a total population of just over 33 million. The number of refugees was over 1.5 million. These are huge numbers, capturing human suffering and distress of the most basic kind.[10]

There exists a string of moral issues that we might discuss here – and indeed should discuss, if the legitimacy of the Iraq invasion in 2003 was our prime concern. But that conversation has recently gone on publicly elsewhere, particularly in London in the wake of the publication of the Chilcot Report on the involvement of the UK government under Tony Blair in the invasion of Iraq,[11] and is not our prime concern. Our prime concern here has to be with important second-order issues – with both the immediate and long-term economic and social fallout from so difficult, controversial and dangerous a military endeavour; and in focusing in on that, the relevant datum is less the cost in human lives (terrible as that cost is) than it is the cost of policy adopted, and policy foregone, because of so large and persistent a military budget. Our focus here has to be on the genuine and calculable *opportunity costs* of military spending, and on the more *general functionality*, or otherwise, of the existence of so large a military-industrial complex at the heart of a liberal capitalist economy.

On the immediate opportunity costs of a large US military budget, we can say this. Money spent on armaments, military personnel, and overseas wars is money that a more peaceful government could spend on better things: better roads, better schools, better healthcare, better rehabilitation programmes for returning and damaged veterans, and so on. We know the cost of keeping a single soldier in Afghanistan for a year: roughly $1 million. We also know the cost of employing extra teachers, extra law enforcement personnel, or extra hospital workers. An extra teacher, for example, costs the school board employing him/her a fraction of the cost to the Pentagon of deploying that one soldier – maybe 17 teachers could be hired if that one soldier was not.[12] Making calculations like this is not rocket science. It is simple common sense. If the US military budget had continued to decline, as it initially did as a peace dividend at the end of the Cold War, the social fabric of American society would now be better resourced. That it is not better resourced, and that the military budget continues to be high, means that in each financial year serious choices have to be made by those who govern us: on whether, for example, to equally sequester discretionary spending and military spending, as in the latter Obama years; or to drastically prune basic social services while inflating military spending, as was proposed in its initial budget by the Trump Administration. And in making that latter choice, the Trump team indicated its willingness to prioritize public spending that has a lower multiplier-effect out into the wider economy than would spending on the social programmes they would prune. In *America in the Shadow of Empires*, we put the multiplier-effect point this way:

> Recent work by Robert Pollin and Heidi Garrett-Peltier would suggest that "investments in the green economy, health care and education will produce between about 50–140 per cent more jobs than if the same amount of money were spent by the Pentagon". So the choices here – effectively between guns and butter – are very real ones, and ones that have been publicly recognized for a very long time. Right now, if Pollin and Garrett-Peltier are correct, $1 spent on the military will generate about 11,200 jobs in the United States, if given directly to consumers to spend will generate 15,100 jobs, and if given to education 26,700 jobs.[13]

The work by Robert Pollin and Heidi Garrett-Peltier cited here brings into sharp relief the bigger and more fundamental question of the *functionality* or *dysfunctionality* of large military budgets for the competitive strength of predominantly civilian-focused economies. That question has long been discussed in the relevant academic literature, and there is more than one view.[14] As far as US military spending is concerned, there are broadly four arguments on the functionality side. The first is that the post-1941 mobilization of large-scale military production runs did lay the foundations for the postwar Fordist-based productivity boom. The second is that, for a large part of the post-1945 period, the R & D expenditure financed by the Pentagon did have important and positive spin-offs for US civilian-focused production. The third, linked to that, is that the US military-industrial complex then drove economic growth across the economy as a whole, acting as the general economic catalyst in much the same manner that the cotton industry did for the original industrial revolution in the UK, and railroad construction did for the US's nineteenth-century leap into industrial growth. And the fourth – that the kind of skilled labour required by the military-industrial sector helped create a powerful postwar US middle class, whose skill sets were then trans-mitted on to future generations. The counterview was and remains just the reverse: that military spending invariably squeezes out more important long-term social investments. That it distorts the distribution of R & D resources, pulling them away from civilian-focused production. That throughout the postwar period as a whole, there was and is more "spin-in" to the military-industrial complex than "spin-out" from the military to the civilian side of the core US manufacturing sector; and that key elements of that sector went competitively soft, particularly after 1980, protected from the need to remain at the forefront of technological capacity and financial rigour by the cost-plus contracts given by a Pentagon keen to sustain a uniquely American capacity to build as well as to bear arms. "Destruction by neglect"[15] is how one set of scholars characterized the fate of the US electronics industry in the 1980s, for example: one of a list of industrial sectors (beginning with steel and ending with semi-conductors) in which a Pentagon-led industrial strategy appeared to fall victim to Japanese competition in that decade, and to its Chinese equivalent two decades later.

When surveying this debate as the new millennium opened,[16] three con-clusions seemed right then, and remain right now. The first is that most of the research data suggests a broadly neutral impact of military expenditure on more general US competitiveness, and at worst a slightly negative one, at least by the 1980s. Certain US industrial regions – the so-called "gun belt" – clearly benefit from Pentagon largesse; and certain categories of employment (particularly high-skilled engineering workers) benefit directly too. But those gains, even at the peak of the functionality between military- and civilian-production, did not thereby lift the rest of the economy to new heights of competitiveness. On the contrary, as US civilian-focused industries ran into stiffer international competition – from Germany in the 1970s, Japan in the 1980s and by extension China after 2000, Sandler and Hartley (the most careful of the relevant scholars) concluded that "the net impact of defense spending on growth was negative".[17]

The second reasonably secure conclusion we can draw in this area is that the functionality of US defence expenditure to US-based capital accumulation generally varied over time. It was highly functional at the beginning of the postwar period, lubricating the spread of Fordist production methods across US industry and, via its negative impact on the US balance of payments, enhancing the global money supply (and hence global levels of demand) at a time when American goods were heavily sought after in world markets. But as we saw in more detail in Chapter 2, as the Fordist settlement unwound, US defence expenditure became less and less functional to continued US industrial supremacy: triggering the collapse of the dollar as the financing of the Vietnam War flooded world money markets with unwanted dollars in the late 1960s and, through the industrial and state policy priorities it generated, leaving US export (and later home) markets vulnerable after the Vietnam War to competitive capture by the retooled consumer goods industries of other major industrial producers. The third conclusion we might draw then is this; that even in its prime, defence spending was an expensive way of creating jobs; and that prime has now passed. The capacity of defence expenditure to generate commercially significant spin-offs has progressively declined; and because it has, it is hard to disagree with the general judgement made by Sandler and Hartley at the conclusion of their extraordinarily thorough study of the relationship between defence inputs and the industrial base: that "defense reallocations are not the desired pathway to growth".[18]

THE LONG-TERM COST OF MILITARY SPENDING

This carefully-anchored scepticism about the economic value of a large and growing military budget can only be reinforced when a set of longer-term and more indirect consequences of such spending are added to the mix. It is not just that certain immediate policy priorities – particularly on the social side of the equation – are invariably downgraded, depleted or lost entirely, the more that military spending rises. It is also that certain patterns of institutional development and cultural change make their own deep contribution to the flawed nature of the capitalism being so stoutly defended by that military effort: and from a list of such long-term consequences, we might here just pick two that are of particularly current significance for the politics of the United States: those of outsourcing and financialization.

But before we do, it is worth noting the upside of being the economically hegemonic power. It is not all bad economic news for empires. Empires attract a lot of subsidy. They find borrowing resources from outside sources easier than it might otherwise have been because the collateral asked of them on such borrowing is invariably low, relative to the borrowing capacity of non-empires. However, even this financial arbitrage comes at a serious long-term price – what Colin Read once labelled "the winner's curse"[19] – in that imperial centres of power come to enjoy a credit-rating that is often too good for their own long-term viability. For that financial arbitrage quickly leaves them disproportionately dependent, for the maintenance of the internal living standards of their home population, on the continued willingness of foreign holders of investment funds to place those funds in the imperial core. And in any event, obtaining things easily because of imperial preference invariably weakens the ability of empires to generate those things for themselves. It frees them from any immediate confrontation with the reality of market forces; and it alters the relative weight within their underlying economy of the sectors that manufacture things and those that merely play with money.

The United States' rapidly changing economic relationship with communist China is a clear case in point. Before 9/11, the annual US trade deficit with China was small: just $10.4 billion in 1991. Twenty-five years later, it was well over $300 billion. When the trade deficit was small, the main US exports to China were manufactured and durable goods, while at home the US-based furniture industry still employed 80,000 Americans and the textile industry 1.5 million. Right now, among the main US exports to China are scrap metal and waste paper – it is as though they sell us the manufactured goods that American consumers need, and we sell them back the packaging in which those goods arrived. As we discussed more fully in Chapter 2, manufacturing employment in the United States has plummeted as Chinese exports of manufactured goods have grown, and although the nature of the causal linkage between those things is a matter of fierce dispute, there is no escaping the fact that since 9/11 the United States has racked up a large and persistent deficit on its balance of trade – particularly with China – a deficit that it can only finance by attracting inflows of foreign direct investment. A lesser power, lacking that capacity, would have been obliged to address its trade deficit directly and immediately: but the United States thus far has escaped that imperative. Whether that will be to its long-term economic cost will depend on the willingness of foreign investors to continue placing their money in Wall Street, but already there is economic dependency here. By indulging in the winner's curse as it has fought its now 16 year-long war in the Middle East, the United States has allowed its economic superiority significantly to wane.

OUTSOURCING

One key element in that waning has been, and remains, the propensity of large US-based companies to relocate more-and-more of their basic production processes to economies outside the United States, where labour costs are lower and growing foreign markets are closer to hand. Safe in a post-Cold War world under the protection and umbrella of US arms, American-based multinationals, which as late as the 1990s were net job creators inside the continental United States itself, have since 9/11 cut employment at home and raised it overseas (by something of the order of 2.9 million in the first decade of the new millennium while adding 2.4 million abroad). Of course, in one sense there is nothing new in this redeployment: American capital went abroad during the Cold War years too, embedding itself in, and helping to reconstruct, economies such as West Germany and Japan at the behest of the American state. But in the post-Cold War years, the imperative to locate production facilities overseas has been qualitatively different. This has been outsourcing driven not by the search for global political stability but by the search for corporate cost-competitiveness; and here the great losers have been American workers, particularly white unionized male workers in the hitherto impregnable Fordist-based semi-automated production systems of the American Midwest. The advocates of outsourcing, and of the associated importation of manufactured goods made outside the United States, invariably insist that the practice has made goods cheaper in US retail stores, and so enhanced the living standards of the American consumer. But those consumers are also workers, and it cannot be emphasized strongly enough that the limited gain brought to American consumers by cheaper imports has been more than offset, since 9/11, by the adverse impact of those imports on general US wage levels – pulling those wages down even before the financial crisis, according to the EPI, by \$2,500 annually for a typical two-income family in 2006, and by 4 percentage points overall for American workers without a college degree. As we discussed more fully earlier, the "hollowing out" of the American middle class has one of its main drivers here: a race to the bottom caused by wage-competition with less well-paid labour forces overseas. The experience of GM workers is symptomatic of this wider trend: "before the 2008–9 recession, a typical GM worker cost the company about \$56 an hour with benefits. Equivalent costs in Mexico were \$7, in China \$4.40, and in India \$1. New hires back in the United States after the recession reportedly started at \$14 an hour".[20]

FINANCIALIZATION

The great winner in all this, by contrast, has been American finance. As we argued at greater length in *America in the Shadow of Empires*, the inward flow of predominantly Japanese capital in the 1990s helped create what Colin Crouch called "privatized Keynesianism",[21] fuelling a Wall Street bull market that raised dramatically the paper-wealth of US asset holders and so financed the Clinton boom years. Similar flows, more from China this time, financed the property bubble during the George W. Bush years that came crashing down in 2008. As Herman Schwartz put it, "during the long 1990s, the U.S. economy avoided the normal trade-offs across domestic consumption, domestic investment, and overseas investment" because "massive foreign lending relieved the normal constraints" and "enabled the United States to enjoy differential domestic growth".[22] Even now, with the US manufacturing and service sectors growing only slowly, the influx of foreign capital has restored profitability to Wall Street, and with it the return of those remarkable bonuses for senior financiers that briefly so outraged American public opinion in the immediate wake of the 2008 financial crash. And of course, "the status of the dollar as the world currency gives the USA, as a debtor country, the unique privilege of being able to borrow from foreigners in its own currency, which means that any depreciation of that currency will both reduce the value of US debt and increase the competitiveness of US exports".[23] Given the scale of debt the United States has now racked up with China in particular, the world's remaining superpower may well in consequence have manoeuvred itself from a position of economic strength in 1945 to one of such financial indebtedness by 2017 as to be now literally "too big to fail". Lawrence Summers, for one, thinks so: writing of "*a balance of financial terror*" in which the US relies on the cost to others of not financing its current account deficit as assurance that such financing will continue.[24]

There is much that is precarious here. For financial empires rest on the confidence of those who control large investment flows (now not simply central banks and multinational corporations, but also increasingly the managers of sovereign wealth funds); and that confidence is necessarily extremely fragile. Partly this fragility derives from the separation of financial circuits from those of industrial and mercantile ones. The more financial institutions make money by trading with each other, the more they become vulnerable to cycles of speculative fever, and the more the transactions they finance become of less and less value to the rest of the economy beyond. Partly the fragility is a product of the inadequate external governance of the financial sector itself, and of the excessive speculation which that inadequate governance allows. Partly the fragility is a product of the centrality of Wall Street institutions to a domestic economy that sustained itself from the 1980s only by substituting rising private debt for stagnant private wages; and partly it can be a product of the disproportionate exposure of even large American financial institutions to the weaker sections of a global economy which is necessarily characterized at its core by processes of combined but uneven development. The American financial system is currently vulnerable to at least three, and possible four, of those sources of fragility. It is fragile by function. It is fragile by governance. It is fragile by the scale of private debt; and it may well be fragile by exposure.

And while Wall Street flourishes, the signs and symptoms of long-term economic weakening are everywhere to be seen, if people are willing to look. The United States was once the best educated society on earth: but not now (the latest PISA scores rank US 15 year-olds seventeenth internationally for reading literacy, twenty-fourth in science literacy and thirty-first in maths). The United States was once the world leader in R & D expenditure, responsible for 38 per cent of total global spending in 1996 – but today, for just 30 per cent. The United States was once the leading economy across a swathe of industrial sectors. It no longer is: leading the pack now only in the more restricted list of computer hardware, software, biotechnology, aerospace and entertainment. The United States was once the society which everyone aspired to join: but no longer. The latest UN survey on human happiness awarded top spot to Norway, and then to Denmark – highly regulated capital-isms with a strong social democratic base. Liberal-capitalist America slipped from third place in 1996 to just sixteenth in 2017, with unhappiness in Amer-ica growing, so the UN report said, because of declining social support and increased corruption.[25] (The detailed report emphasized too the deleterious consequences for US happiness of excessive money in politics, increased income and wealth inequality, enhanced immigration, and the deteriorating quality of the US education system).*

In truth, US underperformance here should come as no surprise. For the guilty secret at the heart of the American empire has long been this. Previous empires have normally enriched their core populations, by drawing into the imperial centre the surplus product of their far-flung possessions. But not this empire: for all that overall American living standards are cushioned by the willingness of foreigners to finance the continuing US trade deficit, the contemporary American version of empire disproportionately enriches just the privileged few, while imposing impossible burdens on military families, and leaving the rest of the US civilian population either financially embattled or actually impoverished. No wonder, therefore, that an electorate has now emerged in the United States that is open to the appeal of a certain kind of right-wing populism. It is a populism which claims that, by resetting the financing and priorities of an American empire whose legitimacy at home remains largely unchallenged, it can bring generalized prosperity back to those many Americans whom the empire, however successful abroad,

---

* The conclusion of the UN report is worth noting, raising as it does themes that here will occupy Chapters 7 and 8. "In sum, the United States offers a vivid portrait of a country that is looking for happiness 'in all the wrong places'. The country is mired in a roiling social cri-sis that is getting worse. Yet the dominant political discourse is all about raising the rate of economic growth. And the prescriptions for faster growth – mainly deregulation and tax cuts – are likely to exacerbate, not reduce social tensions. Almost surely, further tax cuts will increase inequality, social tensions, and the social and economic divide between those with a college degree and those without." (*World Happiness Report*, 2017).

apparently forgot at home. The ultimate cost of American empire right now is nothing less than the presidency of Donald J. Trump – and it is an appalling price to pay.

The long shadow of British imperialism

Empires have gone wrong before, of course: and in both their errors and their demise have thrown a long shadow forward. Part of that shadow is a cultural and ideational one – an inherent sense of imperial superiority in the mindset of the empire's core population that slides easily into a defensive racism when post-imperial economic difficulties intensify and jihadists counter-attack. That shadow – visible now in the contemporary politics of all the major nineteenth-century European imperialisms (French and Dutch no less than Belgian and British) awaits our consideration in the last section of this chapter. What needs to be considered ahead of that however are the other, less dramatic and more institutional, legacies of empire – which in the British case include at least the early loss of manufacturing leadership, the excessive presence of global finance within the contemporary UK economy, and the distorted industrial policy of a globally-preoccupied British state. Each of those legacies helps explain contemporary UK weaknesses in both economy and society; and each, of course, has striking American parallels.

THE LOSS OF MANUFACTURING LEADERSHIP

As we noted briefly at the opening of Chapter 3, the nineteenth-century expansion of the British Empire was made possible by the UK economy's position in the 1860s and 1870s as the manufacturing "workshop of the world" – occupying a global position then of the kind that the US manufacturing sector would enjoy after 1945, and that arguably the Chinese manufacturing sector is beginning to occupy now. But the critical point for us here is not that the UK occupied that position. It is rather that it occupied it only briefly. It is that positions of manufacturing dominance can be lost – and that they certainly were in the UK case. In the wake of German unification in 1871 and the termination of the US Civil War a half-decade earlier, UK-based manufacturing firms incrementally lost their position of global leadership to more modernized producers based in both those countries. Economies catching up invariably follow the best of the practices of the economy they are pursuing, not its average ones: and after 1870 Germany and the United States certainly copied best UK practice, the quicker to surpass it. Then, and as we noted earlier, instead of responding to this rise of high-quality global competition by fundamentally altering their production processes and marketing methods, most late nineteenth-century UK-based firms chose instead to cling ever more tightly to processes and methods they already knew, the ones that had worked in the past; and they retreated into the more protected markets of their own Empire. The result after 1945 was two-fold – and helps explain much of what still ails the modern UK economy.

First, although UK manufacturing industry did increasingly restructure itself – moving from a focus on Victorian industries to post-Victorian ones, going from ships to cars and from coal to electricity – it did so in only a limited and ultimately inadequate fashion. By 1961, the UK car industry was the main employer of manufacturing labour and the most significant source of manufacturing exports – and yet that car industry still manifested the weaknesses of the "flawed Fordism" we briefly touched upon when discussing the fall of the UK's first post-Second World War SSA in Chapter 3.[26] The UK's postwar factories were too small, its ownership structure was too scattered, its level of investment was too low – and it must be said, its workers were too strong on the shop floor – adequately to compete with first German and then Japanese car production as those economies emerged from their brief period of postwar dislocation. The result – the second feature of the UK's postwar manufacturing condition – was that from 1966 (the peak year for manufacturing employment in the postwar UK) the car industry and others began to experience "negative de-industrialization".[27] Like more successful economies elsewhere, the UK economy deindustrialized. Service employment and output came to play a greater and greater role in the construction and delivery of the UK's GDP, as manufacturing employment shrank by 2000 to half its 1966 peak. But unlike those more successful economies, the bulk of UK deindustrialization was increasingly negative rather than positive in form: it was the product of factories shedding jobs because they could not compete, rather than shedding jobs because they were becoming ultra-productive.[28] These days, economies with strong manufacturing bases run large balance of trade surpluses. Those with weak manufacturing bases run balance of trade deficits. The UK moved into a trade deficit on its manufacturing ledger in 1983 and has been in deficit ever since.

THE GROWING BURDEN OF ITS FINANCIAL SYSTEM

Empires like the British – just like the American later – build their dominance on the global strength of their manufacturing sectors and on the quality of their armaments, and initially the parallel growth of financial institutions at the heart of the empire only reinforces that global strength. In the late nineteenth century, UK-based manufacturers needed overseas buyers, and those overseas buyers needed London-provided credit. In the south of the island, the City built its reputation as a global financial centre while away in the north manufacturing firms produced and increasingly exported world-class products (and used their own profits – and not City-provided funds – to sustain their internal investment programmes). In the late-Victorian heyday of the British Empire, sterling acted as the world's global currency and the UK traded manufactured goods for food and raw materials in the manner of modern America. But over time (and indeed quite quickly – certainly well before 1914), all that foreign lending helped key overseas economies catch up and surpass the British in manufacturing capability. It gave London-based financial institutions a set of interests in the success of those economies, rather than in the success of their own; and it established a *gap* between industry and finance that undermined the ability of British manufacturing firms to raise the long-term capital they eventually needed to meet the challenge of all this fierce international competition.

The long-term consequence of that gap was partly economic, leaving in place what London's leading financial journalist, Martin Wolf, recently described as the UK's current strategic nightmare: "a strong comparative advantage in the world's most irresponsible industry"[29] – namely finance. But the long-term consequences of this late nineteenth-century separation of industry and finance ran far wider than that: they were and remain social and political, and not simply economic, in character. For the initial social result of this "two-track development of capital" in the late nineteenth century UK economy "was a marked division within the propertied middle class".[30] The division was partly a geographical one: between a commercial middle class in London and an industrial middle class in the British north.[31] But it was also a political division – a gap of empathy and social standing between an industrial entrepreneurial class located predominantly away from London and a political elite that was still London-focused – one, moreover, still disproportionately staffed by a predominantly southern-based aristocracy whose own income-source was increasingly shifting from rents to interest. For all its mid nineteenth-century domination of global output and trade flows, the UK's industrial owning class never replaced in political influence more traditional elites whose income depended on banking and on land. What the UK's brief Victorian period of global manufacturing dominance then consolidated was not "rule by business" in some modern American sense. It consolidated instead a system of "gentlemanly capitalism"[32] – a fusion of aristocratic and banking interests, and the dissemination of a social culture which prioritized the making of money from money over the making of money from industrial enterprise.

This London-based gentlemanly capitalism sat more easily with the expansion of empire than had the liberal capitalism of Manchester's industrial elite, in part because the imperial project was from its outset – both in personnel and in culture – far more an aristocratic than a middle-class phenomenon.[33] Throughout the nineteenth century, the sons of privilege ran the formal empire.[34] By century's end, the sons of privilege headed the financial institutions of the City; and increasingly over time, the protection of both became the top priority of a political class that was equally privileged. "The pattern of class relations and financial institutions which developed was well adapted for a role of servicing the internationalization of capital, but it was a major obstacle to rapid domestic industrial transformation".[35] The Empire and the City worked together to reorient the priorities of late nineteenth-century politics *outwards*, towards the UK's global role and the strength of its naval military underpinnings. In the process, attempts to reinforce the UK's dwindling manufacturing fortunes – attempts that prioritized an *inward* focus by the UK state – regularly fell foul of the City's need for unfettered commercial and financial access to global markets. In the clash between industrial interests and financial ones, the more the empire grew the more

211

did political weight shift towards the financial, and away from the industrial, lobby. Twentieth-century UK governments regularly put the defence of sterling and the interests of the City before the defence of UK-based manu-facturers and the interests of labour. They did so in 1903, rejecting Joseph Chamberlain's call for imperial preference; and they were still doing so a century later, stoutly defending the autonomy of the City by declining to sub-merge sterling into the euro.

The longevity of this prioritizing of global financial interests over national industrial ones, points to a further consequence of empire that we would do well not to discount in the British case, and which definitely has contem-porary US parallels: namely the degree to which, over time in an imperial economy, industrial interests themselves diverge. It points to the way in which manufacturing industry in imperial economies ultimately splits into a small- and medium-size sector still predominantly dependent on the domestic market, and a series of large firms who are themselves global play-ers. The modern UK economy is a classic case of this, being currently home to a disproportionately large number of such firms – firms that share with the City a commitment to global sourcing, global production chains and global markets. The "hollowing out" of British manufacturing that was such a feature of the post-1961 UK economy was not just the consequence of local under-investment and subsequent negative deindustrialization: although it was predominantly a consequence of that, with all the cumula-tive consequences that flow to firms when they habitually underinvest, underperform, and then lack the surpluses with which to attract the catch-up investment they so desperately need. The other process in play in the hollowing out of modern UK manufacturing we would now recognize as "outsourcing": the shifting by large UK-based firms of their production processes (and markets) more-and-more overseas. The result, potentially devastating to centre-left political forces seeking to harness state power and private enterprise in an alliance for national economic reconstruction, is a new and fundamental difference between UK industry and UK capital. UK capital flourishes – by going abroad. UK-based industry stays home – and flourishes less.

THE IMPERIAL CONCERNS OF A PREOCCUPIED STATE

When the Empire was up and flourishing, its defence was the predominant concern of successive London governments of all political persuasions; and looking back now over the wreckage of empire, it is possible to see the adverse legacy of this prolonged imperial preoccupation. It was not that UK governments kept their distance from all sections of UK-based industry. They did not: on the contrary, funding the best kind of *defence* industries was a constant UK state practice. Shipbuilding industries in the nineteenth century, aircraft industries in the twentieth, the bulk of UK-based science and R & D throughout – all received generous public funding and state direction. But industries geared to *civilian* markets gained no such political priority. Instead, postwar UK governments struggled mightily to protect the global role of the City of London – willingly boosting interest rates and the exchange rate of sterling, the better to bring speculative capital to London. But the cost of that boosting was the steady erosion of the competitiveness of UK-based manufacturing industry in general, and the slippage of UK living standards relative to the best of the rest abroad. While the Empire was there to be extended, or defended, a political culture was consolidated in London in which it was always acceptable for governments to maintain a military-industrial complex, but rarely acceptable for them to develop a sustained industrial policy aimed at any general strengthening of the entire UK manufacturing base.

When examining in detail the impact of this basic policy orientation – what David Edgerton labelled as "liberal militarism" – for the earlier study of *America in the Shadow of Empires,* two conclusions stood out that are worth reproducing here. The first is that well into the post-Second World War period, it made sense to think of the twentieth-century UK state not simply as a welfare state but also as a *warfare state*[36] – one that was quite capable, for example, of rapidly restructuring aircraft production for military purposes (as it did in 1958) even when the political leadership of the UK state was firmly in Conservative hands. Little wonder then that state procurement of weapons, and state funding of military R & D, should have remained such a feature of post-1945 UK political practice; or that the UK civilian economy should have been such a centre of world excellence in militarily-related technologies (not least, aircraft engines) and such an exporter of weaponry. Overall defence

213

spending is now down, back around the 2.5 per cent of GDP that it averaged through the late Victorian period;[37] but even so, and as late as the 1970s, of the major capitalist powers, Britain still "spent the highest proportion of total national R & D spending (approximately 28 per cent), and between 1976 and 1981 the highest proportion of government R & D spending (over 50 per cent), on defense".[38] Even under New Labour in 2005, almost a third of all public spending on research was funded by the Ministry of Defence – at £2.6 billion in total in 2004, far outspending even the NHS.[39] France and Britain may have competed in the 1930s to be the world's largest arms exporter, but more recently the main competition has been with American-based producers; and in both competitions, UK-based arms manufacturers have excelled. UK-based arms manufacturers now regularly capture 20 per cent of the global trade in arms, and in 2010 the UK's BAE Systems actually topped the list as the world's largest arms manufacturer. BAE's arms sales in 2008 exceeded the GDP of at least 100 countries. Moreover, it cannot be without long-term economic significance that from the 1980s, "Britain remained a net *exporter* of armaments, but became a net *importer* of manufacturers".[40] Strong economies would presumably have had those net flows set the other way around.

Then there is this: that with hindsight we can see that for far too long for the competitive health of the UK's manufacturing sector, postwar UK governments attempted to retain the possessions and strappings of empire. For far too long, "both Labour and Conservative governments ... pursued an expensive strategy of keeping Britain's military industries at the leading edge"[41] and for far too long, a disproportionately large proportion of UK R & D, and associated scientists and engineers, remained focused on military, not civilian, production – this at the very time when "countries such as Japan were investing in the long-term technological development of motor vehicles and other manufacturing industries"[42] under strong state leadership. That all this happened was ultimately a consequence of failed political leadership – a genuine postwar "wasting of the British economy".[43] The truth was, as the conservative historian Corelli Barnett put it, "that the world-power men in London simply failed to heed the evidence of the 1930s and the Second World War that the Commonwealth was a strategic *liability* to Britain, *not* an asset" and that "the British Empire was one of the most outstanding examples of strategic over-extension in history".[44] The truth was that those same world-power politicians failed to adjust immediate postwar policy to meet the UK's new economic standing – one in which "Britain, which had once been the world's greatest creditor nation, had become the world's greatest debtor".[45] Writing to the same conference as Barnett, the far less conservative Andrew Gamble put it this way: "the question of decline only makes sense by considering the interrelationship of the relative economic decline and the absolute decline in world power. It was always the absolute decline that mattered most to the British political elite, and measures to stave that off and preserve Britain's traditional global role always took preference over the task of modernizing the British economy and British society".[46] Contemporary Britain continues to play a heavy price for that preference.

Imperial mindsets and populist politics

Empires do more than rule part of the world. They also rule the mind. They create and amplify generalized feelings of superiority in those who run them and of subordination in those who do not; and they justify their existence – both to the ruling population back home and to the ruled populations abroad – by telling misleading stories about what they are doing, and why. Empires then rise and fall, but the justifications linger; and as they do so they provide, to the core populations living through the decline of empire, frameworks within which to understand that decline. Those frameworks are rarely attractive ones.

At the height of their empire, the British told themselves that they were carrying the white man's burden. A sense of white supremacy was written into the entire British imperial project from its outset; and when the British economy was no longer strong enough to sustain that project – when the baton of empire passed to the Americans – the British could still tell themselves that power had remained in some basic sense "with their people", such that the UK political class could settle into a subordinate but close "special relationship" with the new imperial order without experiencing any fundamental crisis of confidence. That subordinate but special relationship left the UK with parts of its imperial structure intact. It left the UK sitting at the top

table of every post-Second World War international institution, and it enabled several generations of UK politicians to persuade themselves (and their
electorates) that the key role of the UK was to act as a bridge between America and Europe.

One major consequence of that, of course, was that from the outset of the
formation of what is now the European Union – the 1956 Treaty of Rome, creating a European common market – the UK political class (and the bulk of its
electorate) remained at best reluctant Europeans. British Conservatives grew
keener on the European project so long as it remained focused on the creation
of a single market. They liked it less as the retitled "European Union" moved
beyond that towards a wider political union; and in that dislike, they were
joined by a residue of Old Labour politicians who had long disliked the Common Market because they had seen it as a capitalist club, and who now saw it
as a neoliberal disaster. More moderate Labourites of the Blair variety, by contrast, warmed to the European project the more it became a political union
with strong social rights for workers: but in each section of the UK political
class – and that included the Blairites – the prior preference remained for
the retention of an independent global (military and diplomatic) role for the
United Kingdom as the USA's special ally.

That preference took Margaret Thatcher into the gamble of the Falklands
War in 1983. It took Tony Blair into the folly of the Iraq invasion twenty years
later: and it kept alive a gap in identity between a significant swathe of the UK
electorate and the European Union that ultimately culminated in the Brexit
vote. South of the Scottish border at least, the main cultural legacy of the
British Empire as it declined was a re-energized and defensive English nationalism – and it was that nationalism, that desire to keep power over policy
back in the UK itself and away from Brussels and the European Union, that
eventually persuaded a narrow majority of the British electorate that the best
way to defend the United Kingdom was to pull the UK out entirely from its
existing treaty obligations to the European Union. Given the likely consequences of cutting the UK economy off from free access to its major European
markets, it is hard to see how such a move will help overcome deep flaws in
the structure and performance of that economy; and given the Scottish electorate's strong preference for remaining within the European Union, it is hard
to see how a London-based government imposing EU withdrawal can in any

way strengthen the political unity of a country whose very title reflects the deep national divisions that persist within it. But the cultural residues of empire often work that way – they induce a mental petulance in those sections of the core population who least benefited from the original imperial project, and who seem – at moments of intense crisis – most inclined to drag the entire population down with them as the ship of state sinks.

Will this then be America's future too? Maybe in some similar form, but not quite yet. For the United States remains a (or arguably, still *the*) major global player, and its internal population remains broadly at peace with the idea of that role, even if not always at peace with specific manifestations of it (say in Vietnam in the 1970s, or in Iraq more recently). The deep patriotism of the bulk of the American electorate is visible in the flags they everywhere fly, and in the Oath of Allegiance they willingly take publicly on every imaginable occasion. This patriotism remains, that is, deeply imperial in character, in the manner of the British before 1945 but definitely not since; and that American patriotism still leaves large sections of the US electorate wedded to an aggressive military role abroad by a country that was attacked by Islamic jihad on 9/11, and with which it has been at war now for more than a decade-and-a-half. Yet the burdens of that war fall back primarily, as we saw, onto the shoulders of the American military, and by association onto the families of those soldiers – and soldiers in America, like soldiers elsewhere, are predominantly drawn from the ranks of the working class. There is, in fact, a double working-class whammy in play here. The American working class is under heavy economic pressure because of the outsourcing associated with empire, and (in many individual cases) also under heavy personal pressure because of the regular redeployment experienced by the members of an armed force that is no longer based on compulsory military service for all. The vulnerability of particularly the white sections of the American working class to the appeals of a political campaign based on the promise "to make America great again" makes perfect sense from where they stand: wanting the Empire to win militarily, and win quickly, to bring the soldiers home; and wanting America to win economically, and to make them less poor, by bringing back the well-paying jobs as well.

In the United States, therefore, as in the United Kingdom, it is proving all too easy to blame foreigners for local problems: to blame immigrants for taking jobs and using up welfare (the Middle Eastern tsunami in the European Union, and the flow of undocumented Hispanic labour in the United States); and to blame foreign governments for taking our money, for free-riding on our defence spending, and for imposing rules from outside on a free people (rule from Brussels in the UK case, and from the UN or Paris in America's). But pointing the finger of blame is not the same thing as locating the genuine causes of the developments to which blame is being attributed. The flow of refugees out of the Middle East has much to do with post-9/11 US military intervention there. The flow of undocumented labour across the Rio Grande has much to do with the impact of the freer trade created by NAFTA on a Mexican agricultural sector increasingly exposed to competition from heavily-subsidized US food producers. Political and economic imperialism lie at the base of so much of what is now driving concerned working-class voters in an authoritarian populist direction; but the one thing which that populism will never challenge – while in the hands of a Donald J. Trump at least – is the underlying imperialism itself.

That is evident in the first budget of the Trump years in Washington – a budget calling for a substantial increase in military spending (some \$54 billion over previously agreed levels[47]) and a culling of civilian-focused regulatory agencies, and a budget linked to a healthcare reform that was supposed to improve on the Affordable Care Act but which visibly is failing to do so. Simultaneously making America great again militarily *and* socially is proving to be an impossible task for a party of the Republican kind; and instead of squaring that circle by curbing military spending, it would appear that, so long as Donald J. Trump is president, any squaring will be done at the expense of further cuts to already inadequate social programmes. It is through this gap between promise and performance in the politics of the contemporary centre-right that the progressive way forward must, therefore, now tread its way: insisting in the American case that it is the cutting of military spending, not the cutting of spending on social programmes and civilian infrastructure, that must become the priority of the day.

Saying that then makes another difference between these two similarly flawed capitalisms crystal-clear. It is that the American centre-left currently faces two awesome political tasks, only one of which it shares with its UK equivalents. The one that is unique to the American agenda is that of getting

America out of the empire business – the critical political task of pulling US troops and covert operations out of the Middle East at the very least, and back eventually to American shores alone.* The task that is not unique to America – the one that is shared – is that of challenging and refuting the austerity politics associated with conservatism at home and imperialism abroad. It is to that task – to an examination of the inadequate politics of domestic retrenchment advocated by centre-right parties in both America and the UK as the imperial nightmare continues – that we need, therefore, now finally to turn.

---

* The case for doing that, and the step-by-step programme that might get us there, are discussed at length in the final chapter of *America in the Shadow of Empires*, and will resurface briefly here in the last chapter's discussion of progressive programmes on both sides of the Atlantic. For the argument in a more abbreviated form, see also http://www.davidcoates. net/2014/12/01/taking-the-imperial-out-of-american-imperialism/.

7

The Folly of Austerity Politics

"Our Congress passes laws that subsidize corporations, farms, oil companies, airlines, and houses for suburbia, but when they turn their attention to the poor they suddenly become concerned with balancing the budget."

Coretta Scott King[1]

"Cuts have almost certainly halted a rise in life expectancy. Our social order is bankrupt. We don't just need a new government, we need a new way to organize society."

Owen Jones[2]

There was a brief Keynesian moment in the immediate aftermath of the 2008 financial crisis, a moment in which the excesses of neoliberalism were so clear, and the adverse consequences of deregulated financial institutions so obvious, that the whole Reagan/Thatcher enthusiasm for free-market capitalism suddenly lost popular support and its political advocates lost electoral credibility. But sadly, it was just a moment – one quickly over-shadowed by the resurgence of self-confidence on the centre-right, and the return to serious austerity politics on both sides of the Atlantic.[3] Since the cutting of public spending in the depths of a recession served only to prolong the recession itself, the return to the economics of neoliberalism only intensified the weaknesses that had generated the crisis in the first place – and in doing so, opened a gap between economic performance and appropriate public policy that thus far the centre-left has failed to close. How that closure might yet occur is the subject matter of the final chapter in this volume. The aim here is simply to demonstrate how real the need for that closure remains.

The Keynesian moment

In the US and the UK, as elsewhere across the advanced capitalist world (and that included China), the first response to the 2008 crash was a reversion to straightforward Keynesianism. Governments spent money, and used quantitative easing, to re-establish credit flows and lessen the recessionary impact of the credit squeeze of September 2008. For some governments, like the New Labour one in London, that response involved no sharp rupture with previous policy; but for others, most notably the Republican one in Washington, DC, it most decidedly did. For the first response of the Bush Administration to the growing evidence of instability in US-based financial institutions in 2007 and early 2008 had been adamantly to insist on the continuation of business as normal. George W. Bush had twice cut taxes on high earners (in 2001 and 2003), arguing that the benefits of making the rich even richer would soon trickle-down to the rest of the economy in the form of job-creating investments fuelled by the tax revenues foregone; and although in 2007 his Administration had discretely switched from this "trickle-down" economics to "trickle-up" – bringing in new tax relief to lower-earners in an attempt to stimulate demand – even so, weeks before leaving office the outgoing president was still telling world leaders that "it would be a terrible mistake to allow a few months of crisis to undermine faith in free markets". The terrible events of September 2008 then changed his mind, totally, leaving George W. Bush by December 2008 telling Congressional leaders that, as he somewhat inelegantly put it, without federal intervention "this sucker is going down".[4] In consequence, and via a truly remarkable volte-face, it was a Republican Secretary of the Treasury, Henry Paulson, who then launched a $700 billion rescue package (his Troubled Assets Relief Program) in a three-page power-grab aimed at locating and absorbing mortgage-backed securities whose value was in freefall. In the event, that volte-face and Treasury power-grab proved too abrupt and too great for Republicans in Congress, who settled instead for revised TARP legislation that included $150 billion worth of tax breaks, limits on executive pay in bailed-out companies, and powers to ease mortgage terms to prevent foreclosure. The US government was, in consequence, already heavily involved in deficit-spending well before the Republican White House stood down in January 2009.

222

The incoming Obama Administration merely picked up the Paulson ball, and ran with it (in the form of the ARRA, the American Recovery and Reinvestment Act). In very quick order, they redirected TARP money into a new programme to help struggling homeowners refinance their mortgages, and into the two GSEs (Fannie May and Freddie Mac) to increase the flow of available mortgage credit. They increased the volume of funds directed to the recapitalization of large-scale American banks, and this time included aid to the struggling automotive industry as well (they even took temporary part-ownership of General Motors); and they put together both a large spending budget financed by public borrowing and an accompanying stimulus package, costing $787 billion in total, that contained $276 billion in tax cuts for low- and middle-income earners and over $500 billion for a series of spending programmes. The resulting budget deficit was projected by the CBO to run at $1.67 trillion in 2009, or 11.9 per cent of US GDP, the vast majority of which derived from Bush policies (tax cuts and war spending) and the downturn in the US economy. That deficit was projected to drop by more than half in the four years to follow, and the Obama Administration – keen to see that happen – moved quickly then to explore ways of cutting the cost of entitlement programmes. In other words, in true Keynesian fashion and very much in line with the later thinking of the administration they replaced, the incoming Obama Treasury team "openly recognized the important role of federal deficit spending as a trigger to private sector growth and employment in the depth of a recession" while also "publicly subscribing to the view that, as that growth returned, a phasing out of the deficit would be both politically and economically necessary".[5]

Meanwhile in London, a New Labour government now led by Gordon Brown took a series of similarly dramatic and large-scale initiatives. Part of the UK banking system was already in public ownership before the 2008 financial crisis broke – the collapse of Northern Rock had already triggered that. So the Brown government did not have a volte-face moment of the Paulson variety, but still it did publicly have to abandon the "golden rule of public spending" religiously followed by Gordon Brown when he was Tony Blair's "prudent Chancellor": namely "over the economic cycle only borrowing to invest and not to fund current expenditure".[6] In its place, and again in very quick order, the UK's Treasury team led by Alistair Darling created an Asset

Protection Scheme through which to buy out toxic assets, introduced a modest Homeowners Mortgage Support Scheme, and (in November 2008) launched a significant stimulus package in the form of £20 billion of tax cuts and government spending.[7] Like the Obama Administration, the UK Government under New Labour had its central bank buy up mortgage-based assets: programmes of quantitative easing that in the UK expanded from £75 billion in 2008 to £200 billion by 2010. (The equivalent US figures were much larger*); and additionally, the two governments together (Brown's and Obama's) emerged as the major advocates at the global level for this deficit-led recovery from the financial crisis and its subsequent deep recession. It was an advocacy that initially carried all before it, but one which over time ran into serious resistance within the councils of the G20, particularly from Angela Merkel's government in Berlin.

A time would come – towards the end of the Obama presidency and long after German resistance to fiscal stimuli had help drive the Eurozone economies into prolonged recession – when Obama's Treasury Secretary could declare victory in the G20s "growth versus austerity" debate.[8] But that was not how the US electorate came to see the immediate legacy of the 2009 stimulus package. On the contrary, while "a month after the law's passage, the Pew Research Center ... found 56 per cent support. Three years later, that number had dropped to 37 per cent".[9] For by then, the Republican opposition to the stimulus package, and to the Administration that introduced it, had managed both to obliterate from the public memory the only slightly smaller stimulus package (of $715 billion) that the Republicans in Congress themselves had passed in January 2009, and to obscure from public view the far

---

* Under the Bush Administration, "Fed-financed injections of yet more credit-guarantees, and central bank orchestrated expansion programs for the financial industry world-wide. $900 billion in loans to banks were made available by the Federal Reserve as early as December 2007, followed by a further $250 billion in March 2008 to encourage mortgage lending, $29 billion to smooth the sale of Bear Stearns to JPMorgan Chase in March 2008, eventually $123.8 billion to bail out AIG, $620 billion in October to help foreign central banks trade foreign currency for dollars, $1.8 trillion to buy commercial paper, and $540 billion to buy assets from money market mutual funds short of cash – these last two again in October 2008. In the last 15 months of the Bush presidency, breath-taking amounts of money were poured into the financial system on a regular basis by the Federal Reserve to keep institutions viable and credit-creation intact." (David Coates, *Making the Progressive Case.* New York: Continuum Books, 2011, p. 15).

greater scale of the recession that would have occurred, had the Obama Administration not acted as it did. Looking back at the trajectory of economic growth seven years on from the financial crisis, Alan Blinder and Mark Zandi estimated that, without the stimulus package, the peak-to-trough decline in GDP in 2008–9 of 4 per cent would likely have been close to 14 per cent; the recession would have lasted probably twice as long; the number of jobs lost (at more than 17 million) would have been twice the loss that actually occurred; and the official rate of unemployment would likely have touched 16 per cent rather than, as it did, 10 per cent.[10] The Obama White House, for understandable reasons, entirely agreed. The Administration's 2014 report claimed that the ARRA saved on average 1.6 million jobs a year for the four years of its operation, and raised the US GDP by between 2 and 3 percentage points from late 2009 to mid-2011.[11] The precise numbers of jobs saved and growth trajectories raised remain matters of controversy, but the broad consensus beyond Republican ranks is clear: that without the 2009 $787 billion stimulus package "the Great Recession would have been far deeper in the United States".[12]

The resurgence of the American right

Which makes it all the more galling that the case for a further stimulus should, in both economies, have fallen by the wayside by the end of 2010. It had fallen off the realistic political agenda by then because, in the UK, the New Labour Government in power throughout the crisis had been decisively defeated in the May general election – to be replaced by a coalition government committed to austerity politics – and because in the United States, the November 2010 mid-term elections had given control of the House of Representatives back to a Tea Party-driven Republican caucus that was equally determined to replace fiscal stimuli with fiscal restraint.

Part of the problem, for those favouring Keynesian-type policies as a solution to recession, was that those policies had never been unanimously accepted by the economics profession nor, in the United States, escaped challenge from well-funded think tanks like the Cato Institute, the Heritage and Petersen Foundations, and the "Fix-the-Debt" public relations campaign funded by Petersen and 127 of America's best-paid CEOs.[13] At the height of the financial crisis, when both the out-going Bush Administration and the incoming Obama one had been united in their desire to stimulate the economy by a mixture of tax cuts and spending programmes, a large group of right-leaning academic economists had publicly voiced their opposition. "Notwithstanding reports that all economists are now Keynesians", they wrote in an open letter to the incoming president, "that is not true ... we do not believe that more government spending is a way to improve economic performance ... Lower tax rates and a reduction in the burden of government are the best ways of using fiscal policy to boost growth".[14] And in "a sign of what was to come", when the Obama Administration introduced the ARRA, "no House Republicans and only three Republican Senators voted for the stimulus bill. Despite Obama's attempts at bipartisanship, the minority leaders in both chambers ... counseled complete obstructionism".[15]

In such a climate, within the new Administration itself more conservative rather than more progressive voices then came to prevail.[16] The initial economic team that Obama called together was heavily influenced by figures from the previous Clinton Administration, and they were no Keynesians. Years later, key members of that initial team would concede the validity of the progressive case made against them at the time, namely that a bigger and better-designed stimulus would have triggered an even faster economic recovery, so undercutting the ability of the Republicans to blame public spending for the slowness of the recovery that actually occurred.[17] (As late as August 2011, 14 million Americans remained involuntarily unemployed – 9.1 per cent of the registered labour force – and one house-owner in four remained "underwater" – trapped in a mortgage larger than the house's current market value.) The result of this initial policy caution was long term and serious: it meant that, even before the 2010 mid-term "shellacking" of the Democrats that opened a six-year period of political gridlock in Washington, DC, the Obama Administration had in effect already surrendered the field to its austerity-advocating opponents. And indeed if that was not enough, the Administration had by then additionally already created its own Greek chorus of doom: setting up in February 2010 the "Bipartisan Commission on Fiscal Responsibility and Reform" chaired by Alan Simpson and Erskine Bowles, who quickly became two further powerful voices close to the Administration, willing repeatedly to advocate cuts in welfare spending as a core response to an ongoing economic crisis that they – and the Republicans – now insisted was the product of too much federal spending rather than of too little.*

But it was the "shellacking" of the Democrats in the 2010 mid-terms that brought the American Keynesian moment to a permanent close. The Republicans in charge of the House were in no mood to tolerate a second round of public spending. On the contrary, they arrived in power on a Tea Party-inspired wave of resistance to further public spending, and dug in to defend the now threatened Bush-era tax cuts, to regularly insist on the repeal of the Affordable Care Act, and to agree to pass Administration-designed policy initiatives only if those were traded for cuts in the federal budget, particularly in discretionary welfare spending. In 2011, Congressional Republicans and the Obama White House clashed initially on whether to renew the Bush-era tax cuts, and then over the raising of the ceiling on the US national debt. Reneging on public debt because of that ceiling was avoided only at the eleventh-hour, by the agreement to cut federal spending by an additional $39.9 billion (hitting education, labour and health programmes most), and to set up yet another bipartisan committee to find ways of reducing the federal deficit over the longer term. This August 2011 deal, the Budget Control Act – made between an embattled Republican Speaker of the House and a gridlocked Democratic President – immediately enacted a further $1 trillion in discretionary spending cuts over the next decade (split evenly between defence and non-defence spending), *and* automatically triggered an additional $1.5 trillion in similarly distributed cuts in January 2013, should the bipartisan committee fail in its task by the start of 2012.

---

* The first Bowles–Simpson report (issued in December 2010) urged a $6 trillion reduction in federal spending over a decade – broadly a 50/50 mix of tax hikes and spending cuts. The second iteration (in December 2012) had much the same total target, but this time relied more heavily on spending cuts. Those cuts included significant changes to Social Security, and cuts in spending on both Medicare and Medicaid. These then alienated progressive voices within the Democrats in Congress, while the proposed tax hikes killed the Commission's plan for Republicans. So deep indeed were the divisions within the US political class by 2010 that the first report never received the full support even of the Commission's members, let alone of Congress. In consequence, the co-chairs acted alone, subsequently issuing – among other options – their own "zero plan" that would, among other things, have phased out most tax allowances and replaced the existing six-bracket individual tax rate schedule with a three-bracket one of 9, 15 and 24 per cent.

And of course, predictably, the "super-committee" did fail: which was why Washington politics in 2013 were initially dominated by the negotiation of yet another eleventh-hour bargain – this one to soften those automatic cuts, and to avoid going over what was hysterically labelled at the time as "the fiscal cliff": partly by delaying the cuts by two months and partly by the signing of yet another modest last-minute tax and spending deal that this time the president won. Then later in the year, concern about the fiscal cliff was replaced by a total breakdown in the cross-party haggling both about spending cuts and the Affordable Care Act, a Congressional failure to appropriate funds for the 2014 fiscal year, and a resulting 15 day-long closure and furloughing of the federal government in October. In the event, this latter proved so wildly unpopular with the American electorate as a whole that the Republicans did not push it again – instead the 2013 stand-off simply set in stone the pattern of budgetary impasse and fiscal crises that was such a hallmark of the Obama Administration's last three years in office. There was another such impasse and crisis in December 2014; one in September 2015, averting which cost the Speaker his job; and yet a third, closely avoided in December 2016. And in the process, as those negotiations and crises played themselves out, a progressive president who had been elected twice on a programme to renew America's infrastructure and to use public funds to ease its social divisions, ended up presiding instead in his second term over cuts of at least $2.4 trillion in public spending between 2013 and 2022 – a deficit reduction that worked out roughly at "$2 in spending cuts for every $1 in revenue increases"[18] – a net zero rate of investment in new infrastructure, and a deepening social crisis of the kind discussed in Chapter 4. Social Security, Medicare and Medicaid spending remained largely protected from these cuts: that much Obama's rearguard action definitely achieved. But his success in defending them simply set up these three pillars of the US welfare state as prime targets for the Republican coalition in 2017, once the road-block of a progressive presidency had been replaced by the authoritarian populism of a Donald J. Trump.

Voluntarily-adopted austerity in Tory-led Britain

In the UK, meanwhile, much the same pattern of retrenchment got under way after 2010, but with literally none of the gridlock or bitterness of the simultaneous American story. In fact, the political interplay was exactly the reverse of that in Washington. In London, a government voluntarily and enthusiastically adopted the austerity route to economic growth, slowed down in its enthusiasm only by a rising chorus of resistance, initially to its social effects and increasingly to its economic ineffectiveness.

The Coalition Government elected in May 2010 had the same finance minister for the entirety of its length – George Osborne – and he entered office as a committed Thatcherite, convinced that scaling back public spending and employment was key to long-term economic recovery. He entered the UK Treasury at what for him was an opportune moment. The UK's projected budget deficit of £163 billion in 2009–10, at 11.6 per cent of GDP, was by far the biggest in the UK's postwar history and the highest in the G7 both for that year and the next.[19] In consequence, the departing New Labour Government was already planning extensive spending cuts – one junior treasury minister even left a note behind, joking that all the money had gone – and Osborne literally took him at his word. He immediately froze/cancelled £10.5 billion of projects announced in the dying days of the Labour government. He followed that with an emergency budget in June 2010 that cut planned public spending by a further £11 billion, with moves in September that cut the benefit budget for the unemployed by £4 billion, and then in October cut again – this time £46 billion from the central departments of government and £7 billion from the welfare budget, including £2.5 billion saved by changes to child benefit. Even the Ministry of Defence found its budget cut – less than other departments but still deep enough to cancel high-profile projects (including a new aircraft carrier) – that cost 42,000 service personnel and civil servants their jobs over a five-year period.[20] Six months into office, and George Osborne had already cut £81 billion off the UK government's projected spending plans, and set in motion policies that would likely reduce total public sector employment by up to 500,000 jobs in total: in order as he put it, to pull Britain "back from the brink" and to bring the UK's fiscal account back into balance by 2015. His underlying rationale is worth hearing in full. It was this:

This is an emergency Budget, so let me speak plainly about the emergency that we face. The coalition Government has inherited from its predecessor the largest budget deficit of any economy in Europe with the single exception of Ireland. One pound in every four we spend is being borrowed ... This Budget is needed to deal with our country's debts. This Budget is needed to give confidence to our economy. This is the unavoidable Budget ... Our policy is to raise from the ruins of an economy built on debt a new, balanced economy where we save, invest and export. An economy where the state does not take almost half of all our national income, crowding out private endeavour. An economy not overly reliant on the success of one industry, financial services – important as they are – but where all industries grow. An economy where prosperity is shared among all sections of society and all parts of the country.[21]

Subsequently, however, things did not quite work out as the Chancellor had hoped. Instead, his claims and calculations struggled for traction as the UK economy continued to teeter on the edge of recession. Lower tax revenues, and greater calls on welfare services for the unemployed, eroded the speed of deficit-reduction in the United Kingdom just as effectively as it had in the United States; and fear of deepening the recession by further public-sector restraint obliged the Chancellor of the Exchequer to hold himself in check through both 2011 and 2012. His budgets in both those years were broadly fiscally-neutral, and his autumn spending reviews were restricted to small-scale but steady welfare erosion (freezing benefits as prices rose, increasing the number of hours that low-income families had to work before becoming eligible for working tax credits, and so on). Even so, the end of 2012 saw a further £10 billion cut in planned public spending, this time achieved by breaking the link between inflation and increases in basic welfare benefits; and by 2013 George Osborne was back to further large-scale cutting again: now altering his projected timeline – promising seven more years of struggle to bring the budget into surplus only by 2020 – and seeking to achieve it by yet more draconian initiatives. These included big cuts on this occasion to both local government and education spending – a further £11.5 billion of cuts in total – including such moves as the so-called "bedroom tax": an obligation of people in social housing to sublet any spare bedroom in their house, or lose 14 per cent of their benefit. Apparently, the Queen – the largest recipient of social housing in the UK, and the person with the largest number of unused bedrooms in the entire kingdom – did not find her sovereign grant payment reduced by 14 per cent if she failed to comply: but every other recipient of social housing did.[22]

Be in no doubt. For all that George Osborne's targets had to be pushed back as deadlines were missed, under his chancellorship and by any reasonable measure, the UK endured what the *New Statesman* later labelled "austerity's cruel pantomime".[23] Deficit reduction can always be achieved in two ways, or in a mixture of both – by cutting spending or by increasing revenue – and deficit reduction can be either rapid or slow, modest or severe. The Osborne austerity drive was both severe and revenue-lite, with reductions "predominantly achieved via curbs on spending. Between 2009–10 and 2021–22", and because of consciously adopted Treasury policy, public sector net borrowing in the UK is currently "forecast by the Office for Budget Responsibility to shrink by 9.2 per cent of gross domestic product. A reduction in spending from 54.3 per cent to 37.9 per cent of GDP is expected to deliver 80 per cent of the envisaged fall in deficit".[24] An Osborne supporter like Norman Lamont might later claim that such spending cuts were "unavoidable" and that what Osborne's policies didn't amount to was austerity – with the term "just another word for living within one's means", but as the editorial in the *New Statesman*, from which these quotations come, put it so well: "Mr. Lamont would do well to put such a claim to the patient waiting more than six months for an operation, the mother struggling to find a school place for her child, or the working family that has lost thousands of pounds in benefit". In the UK under the Coalition Government, austerity policies were a choice, not a necessity; and they came at a real and unevenly distributed cost!

As leading members of the Coalition Government separated before the 2015 general election, George Osborne – free now of coalition constraints – then set out his stall for a second term: his aim being to get public spending down to 35 per cent of GDP by 2019–20 (back to 1930s levels), and the public finances to a £23 billion surplus, by cutting a further million public sector jobs, holding public sector pay in check, and further freezing tax credits.[25] He also set out a plan requiring future UK governments to operate an overall budget surplus in normal times,[26] and used what turned out to be his last spending review to extract yet another £20 billion cut in Whitehall budgets, this one requiring unprotected departments to generate savings plans of between 25 and 40 per cent of their budgets.[27] Only the unexpected defeat of the Cameron-led campaign to remain in Europe stopped Osborne in his tracks – with his successor at the Treasury quietly abandoning these plans under cover of Brexit uncertainty. The Osborne years therefore ended – as most political careers do – in abject personal failure,[28] but two things, important for our purposes here, stand out from them. One is the disproportionate burden that his policies placed on those least able to bear them. The other is that all this pain – voluntarily-inflicted on others as it was – did not in the end fundamentally transform the UK's ongoing economic weaknesses. It did not even hit its own targets on deficit-reduction: the projected UK fiscal deficit in 2016–17 was still £96 billion. The poor suffered, that is, because of Osborne's austerity policies, while the impact of those policies on the UK economy's underlying fundamentals remained itself poor.

Of course, the British Conservative Party and the American Republican Party are not the same political animal. There is a far higher degree of genuine social compassion in the politics of the first than there is in the politics of the second. A long tradition of "one nation Toryism" co-habits with Thatcherite neoliberals in the British Conservative Party, and in any case the Coalition Government in power in London between 2010 and 2015 contained Liberal Democrats for whom poverty reduction was a high and important political objective. All of which helps explain why, as George Osborne pursued his austerity politics, he also regularly softened that austerity with social initiatives that appear nowhere in the parallel Republican austerity songbook. So, for example, in 2015 he funded an extension of free childcare for families on low-income to 30 hours a week, and a year later gave his active support to the introduction of a national living wage for over-25s that would rise to £9 an hour by 2020. And yet in spite of this, in budget after budget and spending review after spending review, George Osborne introduced policies that made life harder and more difficult for one oppressed group within the British population after another. The biggest group – women – took the bulk of the hits,[29] as we saw in Chapter 5: but they were not alone. Policy in different years also targeted the young unemployed,[30] lone parents,[31] families with more than two children,[32] students,[33] those claiming disability benefit,[34] those relying on local council services,[35] and those reliant on housing benefit.[36]

Cuts to, and caps on, this last were particularly burdensome, hitting over 4.8 million households in 2015 according to IFS data,[37] and taking away 30 per cent of income from poor families if the TUC data is similarly sound.[38] As the 2015 general election approached, and academics began to evaluate the full five-year record of the Coalition Government, the most comprehensive of those reports found that "the coalition's changes to benefits and direct taxes [had] hit families with children under five harder than any other group and hurt the poorest more than the better-off". Appallingly, the biggest losers were the children of the poor and near-poor. Calculations released by the IFS in 2015 suggested that progress between the late 1990s and 2010 on reducing child poverty had been reversed under the coalition, with "the number of children living in relative poverty [rising] from 2.3 million in 2010 to 2.6 million in 2014".[39] Austerity politics and child poverty went together in Osborne's Britain, as the government first changed the definition of what constituted child poverty, then abandoned New Labour's goal of eradicating it by 2020, and finally allowed the total number of children in poverty to rise significantly on its watch. Hence the Oxfam projection that, by 2020, "one in four British children will be living in poverty".[40]

It is not that George Osborne and his Conservative colleagues in government were not told about the effects of austerity politics, with all their negativity and pain. They *were* told – in fact, they were told repeatedly – both by their coalition partners and by their critics. They were told and yet they persisted; and in that persistence, lay political and moral responsibility*. Either the Tory ministers chose not to hear, or they chose to ignore, or they chose not to care – it is rather hard to discern which choice prevailed for which Conservative minister on each separate occasion, and no doubt it varied by policy and by individual minister – but the result was the same, regardless of the motive. Life in the UK after 2010 became more-and-more

---

* And it was not just George Osborne. It was also his prime minister. In June 2012, in a major policy speech, David Cameron suggested, among other things, time-limiting benefits, restricting income support and child benefit to single mothers with more than three children, requiring those on jobseeker allowance to perform unpaid voluntary service, and paying more welfare benefits in kind rather than cash. Strong American echoes here!

difficult for more-and-more people because of an austerity politics that was supposed to rapidly generate generalized prosperity for all. But George Osborne's voluntarily-adopted austerity regime did not do that. On the contrary, the Coalition Government's steady pursuit of an austerity route to economic growth failed to generate even the economic growth that the pain of the austerity was claimed to make worthwhile – and what economic growth eventually came, arrived only after (and only because) the Chancellor periodically eased up on the austerity pedal.[41] The result of Osborne's austerity policies was not prosperity for all. It was instead a steady slide by the UK down the international league tables on generalized well-being, to the point of the UK currently languishing in the bottom 25 of the 162 nations surveyed.[42]

That should not entirely surprise us, given that the case for austerity politics in the UK rested on two basic fallacies. The first fallacy was the one Martin Wolf mentioned in an important essay in *The Financial Times* in 2014 – the one that the Chancellor deployed in his Autumn Statement that year – blaming the UK financial crisis and recession on "disastrous decisions on spending and borrowing and welfare that got us into this mess". As Martin Wolf put it in response: "the proposition that the crisis was fiscal has allowed the Chancellor to blame Labour profligacy, rather than a widely-shared failure to appreciate the fragility of an economy based on financial services and soaring private debt".[43] It also enabled him and his allies to frighten the UK electorate with the prospect of Britain without austerity becoming another Greece – financially destitute and unable to provide even basic services. But the problem with the Osborne argument on both the Labour Party and on Greece was, and is, that there was no Labour profligacy before 2008[44] and that the UK is not another Greece. On the contrary: in the ten years between Tony Blair's election victory in 1997 to 2007, the year the subprime mortgage crisis broke, the average budget deficit in the UK was just 1.4 per cent – half the average of that normal under Margaret Thatcher and John Major. The national debt in 2007, at 36 per cent of GDP, was 3.9 per cent *lower* than in 1997; and the debt interest payments, at 2 per cent of GDP, were lower than the Conservatives ever managed between 1979 and 1997.

So if overspending was not the problem, underspending would not be the solution; and it was not. When the austerity drive was in full flow, the UK economy slipped briefly into a second recession, and teetered momentarily on the edge of a third. Growth returned to the UK economy only slowly and moderately as these austerity packages were followed by more fiscally-neutral budgets in 2011 and 2012. Instead of Osborne's tenure as Chancellor of the Exchequer leaving the deficit eliminated and the national debt falling as a percentage of GDP, his tenure actually ended with the budget deficit intact (down from 2010 levels, but still at over 4 per cent of GDP), the current account deficit running at a record 7 per cent of national output, and public debt higher (as a total, and as a percentage of GDP) than in 2010, and rising.[45] In other words, the Osborne focus on austerity as *the* answer at the start of the Coalition Government prolonged the recession rather than speeded its demise – the Office for Budget Responsibility estimated fiscal contraction "to have reduced GDP growth by 1 per cent in both 2010–11 and 2011–12, and ... [that] there are good reasons for thinking this is a conservative estimate". And the Osborne focus on austerity as *the* answer after 2013 kept the Coalition Government's focus for far too long on superficial consequences rather than underlying causes, so that the key underlying issues of low productivity and a sectorally-unbalanced economy remained off the top of the political agenda. The result? "At the end of 2014, UK GDP per person was about the same as it was at the end of 2006, and the UK was about 16 per cent poorer than would be expected on pre-crisis trends".[46] Though the Government "was proud of the fact that UK growth in 2014 was the highest in the G7", that "partly reflected a poor performance elsewhere" and you can only legitimately talk about a genuine long-term recovery "when output reaches the previous trendline". A 16 per cent shortfall doesn't cut it: but it does help explain why "the so-called recovery at the end of the Coalition government's period in office was not a real recovery for much of the working-age population, since it failed to restore incomes and consumption to pre-crisis levels".[47]

The other fallacy that eroded the impact of the Osborne search for an austerity route to prosperity was, and is, a more general one. Like the sixteenth-century search for a northern passage to Asia, the idea of an austerity route to generalized prosperity was easier to sell to the gullible than it was to deliver to the misled. As Paul Krugman wondered as the Coalition Government ended: "is there any good reason why deficit obsession should still rule in Britain, even as it fades away everywhere else?" He thought not.

He thought Britain was not different, and he also thought that "the economics of austerity are the same – and the intellectual case as bankrupt – in Britain as elsewhere ".[48] And on this, he was entirely right, which is why it is to that general intellectual bankruptcy that we now need to turn.

Claim and counterclaim in the battle over spending

This resurgent conservatism on both sides of the Atlantic in the wake of the deepest financial crisis since the 1930s, and one caused by the very neoliberalism to which this resurgent conservatism remained so wedded, is one of the great tragedies of the age. The momentary discrediting of neoliberalism in 2008–9, which at the start of the recession left bankers having to justify their bonuses and Wall Street under siege by an entire Occupy movement, stands in such contrast to the inability of the British Labour Party's then leader, Ed Miliband – in 2015, at the end of the recession – to remind and persuade even a middle-class BBC audience that government spending had been a necessary response to the financial crisis, and not its cause.[49] That shift in popular understanding and attitudes did not occur without orchestration – but nonetheless it did occur, precisely because the orchestration of an anti-Keynesian message was so carefully planned and repeatedly implemented.* Some parts of that orchestrated message were directed at the immediate causes of the financial crisis itself. Other parts were presented as longer-term truths. But whether they were focused on the short- or the long-term, the arguments for a politics of austerity were in each case both damaging and wrong.

THE CASE FOR AUSTERITY POLITICS

To take the resurgent conservative explanation of the causes of the financial crisis first: here the whole weight of the argument was on errors made in the political arena, and on the over-regulation of the private market by the

---

* Simon Wren-Lewis called this *"deficit deceit*: using a manufactured concern about whether the markets will fund the deficit to make otherwise unpopular cuts in public spending." (see his "What Brexit and austerity tell us about economic policy and the media", Sheffield: SPERI Paper No. 36, 2017, p. 3).

public state. In the American case, Republican critics of the ARRA, and then of tighter Wall Street regulation in the form of the Dodd-Frank Act, insisted that the roots of the 2008 financial crisis lay not in the unregulated workings of the US housing market – as so many progressives claimed – but in its politicization, primarily by their Democratic Party opponents.[50] The conservative case here was that it was Democrats, not Republicans, who saw political capital in the giving of subprime loans to marginal groups – often African-American urban voters – and so used the 1977 Community Reinvestment Act, and pressure on the two GSEs to systematically lower the bar on income requirements for house purchase. Moreover, the argument that Wall Street misbehaved because of light/absent regulation and oversight was not one for Republicans. No, for Republicans, recent bank failures were the product of excessive regulation rather than deregulation, compounded by the low-interest rate policy pursued by the Federal Reserve after 9/11. Some libertarian voices on the American Right then even went the further inch: concluding from that mistaken policy that the Federal Reserve itself should be first audited and then possibly closed. Put a central bank into play, they argued, and you necessarily create a financial system that "artificially encourages indebtedness, excessive leverage and reckless money management in general".[51]

For the libertarian strand within the Republican coalition, it was not, therefore, a question of too little government, but of too much. According to them, the Fed driving down interest rates just as emerging economies were beginning to send capital to the United States constituted a form of "pre-emptive Keynesianism", stoking the house price boom and turning the American home from "a castle into an ATM".[52] "US politicians", Johan Norberg wrote at the time, pumped up risk-taking and house prices through deductions, tax benefits for home savings accounts, and restrictions on new construction: while Fannie Mae and Freddie Mac "developed the securitization of mortgages which Wall Street fell madly in love with once the credit-rating agencies – which had been given a legally protected oligopoly by the government – declared them to be safe investments". And "the Fed's safety net and the federal government's deposit insurance made banks dare to take big risks because they could privatize any gains but socialize any losses".[53] "The problem", according to Norberg, was therefore "not that we had too few regulations: on the contrary, we had too many, and above all, faulty ones".[54]

Beneath this set of specific arguments on one single financial crisis lay some deeply held economic and social beliefs of a more general and inherently neoliberal kind. The core one was a faith – and the term "faith" is entirely appropriate here, given the intensity of the way in which the belief was held to and articulated – a faith in the capacity of private enterprise to generate economic growth and generalized wealth if not blocked from its pursuits by either an over-regulating state or a too-assertive labour movement. This, from a string of Republican luminaries in *The Wall Street Journal* in March 2013:

> The country needs a long-term strategy to achieve its common goals of personal freedom, noninflationary prosperity, broad-based economic opportunity and mobility, and national security. With a good strategy as a foundation, sound economic policies will follow. A good strategy must be based on the free enterprise system in which individuals pursue their aspirations with government's role limited to protecting property rights, setting predictable and transparent market rules, and providing a safety net, infrastructure, defence and other functions if the market falls short. Many current government policies are going well beyond such limits, as shown by excessive spending and taxes, growing debt, interventionist monetary policy, and burdensome regulations that have slowed economic growth and job creation.[55]

Throughout the financial crisis and its resulting recession, conservatives in both countries held on to a firm belief in the wonders of trickle-down economics, and therefore to a growth strategy predicated on tax breaks for the rich and limited welfare provision for the poor. Too heavy a tax burden was presented by them as a disincentive to investment. Too generous a welfare net was presented as a disincentive to participation in paid labour – as a failure to differentiate sufficiently sharply between the deserving and the undeserving poor, or between the "strivers" and the "shirkers" as George Osborne put it – with the two presentations linked by an underlying conviction that the Keynesian management of a private economy, or the tight supervision of privately-owned companies by democratically-elected politicians, could only slow the rate of wealth creation and add to the army of the poor. There was even a moment when, in the United States, the Republican leadership in the House of Representatives believed they had an actual number with which to locate the tipping point at which government spending became that barrier: whenever the level of public debt exceeded 90 per cent of GDP, as demonstrated in a widely-acclaimed study of past financial crises by Reinhart and Rogoff.*

For when the government spends, using existing tax revenues, so the standard neoliberal economic argument on both sides of the Atlantic goes, it crowds out private spending. When, alternatively a government spends, printing money to do so, it devalues the currency and brings inflation in its wake. When a government spends by borrowing, it leaves itself (and us, its electorate) in hock to those who finance it (often governments and companies from abroad), and it also leaves a debt-repayment burden to our children and grandchildren, the clearance of which will only slow their economic growth and capacity for wealth creation. So instead of hailing bail-outs and stimulus packages as routes to renewed prosperity, neoliberal critics on the Right in both Britain and America treated them after 2008 as further evidence of a government-led rake's progress. According to them, what the US faced in 2009–10 was not a return to sustained economic growth. What it faced, unless Republicans in Congress stood firm, was a hugely-inflated and ever expanding public spending deficit whose financing would fall on future generations, and not just on the contemporary one. "Sadly", Phil Gramm and Steve McMillin told the readers of *The Wall Street Journal*, "nations generally discover the truth of Albert Einstein's dictum that compound interest is the most powerful force in the universe – not through the happy accumulation of wealth but through the agonizing enslavement of debt".[56] "Fiscal child abuse" was what the Cato Institute's Chris Edwards called it.[57] It was an abuse whose immediate removal was something that responsible politicians and policy-makers ought to prioritize.

---

* The number was entirely discredited when a talented postgraduate discovered that the two economists had seriously miscalculated, due to "selective exclusion of available data, coding errors and inappropriate weighting of summary statistics". On this, see Thomas Herndon, Michael Ash and Robert Pollin, "Does high public debt consistently stifle economic growth? A critique of Reinhart and Rogoff", *Cambridge Journal of Economics* 38 (2014), pp. 257–79.

THE CASE AGAINST AUSTERITY POLITICS

The only problem with all this is that it was quite wrong! It was wrong on the causes of the 2008 financial crisis. It was wrong on the growth consequences of unregulated markets, and it was wrong on the impact of targeted government spending on income growth and distribution. It was all entirely wrong.

There is now a vast literature on the 2008 crisis, much of it discussed and assessed elsewhere;[58] and among the things that any open-minded and careful reading of the US literature makes clear is that the Democratic Party did not cause the housing crisis, and that it was not the Community Reinvestment Act that spread subprime mortgages. Private banks did that, leaving Fannie Mae and Freddie Mac to pick up the pieces. There is no space here to re-establish those truths by examining the evidence in detail. Nor in fact do we need to do so, given that the official Financial Crisis Inquiry Commission has already done this job for us. Their findings stand in stark contrast to the fantasies told about the crisis by those determined to allow private greed and lax regulation no part in it; and include the following (all emphasized in bold in the executive summary of the Report):

> We conclude this financial crisis was avoidable ... We conclude widespread failures in financial regulation and supervision proved devastating to the stability of the nation's financial markets ... We conclude dramatic failures of corporate governance and risk management at many systemically important financial institutions were a key cause of this crisis ... We conclude a combination of excessive borrowing, risky investments, and lack of transparency put the financial system on a collision course with crisis ... We conclude the government was ill prepared for the crisis, and its inconsistent response added to the uncertainty and panic in the financial markets ... We conclude there was a systemic breakdown in accountability and ethics ... We conclude collapsing mortgage-lending standards and the mortgage securitization pipeline lit and spread the flame of contagion and crisis ... We conclude over-the-counter derivatives contributed significantly to the crisis ... [and] we conclude the failures of credit rating agencies were essential cogs in the wheel of financial destruction.[59]

The Financial Crisis Inquiry Commission also found that the two GSEs "contributed to the crisis but were not a primary cause", and that the Community Reinvestment Act "was not a significant factor in subprime lending or the crisis".[60] It is findings like that which remind us that, sadly, part of the case against austerity politics has to be a *negative* one – one consistently demonstrating the falseness of so many of the "truths" presented as axiomatic by those who would cut government spending as *the* route to the restoration of economic growth and generalized prosperity. In the American context, it simply was not the case, for example, that Democratic Administrations created deficits and that Republican ones reduced them. On the contrary, George W. Bush inherited a budget surplus in 2001 and left a budget deficit in 2009 – the vast bulk of the deficit attributed to Barack Obama by his Republican opponents actually stacked up on Bush's watch, the product of two rounds of tax cuts and spending on an illegitimate war – "the result of policies enacted during the Bush presidency coupled with automatic increases in federal spending and decreases in tax revenue triggered by the economic downturn".[61] Which is why people who claim that Obama "tripled the deficit, or increased it, or anything of the sort, are either misled or are trying to mislead. President Obama inherited a budget deficit of $1.4 trillion from President Bush's last budget year – one that was already scheduled to rise sharply – and annual budget deficits have gone down dramatically since".[62] By 2013, those deficits were projected to be *down* by a trillion dollars on their 2009 peak by the time Barack Obama left office. So take away the tax cuts to the wealthy, end the wars, and replace the recession with economic growth, and the US deficit becomes easily manageable again without having to close or reduce a single welfare programme.

Nor was it the case that the Bush-era tax cuts became self-financing over time, by triggering rates of economic expansion and job creation that were impressive when compared to what had gone before or to what has happened since. They did not, and they were not. Trickle-down economics did not work in America the last time it was tried. Rather, and by every important measure – not least GDP growth, investment growth, employment growth and income growth – US "economic performance after the tax *increases* of 1993 outpaced that of the periods following the tax *cuts* of the early 1980s and the early 2000s". In fact, ironically the only major economic indicator bucking that trend, when the three decades are compared, was publicly-held debt, which "rose during both supply-side eras, and fell substantially during the higher-tax period!"[63] Moreover, US corporations are not the most highly-taxed in the western world.[64] Nor are either the United Kingdom or the United States going broke.[65] A country is not like a family whose budget is finite,[66] so the belt-tightening analogy is entirely inappropriate here.* Governments can always print their own money or have their banking system inflate lending – and in the US and UK examples at least, governments running deficits can always attract inflows of foreign capital to help finance them. And we are not leaving unassailable levels of debt to our children. What we are leaving to them, if we spend wisely now, is improved social capital in all its forms; and by borrowing now, we are not burdening future generations: "the burden of reduced consumption to pay for government spending is actually borne by the generation which lends the government the money in the first place".[67] So "No" to a string of what William Mitchell once correctly labelled as "destructive neoliberal myths",[68] whose main purpose was and is to shift the burden of economic reconstruction down onto the shoulders and wallets of those least able to bear it: namely middle-income and low-income families in paid employment or on welfare.

But the specific claims made by the advocates of austerity politics – the ones being refuted here – were no accident. They were the product of deeper weaknesses in the neoliberal case. What united them in part was a profound misspecification of the problem of debt in Anglo-American capitalism. There is undoubtedly such a problem, but not the one prioritized by neoliberals. As we have seen, post-2008, the US and UK economies were both scarred by unprecedented peacetime-levels of three kinds of debt: personal debt, debt on the balance of trade, and public debt (a long-established national debt and a more recent gap between government revenues and spending). It is the first two of those that should concern us most, and certainly not the third.[69] For the evidence is clear that deficit spending by the state – Keynesian style – is a

---

* Robert Skidelsky called this "the Swabian Housewife" fallacy, critiquing German Chancellor Angela Merkel's reported response to the collapse of Lehman Brothers in 2008: "One should simply ask the Swabian housewife", Merkel said, "she would have told us that you cannot live beyond your means." (Robert Skidelsky, *Four Fallacies of the Second Great Depression,* posted on Project Syndicate, 20 November 2013).

key trigger to the recovery of private-sector based economic growth whenever the private sector is, as it was in 2008, heavily in recession. Government spending in such circumstances does not "crowd out" private investment, as the advocates of austerity would have us believe. In a time of recession, government spending generates employment, and rising demand for the products of the private sector – publicly-triggered jobs and spending that then bring the private sector back into more robust activity again. Properly targeted, public spending leaves behind, not debt – the tax revenues inflated by the resulting economic growth eventually more than compensate for the original borrowing – but rather things of value to the present generation, and to generations to come. Public policy leaves behind a more skilled labour force if spent on education; better roads and bridges if spent on infrastructure; and better innovation and competitiveness if spent on basic research and design.

Far from cuts in federal spending helping speed recovery from the post-2008 recession, all the evidence suggests that it was those cuts that slowed the recovery,[70] and kept both economies teetering on the brink of a second recession (or in the UK case, as we just noted, tipping the economy briefly into a second recession, and nearly into a third). In the United States, the failure to follow the first stimulus package with a second one left state governments struggling to sustain social programmes (including education spending) because their own tax revenues were still depleted by a dearth of new local economic activity.[71] The federal sequester created in place of that second stimulus package then compounded the problem. It cost jobs directly, and it prevented public spending from creating more. As the sequester began, the CBO estimated the likely job losses associated with it at 750,000, and that at a time when the total number of federal, state and local government employees was already 500,000 down on its pre-crisis 2007 peak.[72] Indeed as late as October 2016, the US public education system was still employing 214,000 fewer people than in 2008[73] – some of the "roughly 650,000 fewer public sector employees than there were before the crisis: normally, we would have expected some two million more".[74]

As Paul Krugman has convincingly argued, the financial crisis of 2008 and subsequent recession left the US economy caught in a "liquidity trap" – one in which, with interest rates at rock bottom, just easing credit-terms

FLAWED CAPITALISM

would not rekindle growth. On the contrary, and because of the debt-based nature of the economic growth that preceded it, any easing of credit-terms would first be used by private citizens to lower their own debt levels, reinforcing tendencies to secular stagnation in the wider economy as they did so. In such a context, extra government spending was not an indulgence. It was a necessity, if the general rate of economic growth was ever to return to its higher pre-recession trajectory.[75] But tragically, post-2010 that extra spending did not happen. Just the reverse, in fact. For the US economy, Josh Bivens later put it this way, in exploring "Why is recovery taking so long – and who's to blame?":

> The ability of conventional monetary policy to spur recovery following the Great Recession was more limited than in any other postwar recovery. Given the degree of damage inflicted by the Great Recession and the restricted ability of monetary policy to aid recovery, historically expansionary fiscal policy was required to return the US economy to full health. But this government spending not only failed to rise fast enough to spur a rapid recovery, it outright contracted, and this policy choice fully explains why the economy is only partially recovered from the Great Recession a full seven years after its official end ... By far the biggest drag on growth throughout the recovery from the Great Recession has been fiscal policy forced upon us by Republican lawmakers in Congress and austerity-minded state legislatures and governors.[76]

John Weeks' judgement on the causes of the slow recovery of the UK economy was entirely at one with this: namely that the "numbers imply that over almost seven-years Conservative chancellors took a net £100bn out of the economy, an extraction [he labels] as 'fiscal drag'".[77] So too was Simon Wren-Lewis: "the delay in the UK recovery over the first part of the Coalition government's term is at least in part a result of the government's fiscal decisions ... It will be many years before we can settle on a figure for the total cost of that mistake, but measured against the scale of how much governments can influence the welfare of its citizens in peacetime, it is likely to be a large cost".[78]

What the evidence of the post-2008 decade also makes clear is that, left to themselves, unregulated private markets generate outcomes that are far from socially optimal. Unregulated markets generate inequalities of income and wealth that become self-sustaining, if not offset by policies of income redistribution and the renewal of social capital. They generate externalities that erode the general context of life for future generations, if not subject to policies of environmental control and improvement; and they deindustrialize economies with decent wages and strong labour movements, unless policies are in place to generate a global race-to-the-top rather than a race-to-the-bottom. The basic case for Keynesianism is short term, and focused on recovery from recession; but the basic case for the public regulation of private market forces – the democratic case – is longer-term, and focused on the establishment of a fairer balance of resource-use and resource-access within and between generations. Without the active intervention of a Keynesian-inspired democratic state, the biggest threat now facing both the American and British economies in the middle-term is *secular stagnation* and over the long-haul is *serious environmental degradation*; and no sensible person ought to be comfortable with the prospect of either.

The consequences of cutting back on the welfare state

If that were not enough, there is more. What well-targeted public spending does, in both the United States and the United Kingdom, is help alleviate poverty; so that ultimately the most offensive of the claims made by those who would cut that spending is that they are cutting welfare programmes to help the poor. They are not. If they genuinely think they are, they are misinformed; and if they are not misinformed and still advocate what they euphemistically refer to as "welfare reform", then what they are guilty of is waging war on the poor behind a smokescreen of neoliberal economic theology. Misinformation seems to explain much of the anti-poverty stance of those advocating austerity politics in the UK – the key welfare minister involved (Iain Duncan Smith) was clearly well-intentioned, although hopelessly incompetent[79] – but it is hard not to be struck by the protection of class privilege and by the hidden racism that so infects the parallel arguments in the United States. Either way, whether well-intentioned or deeply cynical, cutting welfare to help the poor must stand in the modern age as the ultimate form of oxymoronic politics.[80]

The conservative concern to balance the books whenever welfare spending is discussed stands in such stark contrast, as Coretta Scott King rightly observed, to their enthusiastic advocacy of corporate welfare: of tax cuts for the rich, and government subsidies for the companies they own and manage. In early 2017, the siren voices were out again in force, warning of the dangers to long-term prosperity of excessive government spending. "Without changes to the federal budget, we are on a path to fiscal crisis with spending, deficits and debt continuing to balloon out of control",[81] according to the chair of the Republican Study Committee, the main voice for House conservatives. "Long term, that continued growth, driven by our tax and spending policies, will create the most significant fiscal challenge facing our country", Paul Volker and Peter Petersen agreed.[82] No mention by any of them of the fact that the flow of funds to corporate America continues apace,[83] or that post-Brexit the Conservative government is developing an industrial strategy that will do the same for corporate UK.* And no mention by any of them that public borrowing is as inexpensive now as it has ever been, or that a failure to spend and borrow now will directly (and adversely) impact the American and British poor. All the serious commentary at the time showed that the greatest burden of the 2013 US sequester fell on the shoulders of the American poor,[84] just as now all the serious commentary is anticipating an intensification of income inequality and poverty in the UK because of the upcoming impact of George Osborne's last austerity budget.[85]

---

* Corporate welfare is not just a US issue. This, on the UK. "Corporate welfare is worth between £93bn and £180bn per year. The lower figure is enough to wipe out the UK deficit for 2015. The higher figure would make a significant dent in the national debt. The cost of corporate subsidies is higher than unemployment benefits. And capital grants are worth more than subsidies. Meanwhile corporate tax cuts have reduced revenues by over £12bn since 2005, enough to halt the planned cuts in the unemployment benefits of the poorest and most vulnerable individuals in society." (Kevin Farnsworth, "The British Corporate Welfare State: Public Provision for Private Businesses", Sheffield: SPERI Paper No 24, July 2015, p. 36). Fabian Society research suggests "the wealthiest 20% of Britain's earners will receive almost as much support from the state through the 'shadow welfare' of generous tax breaks by 2020 as the poorest fifth take home in benefits." (Heather Stewart, *The Guardian*, 1 April 2016).

The Conservative Party election manifesto in 2017, and the subsequent policy-deal with the Democratic Unionist Party that kept the Conservatives in office, both suggest that the prospect of Brexit may well be forcing a slight moderation of austerity politics in the UK: as government ministers struggle to strengthen an already weak economy that may soon be obliged to survive without easy access to EU markets and EU funds; and as the prospect looms of record levels of UK taxation if the economy slows and as the population continues to age.[86] Certainly the Tories went to the country that year behind a leader determined, as she put it, to leave behind "untrammelled free markets and selfish individualism" in favour of "a belief not just in society but in the good that government can do".[87] They also went to the country facing an electorate in which, rather unexpectedly as it turned out, "popular support for higher taxes and increased public spending was stronger than it had been for more than a decade". Indeed, that unexpected resurgence of popular antipathy to full-blown austerity politics was one major reason why the snap election that Theresa May called in June 2017 backfired so spectacularly against her!

But we can anticipate no equivalent moderation of austerity politics in the America of Donald J. Trump. On the contrary, Congressional Republicans and their Tea Party base have waited for too long for an opportunity to implement their full austerity programme to pass up their opportunity now, when they find themselves facing a president who is partly sympathetic to their programme and partly too spineless politically to break with them on the bits he dislikes. Indeed, Republican lawmakers in the House of Representatives moved quickly, in the wake of the Trump inauguration, to bring in a budget plan that "set the stage for a potential $203 billion rollback of financial industry regulations, federal employee benefits, welfare spending and more".[88] Those same House Republicans may yet – in an entirely unprincipled way – tolerate higher levels of public debt under Trump than they did under Obama, in return for a further run at the repeal of the Affordable Care Act and the further restriction of abortion rights. But even so, there will doubtless be a second coming of trickle-down economics and welfare reform in Trump's America – "history once as tragedy and twice as farce", as Karl Marx once observed of a similarly narcissistic charlatan on the throne of a major power[89] – and if there is, it will be the American poor who will bear the brunt of the adverse fallout from yet another iteration of a morally bankrupt and economically defective philosophy.

How long they will have to bear that brunt will turn critically on the ability of the American centre-left to regain political traction again, just as in the UK the drip-drip of Tory-induced austerity will no doubt continue to eat away at the viability of the stronger UK welfare support-net unless the Labour Party can consolidate and expand its currently rising level of popular support. Quite how to achieve an effective centre-left renaissance on both sides of the Atlantic, and how to do it with all requisite speed, is for that set of reasons the central concern of the final chapter that now follows.[90]

PART IV

Conclusion

8

Towards a Better Future

"For all the work that remains, a new foundation is laid. A new future is ours to write. It must be one of economic growth that's not only sustainable but shared. To achieve it, America must stay committed to working with all nations to build stronger and more prosperous economies for all our citizens for generations to come."

Barack Obama[1]

"We label the current era 'the Great Uncertainty' and suggest, by the deliberate use of that term, that the present conjuncture is being shaped by a remarkable, and hugely challenging, coalescence of three major processes ... financial crisis ... shifting economic power ... [and] environmental threat ... processes of change all taking place now and arguably coming to a head at broadly the same time."

Colin Hay and Tony Payne[2]

Whether the new foundation laid in the Obama years is as solid as the former president asserted is now the governing question in the America of Donald J. Trump. But what we have already seen is that those foundations were not as strong, nor their outcomes as adequate, as the Obama reflection implies. In his defence, of course, it should be immediately said that he knew that too. The words quoted at the top of the page came at the end of a powerful and reflective essay focused on what remained still to be done: for Barack Obama, in the last months of his presidency, this included "boosting productivity growth, combatting rising inequality, ensuring that everyone who wants a job can get one, and building a resilient economy that's primed for future growth".[3] That was difficult, he implied, because of things specific to the

251

United States – not least political gridlock, social complexity, and global responsibilities. But as the quotation from Colin Hay and Tony Payne suggests, those specificities look rather different, and even more intractable, when seen as part of a bigger and more general picture – one overwhelmed in the moment by the impact of a financial crisis "brought about by neoliberal excess", by a new international division of labour "characterized by the rise of countries like China, India and Brazil", and by a pattern of climate change that is both "real and accelerating" and raising serious questions about "the ongoing viability of traditional notions of economic growth and indeed the good society itself".[4]

This final chapter starts with these two quotations because they throw into relief the importance of dealing with our modern condition at these two different levels simultaneously. Those of us in possession of progressive values and ambitions need to find a politics that can address nationally specific economic weaknesses and their associated social problems, while recognizing the anchorage of those weaknesses and problems in wider sets of economic and social trends.[5] The economies and societies studied here have been treated as "flawed capitalisms": and certainly, they are flawed. Indeed, it is because they are so flawed that progressives in both countries find themselves with so long and daunting a list of reforms to be made. But these two economies are also capitalisms, so making that progressive "to-do" list very difficult to achieve. The list is difficult to achieve both because the weaknesses the economies contain are deeply rooted, and because the reforms required to resolve them will directly challenge existing patterns of power and reward. Any incoming progressive administration attempting to reform a flawed capitalism therefore will not only face problems. It will also face resistance.

Yet that is not an argument for abandoning the attempt. Just because something is difficult, it does not mean that it should not be tried. On the contrary, what it actually means is that progressive reform requires courage as well as insight. It means that, as the Independent Labour Party leader Jimmy Maxton said to his left-wing colleagues in the UK long ago, "if you can't ride two horses at once, you shouldn't be in the circus!" Getting to grips with the flaws in any one national context has always required getting to grips as well with the wider capitalism into which those flaws are embedded; and with capitalism now so globalized, that requirement is as prescient as it has ever been. Indeed, the underlying critique of the neoliberal alternative, of the kind just laid out in Chapter 7, ultimately always comes down to this single point: *that neoliberalism intensifies the flaws it pretends to remedy by failing to address the deeper weaknesses of the capitalism that generates them.* When the ocean is sending you a tsunami, you don't survive by jumping in and swimming stronger. You survive by jumping out and building a stronger defence. That is the task of the contemporary centre-left: to build a new and stronger defence, so that swimming becomes safe again – for everyone.

Local stock-taking

The picture drawn here of both the US and the UK is not a pretty one. The over-arching argument of this volume is that we are living through the death throes of the second great social settlement that surrounded (and facilitated) successful postwar economic growth on both sides of the Atlantic. We are having to live through those death throes because the second social settlement – the Reagan/Thatcher one – is not going into its dark night quietly, any more than did the first social settlement as that collapsed in the 1970s. We are in a period of transition, one in which the advocates of a less-regulated capitalism are attempting to hold the line on the Reagan/Thatcher settlement that worked so well for many conservatives until 2008. Holding that line is both easy and difficult for them. It is easy to the extent that more progressive forces fail to generate a credible alternative model and programme to the one now so seriously discredited by the fall-out from the global financial crisis that neoliberalism spawned; and yet it is simultaneously difficult because of the scale and character of the fall-out itself.

In the first two parts of this volume, that fall-out was documented first for the United States and then for the United Kingdom. The US story, as far as the economy was concerned, was (and remains) one of slow and uneven recovery, until very recently stagnant real wages, and hidden under-employment. In the American case, those economic difficulties were (and still are) accompanied by a set of social problems that are also entrenched and daunting – problems made worse by the economic underperformance itself. These include a squeezed middle class, an embedded racism, a large underclass of the

253

permanently poor, and a welfare net that is so limited that it does little to alleviate poverty, and even less to enable an increasingly hard-pressed generation of millennials to establish an adequate work–life balance. Meanwhile, across the Atlantic, the UK continues to struggle with a similar pattern of low and uneven economic growth, wage stagnation, and even lower labour productivity. The UK and US differ in the positioning of racial tension in their social mix, but in the UK too social problems abound. From a litany of possibilities, Chapter 5 focused in on the threatened living standards of the middle class, the persistence of poverty (particularly in urban areas), the depth of gender inequality, the difficulties of striking an adequate work–life balance, and the growing crisis of access to affordable housing. Neither of the social chapters was able – for reasons of space – to cover all the ills now besetting each society in turn, but the hope is that each chapter did enough to demonstrate the depth and character of the social flaws now in place around us.

Additionally, both these economies and societies share at least two other features that set them apart from their own immediate past. One is their current retreat from "politics as normal" – the rise in both countries of a right-wing populism that balks at free trade, opposes the free movement of people, and looks to strengthen the national economy by pulling back (or in the UK case, entirely breaking from) existing international agreements and institutions. The other is the way in which – in both countries – the burden of current economic underperformance and past social divisions is falling particularly heavily on the shoulders of the millennial generation, so that options taken for granted about trajectories of life over time are being increasingly eroded and constrained in what were once the two most successful capitalist economies on earth.

Of course, none of these problems are uniquely American or British. There are elements of right-wing populism and millennial distress in every advanced economy in the global system – indeed in some of those economies, not least those on the Mediterranean rim, the distress has been even more severe – because in each of those economies the social settlements that once guaranteed prosperity have now eroded, and because the millennial generation is everywhere paying the price of the resulting slower rates of GDP- and labour productivity-growth.[6] But both these ruptures with the immediate past – the one political, the other economic – are such defining features of contemporary

254

life in both America and Britain that they deserve our particular attention here. What passed as "the American Dream" for at least the white sections of the US working class until as late as the 1980s no longer cuts muster with the children born in or after that decade; and even in the UK – where no such "dream" ever formally developed – the data are equally striking. Unless things dramatically change, people now in their 20s in Britain face a lifetime of lower wages, longer working hours, less job security, more expensive accommodation, and less generous pensions than did their parents or grandparents. In both countries, middle-class members of the baby-boomer generation have lived – and indeed continue to live – the good life, but now seem increasingly incapable of passing that good life on to the generations that follow.

General headwinds

The American economic historian, Robert Gordon, has recently labelled those common problems "headwinds", and has used that imagery to predict very constrained economic times ahead for the United States at least. The Gordon thesis is that the US economy in particular now faces "a set of four headwinds, all of them widely recognized and uncontroversial": demographic shifts that will reduce working hours per capita; stagnation in US educational attainment levels, "as the US sinks lower in the world league tables of high school and college completion rates"; rising inequality, and "a long-term increase in the ratio of debt to GDP at all levels of government". Combining that with a recognition that each of the three industrial revolutions* that have raised generalized living standards from the 1750s have each run their course more quickly than the one before, Gordon has argued convincingly that whereas "the United States achieved a 2.0 percentage average annual growth rate of real GDP per capita between 1891 and 2007", rates of growth "in the 25 to 40 years after 2007 will be much slower, particularly for the great majority of the population".[7]

---

* "IR#1 (steam, railroads) from 1750 to 1830; IR#2 (electricity, internal combustion engine, running water, internal toilets, communications, entertainment, chemicals, petroleum) from 1870 to 1900; and IR#3 (computers, the web, mobile phones) from 1960 to the present." (Gordon, NBER Working Paper 18315, August 2012).

The Gordon thesis on supply-side blockages stands alongside, and is entirely compatible with, the other thesis currently being widely discussed on the Anglo-American centre-left – namely that on "secular stagnation" developed by Lawrence Summers among others. Here the argument, focusing on the demand side of the economic equation, is that "without rapid asset-price inflation or exceptionally aggressive monetary policy, it has proved impossible to generate enough demand to absorb potential global supply".[8] On this view, the economies of the industrial world "suffer from an imbalance resulting from an increasing propensity to save and a decreasing propensity to invest, [leaving each] stuck in neutral".* Joseph Stiglitz put it this way:

> The economics of this inertia is easy to understand, and there are readily available solutions. The world faces a deficiency of aggregate demand, brought on by a combination of growing inequality and a mindless wave of fiscal austerity. Those at the top spend less than those at the bottom, so that as money moves up, demand goes down. And countries like Germany that consistently maintain external surpluses are contributing significantly to the key problem of insufficient global demand.[9]

Neither thesis is without its critics, particularly Robert Gordon's,[10] but even critics are obliged to concede the force of the trends being alluded to in this important and ongoing conversation about wage stagnation, economic slow-down and productivity dearth. For whether we like it or not, we would appear to be caught up in "an age of global oversupply". As Daniel Alpert put it, "an oversupply of global labour (hence high underemployment); an oversupply of global productive capacity (hence ultra-low inflation); and an oversupply of global capital (hence low interest rates)".[11] It is an age of oversupply which the politics of austerity then make significantly worse – particularly in the Eurozone. "Stupid ... politics and policies that choked off

* Quite why, and quite why now, remains a matter of debate – one characterized in this way by Larry Summers. "Other explanations have been proposed, notably Kenneth Rogoff's theory of a debt overhang, Robert Gordon's theory of supply-side headwinds, Ben Bernanke's theory of a savings glut, and Paul Krugman's of a liquidity trap. All of them have some validity, but the secular stagnation theory offers the most comprehensive account of the situation and the best basis for policy prescriptions." ("The Age of Secular Stagnation", *Foreign Affairs*, March/April 2016, p. 3).

demand", as a frustrated Joseph Stiglitz put it in 2015. "In the absence of demand, investment and jobs will fail to materialize. It is that simple".[12]

Regardless of where we stand on the relative importance of demand-side and supply-side barriers to rapid economic growth, there is no avoiding the underlying truth to which Summers and Gordon both direct our attention: namely that dominant trends in contemporary capitalism are generating new difficulties for centre-left parties in advanced capitalisms seeking full employment and rising living standards for the bulk of their labour forces. One adverse trend is anchored in the *globalization of industrial production*: the spread of capitalist wage relationships into what was once the closed world of global communism and the third world of colonial dependency, and – what goes with that – the increasing propensity of large US- and UK-based firms to indulge in outsourcing and subcontracting (so creating what David Weil recently called "the frissured workplace"[13] – one in which numerous tasks, previously performed by direct employees, are the subject of arms-length contracts). As we saw earlier, social settlements fixed in the West during the Cold War years are now under challenge precisely because less well-paid labour forces are suddenly available for exploitation in authoritarian regimes like China and Russia, as well as in struggling democracies that were once military dictatorships (particularly in South and Latin America). The resulting outsourcing of middle-ranking industrial jobs is then reinforcing a second adverse trend: job polarization in northern labour markets brought into being by *patterns of technological change* that are – sometimes entirely, sometimes only partially – replacing manual labour with robotic production in many previously only semi-automated production systems.* Globalization and technological change are currently combining, that is, to squeeze

---

* The future impact of robotics on employment is a matter of huge importance and, for the moment at least, huge uncertainty. On the worst scenario, technologically-induced unemployment might drown out everything else discussed here. Less dramatically, it might significantly improve productivity while dislodging employment up and down the employment hierarchy. For the worst-case scenario – 670,000 manufacturing jobs lost in the US between 1990 and 2007, with more job losses expected as robot-use quadruples, see Daron Acemoglu and Pascual Restrepo, "Robots and Jobs: Evidence from US Labor Markets". NBER Working Paper No. 23285, March 2017. Parallel calculations by the IPPR for the UK suggest a possible robot-induced loss of one job for every three over the next two decades. (For a counterview, see Lawrence Mishel and Josh Bivens, "The zombie robot argument lurches on". Washington, DC: EPI, 24 May 2017).

traditionally-generated middle-class earnings and job security out of the heart of advanced capitalisms, and to leave labour markets there increasingly divided between high productivity (and high-waged) labour on the one side and low productivity (and low-paid) labour on the other – with far more of the latter than of the former. In this sense, what centre-left parties now face is the task of raising productivity and living standards in economies that have deindustrialized to a significant (and many claim, permanent) extent, with one core dividing fissure in their labour markets and their electorates being that between a restricted group of top-salary earners and a growing body of the full-time working poor.

Of course, not all advanced capitalist economies are equally deindustrialized. Nor are all of them subject to exactly the same low-productivity drivers. Instead, national specificities here relate back in a strikingly direct fashion to the general global role of their dominant classes, and so to the different degrees to which their national economic fortunes are linked to imperialism.[14] (The US and UK economies are, therefore, particularly vulnerable in consequence.) But whether facing a fully deindustrialized economy, or one only partially transformed into a service-dominated entity, centre-left politics in each major national capitalism now has to operate inside (and against the background of) a new (and from a progressive standpoint, more adverse) *balance of forces between capital and labour* on the global scale: with capital's freedom of manoeuvre enhanced globally, and with the defensive power of labour movements (and the labour share of GNP) threatened inside core capitalisms themselves.[15] In fact, "bargaining and market power have become more concentrated both between companies and within them, fueling a dynamic of ever-greater income and wealth inequality" as they do so. In Ben Casselman's words, "it's not manufacturing jobs that Americans miss. It's unionized jobs".[16] Or as the Nobel Prize-winning economist Robert Solow recently put it, with his usual care and caution:

> The suggestion I want to make is that one important reason for the failure of real wages to keep up with productivity is that the division of rent in industry has been shifting against the labour side for several decades. This is a hard hypothesis to test in the absence of direct measurement. But the decay of unions and collective bargaining, the explicit hardening

of business attitudes, the popularity of right-to-work laws, and the fact that the wage-lag seems to have begun at the same time as the Reagan presidency, all point in the same direction: the share of wages in national value-added may have fallen because the social bargaining power of labour has diminished.[17]

In consequence, the contemporary centre-left now faces a world in which growth models have emerged, and prevailed, that are characterized by widening levels of income and wealth inequality which – if Thomas Piketty is right – will become self-sustaining unless public policy acts to redress the trend. The generation of that kind of counteracting public policy is then only made more difficult, of course, by the institutional embedding of neoliberal principles and practices, and by the systematic and deliberate weakening of institutions and social forces committed to greater economic equality and social justice – particularly trade unions. The backcloth to both the US and UK centre-left's search for an effective growth strategy is the emergence, that is, of what Robert Reich called "the share-the-scraps economy" in which "almost all profits go to the … owners" and in which just "the scraps" go to labour that is increasingly deployed only on demand.[18]

If those were not problems enough for those of us committed to progressive politics, then let us also add demographic and welfare issues of the kind mentioned by Robert Gordon. It is conventional in much of the literature on comparative welfare politics to recognize the existence of a *generalized crisis of the welfare state* – a crisis differentially impacting (but common to all) the various types of welfare system now embedded in the advanced capitalist world. Prior to the 2008 financial crisis, problems of welfare provision in such economies were largely a product of the systems' successes: people living longer, expecting better healthcare, looking for a more equitable work–life balance, and so on. Pre-2008, it was the growing weight of welfare provision on even successful economies that was producing tax rebellions, a degree of recommodification of welfare services, and the recalibrating of many welfare programmes.[19] But post-2008, it has been the underperformance of the underlying economies that has taken the crisis of the welfare state to a new level. Aging baby-boomers, growing numbers of the poor and underemployed, and escalating healthcare costs now all have to be sustained from tax revenues depleted by low rates of economic growth, poor productivity performances, and growing opposition to increased taxation. The politics of reform are always easier when rates of economic growth are high: but post-2008, those growth rates have simply not been available to us. On the contrary, the global economy now looks set – for the foreseeable future at least – to be locked onto a growth trajectory lower than that sustained through the peak years of the Keynesian settlement, or through the peak years of the neoliberal one that followed – a growth trajectory that Christine Lagarde, the Managing Director of the IMF, recently labelled "the new medio-cre". The need for a new social settlement is high precisely because the conditions that would facilitate its easy introduction are visibly absent. But then, as the earlier comment from Jimmy Maxton implied, in a capitalist circus, riding horses in a left-wing direction requires a very high level of skill. If the thing had been easy to do, it would already have been done. People go to the circus to see difficult performances made easy; which is why, in our contemporary circus of flawed capitalisms, if the centre-left wants to regain the support of its old electorate again, it is now time for progressives to begin once more to effectively perform!

Top priorities

The unexpectedly strong showing of the Labour Party in the UK's snap general election in June 2017, on the Party's most radical manifesto for at least three decades, does suggest that – in the UK at least – progressives are at last beginning to perform more effectively again. But one swallow does not a summer make, nor did the strong showing produce a Labour majority: which is why, even in the UK case, it seems wisest to assume two linked things: that we shall have to wait some time yet for the successful election of a centre-left government in either the US or UK; and that one way of curtailing that delay is to establish an honest recognition now of the problems that any such government will face, and need to be equipped to resolve.

Of the major headwinds they are likely to face, the main *economic* ones are likely to be rooted either in the short-term consequences of *secular stagnation* or in the longer-term problems generated by *low labour productivity*. Issues of globalization and technological change will no doubt then compound those economic difficulties (so making the issue of a basic income for citizens, regardless of their employment status, now worth discussing fully[20]), but they will not create them. The main and parallel *social* problems confronting such governments are likely to be the results of inherited *inequality in all its forms* (inequalities of class, gender, ethnicity, and sexual orientation), compounded by the resulting starkly differential access to available economic and social resources between and within generations. The capacity of any incoming progressive UK government or US administration to deal effectively with such entrenched problems will then, in its turn, depend heavily on the degree to which a new generation of centre-left politicians has by that point openly embraced this one basic truth: that *only by seriously addressing the social agenda (of inequalities and generational injustice) will they be able to simultaneously resolve the economic one (of low productivity and inadequate demand)*. The route out, that is, from here to a better future will require of the centre-left nothing less than *the construction of an entirely new and progressively-grounded social structure of accumulation* – one within which economies can grow rapidly again, and the pressures on emerging generations begin once more to ease.

On the productivity front of that new SSA, the need for strategic interventions by a progressive democratic state will be particularly acute in the UK case because, as we saw in Chapter 3, the UK's productivity problem is now both deep and entrenched. But not just in the United Kingdom: in the United States too, we are now downwind of a growth strategy that relied heavily on private sector-provided, low-productivity service sector expansion. That strategy too pulled overall labour productivity down. So, in both economies and at the very least, new forms of industrial policy will be required to develop high-productivity service sectors, and the high-skilled and high-wage labour force that alone will be capable both of providing those services as workers and of sustaining them as consumers. It may be, of course, that to some difficult-to-establish degree, existing levels of labour productivity are higher than currently recorded – because measuring labour productivity through crude output indices underplays growth in product quality and in what economists now call "consumer surplus" – the services we get, for example, from the apps on our phone for free.[21] But as Kemal Derviş and Zia Qureshi recently noted, "these two types of mismeasurement explain only a relatively small share of the slowdown in economic gains" and "have existed for a long time". Nor do they "seem to have increased substantially in recent years";[22] and because they have not, "the conclusion is clear: the productivity-growth slowdown is real".[23] And being real, it gives force, therefore, to Anne Wren's observation that "without a thriving set of high value-added sectors to finance them, expansive public services ... are ultimately unaffordable"; and gives even greater force to her associated prescriptions for rectification – solutions that include an increased supply of "college educated labour ... public investment in education as early as the pre-primary level" and moves to "facilitate women's participation in the labour market".[24]

Then this: one recurrent theme in the ongoing discussion on the current productivity shortfall across advanced industrial economies – including in both the US and the UK – is that productivity growth remains low in part, *not* because innovations do not happen (they do, and sectors and companies at the forefront of technological change continue to show significant productivity growth) but because those innovations are *slow to spread* widely.[25] This key process of dissemination is now apparently held in check by a lack of demand created in large measure by the growing inequality of income and wealth that has accompanied this shift from an industrial to a service-based economy. It is held in check too, as Robert Gordon noted, by the way in which low incomes and low capacities for reskilling also go together. In other words, low productivity and high-income inequality are intimately interrelated, such that solutions to the first necessarily require reductions in the second. Dervis and Qureshi put the inequality-skills point this way:

Any strategy to address the problems underpinning low productivity growth – from inadequate technological diffusion to income inequality – must address skills constraints and mismatches affecting the labour market's ability to adjust. As it stands, workers, particularly from lower income groups, are slow to respond to demand for new high-level skills, owing to lags in education and training, labour market rigidities, and perhaps also geographical factors. These factors, together with rent capture and winner-take-all markets, can entrench inequality and blunt markets' competitiveness.[26]

One other specificity too is worthy of note: that there is currently an acute need to rebalance both the UK and US economies: rebalancing out of an excessive concentration on military production in the US case while getting out of the empire business; out of an inflated financial sector in the UK; and back towards civilian-focused industrial and manufacturing renewal in both. For the case remains strong that the multiplier effect on the rest of the economy of investment is greater when production is geared towards the provision of civilian goods rather than of armaments in all their forms.[27] The case also remains strong that the steady increase in the weight of financial services in the overall GDP acts as a multiplier of income inequality in the society that surrounds them, becomes a major source of regional imbalances in wealth and income, and leaves over-financially dependent economies vulnerable to prolonged deficits on their overseas balance of trade.[28] And the case remains strong too that manufacturing industries – if properly reconstituted – help sustain a higher general rate of labour productivity, and associated improvements in real rates of pay, in the wider economy they service.[29] The case for reindustrializing at least part of the base of both the US and UK economies remains, therefore, a powerful and a compelling one. There is a very real sense in which now – just as in the 1980s when the matter was first extensively discussed on both sides of the Atlantic – *Manufacturing Matters*;[30] and certainly, if centre-left political parties are ever to extract white working-class voters from their current infatuation with right-wing populism, partial reindustrialization will have to be part of any progressive programme in opposition and performance in power.

None of that will happen while existing trade rules apply. Donald J. Trump is quite right on that; but it will also not happen if capital continues to be strengthened and labour consequently weakened – and on that, Donald J. Trump and his Republican friends could not be more wrong.[31] For it is not simply, as we argued in Chapter 7, that the austerity route to generalized prosperity favoured by Republicans is a mirage. It is also that there is now growing evidence, not least from international agencies that once stood at the heart of the neoliberal settlement,[32] that at this stage of capitalist development, economic growth and social inequality are increasingly incompatible; and that any long-term successful growth strategy has, therefore, to be based on reduced levels of inequality, and on the full development and mobilization of all levels and forms of human capital.[33] The well-paid boss in the top office is no longer – not that in truth that s/he ever was – sufficiently significant as to be able to trigger prolonged economic growth by his/her initiative or genius alone. The reality is beginning to dawn, in key sections of the international governing strata, that because production is inherently a social process its success over the long term requires the full motivation of all involved economic players. On the demand side of the economic equation, those players require a capacity to buy goods and services from the wages they earn rather than from the credit they borrow; and on the supply side of the equation those same players need to be able to sustain over the long period high-quality inputs into the creation of goods and services that others buy, and so require among other things working environments and work–life balances that will enable them – and motivate them – to do so.

What has ultimately to replace the neoliberal politics of austerity, therefore, is a progressive resetting of public policy and the social order in ways that stimulate the full use of existing productivity capacities in both economies. It may be that help for this will come from a new generation of technologies – software, automation, robotics and the like – to balance out the pessimism of the Gordon thesis. But if (as is likely) we now face a sustained period in which there is no systemically-induced new technology to lift productivity up across the entire economy, any incoming progressive government in either London or Washington will need to lift that productivity by fully-utilizing the productive potential that is already there. It is only possible to stimulate greater labour output per hour across the entire economy in a limited number of ways. Some of these ways, like intensifying the work process by managerial dictat, or lengthening the working day,[34] are neither possible in the present conjuncture nor progressive in any conjuncture. But other ways are both those things – possible and progressive.

- Productivity in key sectors can be raised by *increasing the volume of investment*, breaking the syndrome of low demand and looming deflation by borrowing now, when investment funds are so cheap (a solution favoured by, among others, Paul Krugman, to end what he termed "the Great Capitulation"[35]).

- Productivity can be increased in key manufacturing sectors by *improving the underlying quality of the STEM economy*, by attracting highly-skilled immigrants or funding STEM education at sub-college level (as favoured by, among others, the Brookings Institution's Metropolitan Policy Program[36]).
- Productivity can be raised by *improving the "innovation diffusion machine"* (the current OECD position, not least by more effectively allocating human talent to jobs, and reallocating scarce resources to underpin the growth of innovative firms).
- Productivity can be raised, across an entire economy, by *rebalancing the distribution of labour* from low-productivity to high-productivity sectors (the traditional Swedish model solution, now requiring both active industrial policy and an active labour market one).
- Productivity can be raised by *fully employing the entirety of its labour force and increasing its skill level* (the traditional left-Keynesian solution, now requiring quantitative easing as well as long-term public spending or borrowing[37]).
- Productivity can be raised by *fully mobilizing the existing set of economic skills, a set now so heavily skewed by gender*[38] (the solution currently favoured by both the EU Commission and the former US Fed chair, Janet Yellen).

This last source – the full use of an educated female labour force – is especially important, given the clear and readily available evidence that advancing women's equality can add trillions of dollars to global growth.[39] The deconstruction of patriarchal structures for progressive purposes should be a "no-brainer", but it is not: women now out-perform men in systems of higher and further education across the advanced capitalist world, acquiring as they do so bodies of knowledge and sets of skills, only to have those remain seriously under-utilized in societies and economies that are still riddled with sexist cultures and still structured around a variety of glass ceilings. Tapping this huge productive potential for progressive ends requires the adoption by parties of the centre-left of a new and gender-focused set of social policies – the creation, indeed, of an entirely new social settlement focused on the needs of working families, and particularly on the needs of the women within them. In this last route to sustained and progressive productivity growth, policies on equal pay, on flexible working hours, on affordable child care, and on the de-gendering of family responsibilities need to move centre-stage: no longer to be add-ons to be cut the first time the national budget has to be balanced, but rather the first thing to be funded to make sure that the budget balances at a higher and a more generous level.

All of which means that, on both sides of the Atlantic, a progressive growth strategy will only come from political parties committed to *managing capital in the genuine interests of labour*, and one equipped with an intellectual framework that recognizes the vital role of progressive social settlements in facilitating economic growth. At its core, any turn to the left will require the progressive remanagement of capital: internationally, through new trade rules and capital controls; internally, through new policies of public ownership, progressive taxation, and industrial democracy – all underpinned by strong trade unionism. It will require the state-led reconstitution of both economies' manufacturing base, and a fully revamped and better-funded education and training programme. It will require state financing of research and development geared to the greening of the economy, with environmental regulations being used as a beachhead to establish the legitimacy of the more general regulation of private industry by the democratic state. It will require a generous living-wage at the base of the income ladder, and sharply progressive taxation to keep that ladder short; and it will require a resetting of the relationship between work and family – the privileging of policies addressed to the new reality of a two-income family unit in which the vast majority of both men and women are heavily engaged in paid work.

Good news and bad news

The good news is that the kinds of political programmes needed to implement the transition from one kind of Anglo-American capitalism to a better and more progressive one are already available, and in some volume. The bad news is that the main political agencies charged with their delivery are currently struggling mightily to meet their obligations in this matter.

We shall get to the question of agency later. Let us first be clear here about the validity of the claim on available programmes. In fact, there are so many of them now around – all broadly similar in content and underlying premises – that they are readily to hand. They come from individual politicians, particularly in the United States where that form of policy-generation is so entrenched.[40] They come from centre-left think tanks on both sides of the Atlantic: including Compass,[41] NEF[42] and the RSA[43] in the UK; and the EPI[44] and the Center for American Progress[45] in the US. And they come from a swathe of outstanding public intellectuals – from such figures as Will Hutton[46] and the late Tony Atkinson[47] in the UK; and from Joseph Stiglitz,[48] Heather Boushey,[49] Robert Gordon,[50] Dean Baker and E. J. Dionne,[51] among others, in the US.

In the US case, for example, as we argue in more detail in the parallel publication to this one, *Reflections on the Future of the Left*, the 2016 presidential campaign witnessed the incremental development of a string of policy proposals, each slightly more radical than the one before, which collectively brought into public view a developing map of how best to reset the US economy and society in ways that strengthen the first and enrich the second. In US progressive circles, the most moderate demand on the table after 2008 was for *demand-maintenance through public spending and managed public debt*:[52] for growing the US economy, as President Obama put it, from the "middle out". Another common theme in the US progressive rethink after 2008 was what was later dubbed "the infrastructure route to growth": the call for a regeneration of economic growth and greater international competitiveness through federal spending on the *modernization of the US economy's physical infrastructure* (roads, bridges, rail and internet).[53] Other, more radical voices, also added a demand for *progressive taxation* to redress the "theft" of wealth by the top US income earners, to slow the rate of growth of (or reverse) the trend to income and wealth inequality, and to generate demand for goods and services across the entire US economy by concentrating extra purchasing power in the hands of those most likely to spend it – the American middle class and the American poor. Such demands for progressive tax reform also now tend to be accompanied in the US by a call for *universal access to high-quality education and greater spending on training and skill upgrading*,[54] for a *higher minimum wage*, for *more generous earned-income and child-tax credits*,[55] for *renewed trade union rights, for greater rights for women and minorities at work*, for *a bigger federal pension* (increasing Social Security for all but high income earners), and for policies designed to *reverse the outsourcing of well-paid American jobs*. In certain hands, these policies are gathered in a call for a new "twenty-first century social contract";[56] and in yet others, more radical still, that last demand is often linked to one calling for less spending on the US military – a call for a redistribution of resources and efforts into more nation-building at home and less overseas – and for the use of public procurement policies to strengthen home-based manufacturing industry. Although the extension of public ownership still has yet to surface as a major progressive demand in the post-2008 United States, the demand to either more *tightly control* or *actually break up large financial institutions* certainly has; as too has the demand for the placing of a *green agenda* at the heart of any future US progressive growth strategy.

In the United Kingdom, the most recent policy rethink (the one after the election defeat of 2015) initially went more slowly and covered less policy distance than in the United States. It covered less distance partly because it had less distance to go (much of what Bernie Sanders, for example, advocated as "democratic socialism" was pretty-standard European social democratic stuff, as he himself openly acknowledged). It went more slowly because unlike Bernie Sanders, Jeremy Corbyn and his new team had a whole parliamentary party to bring on board behind them, significant sections of which remain unenthusiastic at best, openly hostile at worse. Yet there were signs from the outset of the Corbyn leadership of new policy emerging from his post-New Labour party: *ending support for the UK nuclear deterrent*, for example, or *renationalizing the basic railway system, abolishing fees for attending university or college, and resetting the industry department* into what the Shadow Chancellor, in his first party conference address in that role, called "a powerful economic development department, in charge of public investment, infrastructure planning and setting new standards in the labour market".[57] And although this process of policy innovation was cut short by the calling of an unexpected general election in June 2017, the Labour Party was still able to go to the country in that election with its most radical set of proposals since 1983: renationalizing not just the railways but also the Post office and energy and water companies; providing free childcare for all two years olds, and 12 months maternity leaves for their mothers; committing to the creation of 100,000 council and housing associations new homes per year;

and paying for a stronger NHS and student maintenance grants by raising corporation tax, taxing derivative trading in the City, and taxing high earners (those earning £80,000 a year) at new income tax rates of first 45 and then 50 per cent.

This self-conscious shift by the Corbyn-led Labour Party towards the creation of a Mariana Mazzucato-type "Entrepreneurial State",[58] and to the parallel *restoration and extension of trade union and worker rights*, built on the incremental movements away from the New Labour paradigm that had begun under Ed Miliband after 2010. The Miliband-led Labour Party fought (and lost) the 2015 general election on a policy platform that remained committed to the rapid balancing of the public accounts, so retaining one foot in the old policy camp. But it also went to the country committed to a modest increase in top rates of tax, a higher minimum wage, new labour rights, more free childcare, protected funding for the NHS and for publicly-provided education and skills training, enhanced infrastructure investment, a state-run investment bank, and proactive policy to slow down climate change. At the heart of those policies were social ones facilitating individual opportunities (things like funding preschool education and providing paid parental leave), labour market ones strengthening trade unions and individual worker rights, and economic ones focused on the regulation of finance and business. Cumulatively, these policy developments inside the Labour Party, when supplemented by others canvassed but not yet adopted (not least, a much shorter working week[59] and the possibility of a basic income for all[60]), potentially constitute the core elements of what Colin Hay and Tony Payne recently termed "civic capitalism",[61] – policies, that is, which if implemented are capable of taking the UK towards a new growth model based on "inclusive growth".

Whether these changes are harbingers of a permanent policy realignment in Anglo-American progressive circles remains to be seen. But let us hope so. Let us hope that the next iteration of the US and UK centre-left is built around a set of integrated policies: policies designed to strengthen the economy's manufacturing base and skill-sets (its source of productivity and high-paying jobs); policies designed to create a new, more socially just and family-focused social settlement; and policies designed to regulate privately-driven market-processes, the better to maintain basic social rights and to protect the environment over time. For policy design is not our problem here. As a first rudimentary move, all we need do, in order to create the progressive policy-package required, is put the American and British centre-left policy trajectories together: in the process quickly generating a list that looks like this – so organized here in a form that puts moderate progressives in the middle of the list, with more radical proposals as you move out to the list's top and bottom edges.

1. Public sector-led shift to a green economy.
2. Public ownership of troubled industries and companies, including the break-up of large banks.
3. More public spending on domestic needs, less on the US military: including employment growth via federally-funded infrastructure improvement.
4. Policy to prevent the "outsourcing of jobs" and the strengthening of domestically-based manufacturing industry, not least by refusing to sign free-trade agreements weak on labour standards.
5. Legal support for trade unions and new worker rights.
6. Stimulation of demand via public spending.
7. Public institutions and policies to strengthen economic competitiveness.
8. Public institutions and policies to reduce/remove uneven economic development.
9. State encouragement of new industries based on publicly-funded R & D.
10. Fully developed welfare programmes to protect against involuntary unemployment, ill-health and poverty in old-age: including free basic health care for all, and increased Social Security.
11. Progressive taxation to spread the cost of welfare provision to those best able to bear it.
12. Increased spending on education and reskilling.
13. Higher minimum wage to help low-wage workers, and free college tuition to help middle-class families.
14. Publicly-funded childcare provision, and paid parental leave, to help both parents participate fully in labour markets.

15. Shorter working week, and establishment of a more family-friendly work–life balance.

16. Closing of race and gender inequalities, and ending of mass incarceration.

17. The possibility of developing a basic income for all.

A fully radicalized political movement might operate on all 17 fronts at once. More moderate ones might begin with policy proposals 6–10, governing under pressure from more radical progressives to widen their policy scope to take in the rest. The good news, therefore, is this. The fact that the list exists at all shows us the possibilities of significant progress going forward. The less good news that accompanies this? The fact that the list is currently fractured between a moderate centre and a radical edge, and is so because of the persistence of divisions on the centre-left about the scale of transformation required. Progressive policy is readily available – that much is now clear – and fundamental change is therefore possible: but only if the political agency can be forged, and the political strategy found, that will enable the speedy and unalloyed implementation of an entirely new social structure of accumulation. The main problems currently facing the Anglo-American centre-left, therefore, are not weaknesses within flawed capitalisms. Even on one of their good days, flawed capitalisms recruit for the Left. The main problems facing the Anglo-American centre-left are weaknesses within itself.

Agency

It is one of the tragedies of the age that, in both the United States and the United Kingdom, the obvious political vehicles for the delivery of a new and more progressive settlement around each flawed economy should be currently struggling electorally; but sadly they are, although with differing degrees of short-term success. Things are particularly tough in this regard in the United States right now, where the Democratic Party has spent the last eight years struggling down-ballot to hold onto, let alone to increase, its representation at state and local level, a struggle obscured from general public view during the Obama years by the presence of an outstanding Democrat in the White House. But with him gone, the Party is now entirely out of power in Washington, DC, and in the vast majority of US state capitals. The British Labour Party, for its part, spent the bulk of those same Obama years in an even greater political wilderness: blocked entirely from power by a coalition government after electoral defeat in 2010, and by a Conservative one after a similar defeat five years later. In that election, the Party managed to lose all but one of its Scottish seats to the Scottish National Party, and south of the border to face a UKIP challenge that garnered the Independence Party some 4 million votes. But things have now changed. The Party has changed – going to the left; and the electorate has changed: abandoning the UKIP brand of English nationalism completely, and retreating from Scottish Nationalism to a sufficient degree as to let Scottish Labour back in. There is an electoral tide moving in Labour's favour as this volume goes to press; so that the question in the UK is – for the moment at least – no longer how to create that tide, but how to both consolidate it and to make it grow.

The detailed answers to that question – and to parallel ones about the United States – are more fully developed in the companion volume to this, *Reflections on the Future of the Left*, but at least four broad observations seems relevant here.

The first is that progressive politics will not be advanced in either country, nor will any immediate electoral rot be stopped, by mainstream centre-left parties tacking to the right. Modern electorates know well enough that if they want conservative policies in place, parties on the Right will provide those with greater certainty than any blue-dog Democrat or Blairite centrist will ever do. The centre-left in both countries is out of power now, not because it was too radical in the past, but because it was too associated with a neo-liberal common sense that is now increasingly questioned by more-and-more thinking people. If the centre-left is ever to return to power in either London or Washington, it will only do so by making a fundamental break with neoliberalism in all its forms, and by making what goes with that – namely a fundamental break with its own recent "third way" past. That fundamental break is not easy to make for a generation of politicians, many of whom were part of the earlier third way accommodation to neoliberal orthodoxies; which is why the return to power of an effective centre-left coalition may indeed take a generation to effect. In that downtime, the pressure will always be on to tack to the immediate electoral wind, the better to exploit temporary right-wing distress and slip unexpectedly into power again. But that power will not be worth winning, if it is not won on a programme of fundamental rupture. As R. H. Tawney observed of a similar dilemma, in the British Labour Party after the trauma of 1931, "it is objected that such methods involve surrendering for a decade the prospect of office. It may be replied that, if so, impotence out of office is preferable, at any rate, to impotence in it".[62]

The second is that there is a huge electoral army, out there, waiting for the emergence of a genuine progressive alternative to the political status quo – and it is not only a huge army. It is also a young one: an army for the future as well as for the past. "The Millennials", as John Judis recently observed, "are moving left". Bernie Sanders, he reminds us, won more primary votes in 2016 among 18–29-year-olds than did Hillary Clinton and Donald J. Trump combined; and in June 2017, "Labour candidates won 63 per cent among voters 18–34 years old. The Tories took a dismal 27 per cent".[63] The electoral potential for a revitalized progressive politics is especially clear in Republican-led America, where the very extreme nature of Republican policies currently leaves a large gap in the centre of US politics that is available for progressives to pull to the left. Sixty three million people voted for Hillary Clinton. More than 70 million voted for candidates other than Donald J. Trump; and that voting was not just token. It was real – so real in fact than more than half-a-million of them, the bulk of them well under 35, flowed into Washington, DC the day after the Trump inauguration, to protest against the man and his policies. But what took so many of us to Washington, DC that day was not just revulsion against the narcissism and homophobia of Donald J. Trump. It was also genuine anger about the many policy proposals that he and a Republican-controlled Congress were likely to effect – policies that can only intensify the worst excesses already put in place by a flawed capitalism. The list is long and deeply distressing: greater inequalities of income and wealth; even more sustained pressure on middle-class living standards; persistent poverty, racial tension and gender discrimination – and even more difficulties for a new young generation of adults trying to balance work and family, trying indeed even to afford housing as adequate as that enjoyed by their parents before them.

The rise of Donald J. Trump demonstrates that American conservatives at least recognize that, in these troubled times, "politics as normal" will not do; but hopefully, all progressives recognize something too that conservatives most decidedly do not. We recognize that – if the arguments developed here have any validity – the right-wing policies now being touted in Washington, DC will quickly discredit themselves. Donald J. Trump is a huge own goal for the American Right, as many conservatives are beginning to recognize; and Brexit is similarly likely to be a long-term disaster for British Conservatism. We can expect buyers' remorse to grow on each side of the Atlantic, as the Left's political opponents lean over backwards to make the return of the Left possible again. Which makes it all-the-more vital that this moment of rupture, as it opens up before us, is not wasted by progressive forces in either the US or the UK. Facing such entrenched conservative opponents selling such problematic politics, now is the key moment for the Left to really lift its game.

The third general observation that follows is therefore this. "Lifting its game" by the centre-left means nothing less than playing full-scale counter-hegemonic politics. It means making clear to every would-be voter now that the next time the centre-left is in power, an entirely new social settlement will be wrapped around each country's troubled economy. Of course, it is not that any government, even a fully-armed progressive one, can immediately effect total social change of so fundamental a kind – and that should not be promised. But a centre-left government armed with genuinely progressive principles can set out the path. It can be clear about the nature and novelty of the path chosen. And it can – and should – organize its early days in office on the recognition that the protection of that path requires the incremental but immediate embedding of new ways of running an economy and organizing a society – ones that can then become self-sustaining over time. Margaret Thatcher, long ago, keen to embed and protect her guiding principle of "free markets", moved quickly to break up big publicly-owned industries into sep-arate parts, each owned by different people: so that any move back towards full public ownership would be that much harder to implement. There is a lesson there for those of us keen to control those markets in the interests of a greater good. We too need to embed and protect our principles quickly when first in office.

That is why, in the transition from the old to the new social settlement, any incoming centre-left government would do well to move quickly to ease the work–life balance of today's two-income families by designing a growth strategy that has flexible working hours, readily-available childcare and strengthened worker rights at its core – not as add-ons, but as the spine of its whole strategy. That same government would also do well to immediately establish a new social and industrial contract based on the notion of an empowered citizenry: empowered at work by a new mixture of individual and collective rights: to unionize, to be consulted, and to enjoy a high basic wage; empowered socially by a fairer distribution of income, free education from preschool to college, and more generous welfare payments to those caring for the young, the sick and the old. Speed and radicalism will need to go together here: to let people in each of the centre-left's key constituencies experience improvements in their well-being directly linked to this new settlement, and to give them the associated incentive to defend those improvements when they are challenged.

For that is the fourth and final matter to bear in mind here: that so funda-mental a resetting of the social settlement surrounding each economy will inevitably be challenged, and will prevail only if it is already well understood and supported long before the moment of its inception. Effective counter-hegemonic politics, of the scale now required if neoliberalism is ever to be finally put to rest, requires that progressive politicians actively shape their electorate *ahead of time*, so that the election is the culminating moment of a long prior period of mobilization, education, and empowerment. To that end, the centre-left must not present itself as just another political party, as inter-changeable as the rest. It must present itself rather as part of a broader crusade for social justice. It must insist that its task is nothing less than the creation of a new social settlement of a truly progressive kind, one similar in scale but superior in quality to its Attlee/New Deal and Thatcher/Reagan predecessors. And it must then call people to join it in creating that new set-tlement, by their full mobilization at every level in the economy and society that we all share. As R. H. Tawney said long ago, when trying to lift the British Labour Party up from its electoral drubbing in 1931, if the Left "is to tackle its job with some hope of success, it must mobilize behind it a body of con-viction as resolute and informed as the opposition in front of it". He said this too: and it remains as true today as it was then – that the function of a progressive party:

> ... is not to offer the largest number of carrots to the largest possible number of donkeys. It is not to prophesy smooth things: support won by such methods is a reed shaken by every wind [...] It is to ask the question; Who is to be the master? It is to carry through at home the measures of economic and social reconstruction which, to the grave injury of the nation, have been too long postponed [...] It is not to encourage adherents to ask what they will get from a Labour Government, as though a campaign were a picnic, all beer and sunshine. It is to ask them what they will give. It is to make them understand that the return of a Labour government is merely the first phase of a struggle, the issue of which depends upon themselves [...] To kick over an idol, you must first get off your knees.[64]

If the desperate legacies of the past are not to destroy the glorious possibilities of the future, there is important work to be done; which is why, more than ever, it is now time for progressives to reassert their commitment and their confidence, to get off their knees, to stand tall and confident, and to ask the ultimate political question: "Who is to be the master here?" Let us hope, for the good of our children and grandchildren, that ultimately it will be them.

Endnotes

INTRODUCTION

1. Daron Acemoglu *et al.*, *The rise of China and the future of US manufacturing*. Posted on Vox: CEPR's policy portal, 20 June 2016.
2. Jeff Guo, "The shocking pain of American men", *Washington Post*, 13 October 2016.
3. Martin Sandbu, "Jobless recoveries and wage-less job booms", *Financial Times*, 29 July 2016.
4. Gemma Tetlow and Sarah O'Connor, "UK workers face worst decade for pay in 70 years", *Financial Times*, 25 November 2017.
5. Conor Darcy, "May must stop these grim economic forecasts becoming reality", *Prospect Magazine*, 24 November 2016.
6. Larry Elliott, "UK productivity gap widens to worse level since records began", *The Guardian*, 18 February 2016.
7. Simon Tilford, *Brexit Britain: The Poor Man of Western Europe?* London: CER, September 2016, p. 1.
8. Larry Elliott, "Bank of England warns of complacency over big rise in personal debt", *The Guardian*, 24 July 2017.
9. Martin Sandbu, "Who are the left-behind?", *Financial Times*, 27 July 2016.
10. R. W. Johnson, "Trump: some numbers", *London Review of Books*, 14 November 2016.
11. The UK classic here is undoubtedly Will Hutton's *The State We're In* (London: Cape, 1994). The US equivalent most potently lies in the post-Clinton era writings and commentary of Robert Reich, and of his colleagues on the editorial board of *The American Prospect*.
12. On this, see David Coates, "Riding the Tiger: Towards a New Growth Strategy for the Anglo-American Left", Sheffield: SPERI Working Paper 32, September 2016.
13. Ben Clift, "Brexit, May & Trump: the dangerous illusion of 'taking back control'". Posted on speri.comment, 30 November 2016.

1. THE ANGLO-AMERICAN CONDITION: SIMILARITIES AND DIFFERENCES

1. Quoted in "Anglo-Saxon attitudes", *The Economist*, 28 March 2009, p. 71.
2. Johnna Montgomerie, "Household debt: the silent dimension of the financial crisis", posted on speri.comment, 28 August 2013.

3. Andrew Gamble, *Between Europe and America: The Future of British Politics* (London: Macmillan, 2003).

4. James Cronin, "Convergence by Conviction: Politics and Economics in the Emergence of the 'Anglo-American Model'", *Journal of Social History* 33:4 (2000), pp. 781–804.

5. Peter Hall and David Soskice (eds), *Varieties of Capitalism: The Institutional Foundations of Comparative Advantage* (Oxford: Oxford University Press, 2001).

6. David Coates, *Models of Capitalism: Growth and Stagnation in the Contemporary Era* (Cambridge: Polity, 2000).

7. David Coates, *America in the Shadow of Empires.* (London: Palgrave Macmillan, 2014).

8. On this, see the essay by Leo Panitch and Sam Gindin, "Class, Party and the Challenge of State Transformation" in David Coates (ed.), *Reflections on the Future of the Left* (Newcastle upon Tyne: Agenda Publishing, 2017).

2. THE RISE AND FALL OF AMERICAN ECONOMIC LEADERSHIP

1. George Bernard Shaw, *The Political Madhouse in America and Nearer Home* (London: Constable, 1933), pp. 40–1.

2. When accepting the Nobel Peace Prize in 2009.

3. See David Kotz *et al.*, *Social Structures of Accumulation* (Cambridge: Cambridge University Press, 1994).

4. Jeff Maddick, *The End of Affluence* (New York: Random House, 1995), pp. 34–5.

5. David M. Gordon, "Chickens Coming Home to Roost: From Prosperity to Stagnation in the Postwar US Economy" in Michael A. Bernstein and David E. Alder (eds), *Understanding American Economic Decline* (Cambridge: Cambridge University Press, 1994), p. 37.

6. Robert Gordon, *The Rise and Fall of American Growth* (Princeton, NJ: Princeton University Press, 2015), pp. 564–5.

7. Robert Reich, "The truth about the American economy", posted 30 May 2011.

8. David M. Kotz, *The Rise and Fall of Neoliberal Capitalism* (Cambridge. MA: Harvard University Press, 2015), p. 63.

9. Ricardo Parboni, "The Dollar Weapon: From Nixon to Reagan", *New Left Review* 158 (1986), p. 5.

10. Julian Germann, "State-led or Capital-driven? The Fall of Bretton Woods and the German Currency Float Reconsidered". *New Political Economy* 19:5 (2014), pp. 769–89.

11. Robert Reich, *The Next American Frontier* (New York: Penguin, 1983), pp. 174–5, 198.

12. M. I. Dertouzos *et al.*, *Made in America: Regaining the Productive Edge* (Cambridge, MA: MIT Press, 1989), p. 44.

13. Michael Porter, "Private Investment" in Bill Clinton (conductor), *President Clinton's New Beginning* (New York: Donald I. Fine Inc., 1992), p. 41.

14. Michael Porter, *The Competitive Advantage of Nations* (London: Macmillan, 1990), p. 532.

15. Dean Baker, *The United States Since 1980* (Cambridge: Cambridge University Press, 2007), pp. 45–6.

16. Fred Block, "Crisis and Renewal: The Outlines of a Twenty-First Century New Deal". *Socio-Economic Review* 9 (2011), p. 39.

17. Robert Brenner, "The World Economy at the Turn of the Millennium: Towards Boom or Bust?". *Review of International Political Economy* 8:1 (2001), pp. 21–2.

18. Block, "Crisis and Renewal", p. 39.

19. Baker, *The United States Since 1980*, p. 148.

20. Emad El-Din Aysha, "The United States Boom: 'Clintonomics' and the New Economy Doctrine: A Neo-Gramscian Contribution". *New Political Economy* 6:3 (2001), pp. 341–58.

21. Fred Moseley, "The United States Economy at the Turn of the Century: Entering a New Era of Prosperity?". *Capital & Class* 67 (1999), p. 34.

22. Josh Bivens, Elise Gould and Lawrence Mishel, "Raising America's Pay". Washington, DC: Economic Policy Institute, 2014, Briefing Paper #378.

23. David Coates, *Capitalism: The Basics* (London: Routledge, 2015), p. 70.

24. Grahame Thompson, "The US Economy in the 1990s: The 'New Economy' Assessed" in Jonathan Perraton and Ben Clift, *Where Are the National Capitalisms Now?* (Basingstoke: Palgrave Macmillan, 2004), p. 27.

25. Danny Vinik, "Workers' Wages Have Barely Grown in Decades. Here's What Obama's Doing About It", *New Republic*, January 2015.

26. Monique Morrissey, "Working hard or hardly working?", *Economic Snapshots,* Economic Policy Institute, 12 November 2008, p. 1.

27. Robert Reich, "The Truth About the American Economy", 11 May 2013. Available at http://www.robertreich.org/post/5993482080..

28. David Brennan, "Too Bright for Comfort: A Kaleckian View of Profit Realization in the USA, 1964–2009". *Cambridge Journal of Economics* 68 (2014), p. 252.

29. John Schmitt, *Inequality as Policy: The U.S. since 1979*. Washington, DC: CEPR, October 2009.

30. Block, "Crisis and Renewal", p. 43.

31. Coates, *America in the Shadow of Empires*, p. 12.

32. *Ibid.*, p. 23.

33. David Coates, *Making the Progressive Case: Towards a Stronger US Economy.* (New York: Continuum, 2011), p. 71.

34. Porter, *The Competitive Advantage of Nations.*

35. CRS Report for Congress, *America COMPETES Act: Programs, Funding and Selected Issues.* 22 January 2008, p. 7.

36. Coates, *America in the Shadow of Empires*, p. 23.

37. Josh Bivens and John Irons, "A feeble recovery: the fundamental economic weaknesses of the 2001–7 expansion". Washington, DC: Economic Policy Institute, Briefing Paper #214, May 2008.

38. Lawrence Mishel, Jared Bernstein and Heidi Shierholz (eds), *The State of Working America 2008/2009*. Ithaca, NY: ILR Press, 2009, p. 361.

39. Coates, *America in the Shadow of Empires*, p. 209.

40. Robert J. Schiller, "The best, brightest, and least productive?", posted at Project-Syndicate, 24 September 2013.

41. John Cassidy, "What Good is Wall Street?". *The New Yorker*, 29 November 2010.

42. David Coates, *Answering Back: Liberal Responses to Conservative Arguments* (New York: Continuum, 2010), p. 257.

43. Coates, *Making the Progressive Case*, p. 173.

44. *Ibid.*, pp. 12–23.

45. BBC, "US economic activity falls sharply", 30 January 2009.

46. Josh Bivens, "Worst economic crisis since the Great Depression? By a long shot". Washington, DC: Economic Policy Institute, Snapshot, 29 January 2010, p. 1.

47. Josh Bivens, *Failure by Design: The Story behind America's Broken Economy* (Ithaca, NY: ILR Press, 2011), p. 17.

48. Henry S. Farber, "Job Loss in the Great Recession". Cambridge, MA: NBER Working Paper 17040, 2011.

49. Robert E. Hall, "Quantifying the Lasting Harm to the U.S. Economy from the Financial Crisis". Cambridge, MA: NBER Working Paper 20183, 2014.

50. John G. Fernald *et al.*, "The Disappointing Recovery of Output after 2009". Cambridge, MA: NBER Working Paper 23543, June 2017, p. 41.

51. Neil Irwin, "Is the U.S. economy too dynamic, or not dynamic enough?", *New York Times*, 4 February 2017.

52. Council of Economic Advisers, 2016, p. 91.

53. Laura Tyson, "Closing the Investment Gap", Project-Syndicate, 19 February 2016.

54. Cited in Martin Sandbu, "Debt and demand", *Financial Times*, 6 October 2016.

55. Richard Vague, "The Private Debt Crisis", *Democracy Journal* 2, Fall 2016.

56. Robert Samuelson, "Solving the productivity mystery", *Washington Post*, 3 April 2016.

57. David Wessel, "Spending on our crumbling infrastructure". Brookings Institution, 10 March 2015.

58. Robert Wright, "US infrastructure: broken system", *Financial Times*, 28 April 2014.

59. William A. Galston and Robert Puentes, "What the presidential candidates need to know about infrastructure: issues and options". Brookings Institution, 18 November 2015.

60. Thomas Edsall, "Why Trump now?", *New York Times*, 1 March 2016.

61. Justin R. Pierce and Peter K. Schott, "The Surprisingly Swift Decline of U.S. Manufacturing Employment". Washington, DC: NBER Working Paper 18655, 2012.

62. Damon Acemoglu *et al.*, "Import Competition and the Great U.S. Employment Sag of the 2000s". Washington, DC: NBER Working Paper 20395, 2014.

63. Murat Tasci and Caitlin Treanor, "Labor Market Behavior during and after the Great Recession: Has It Been Unusual?". Federal Reserve Bank of Cleveland, Economic Trends, 13 October 2015.

64. Alejandro Reuss, "America has a triple-decker jobs crisis", posted on Alternet.org, 10 September 2013.

65. Heidi Shierholz, "Six Years from its Beginning, the Great Recession's Shadow looms over the Labor Market". Washington, DC: Economic Policy Institute, 2014, Issue Brief #374.

66. David Wessel, "America isn't working: more than one in six men between 25 and 54 is without a job". Brookings Institution, 6 February 2014.

67. Elise Gould, "2014 continues a 35-year trend of broad-based wage stagnation". Washington, DC: Economic Policy Institute, 19 February 2015.

68. Brookings, "The closing of the jobs gap: a decade of recession and recovery". Washington, DC: Brookings Institution, 4 August 2017.

69. Emily Badger, "U.S. job growth is coming in all the wrong places", *Washington Post*, 28 April 2014.

70. Paul Buchheit, "The shocking reality of a future of shrinking jobs", posted on Alternet. org, 20 April 2017.

71. On this, see Josh Mitchell and Austin Nichols, "Job Polarization and the Great Recession". Washington, DC: Urban Institute, October 2012.

72. On this, see Lonnie Golden, "Irregular Work Scheduling and Its Consequences". Washington, DC: Economic Policy Institute, Briefing Paper #394, 9 April 2015.

73. Jim Puzzanghera, "Average full-time workweek is 47 hours, Gallup says", *LA Times*, 2 September 2014.

74. Steven Greenhouse, *The Big Squeeze: Tough Times for the American Worker* (New York: Anchor, 2008), p. 10.

75. Lydia Saad, "The '40-Hour' work week is actually longer – by seven hours", Gallup, 14 August 2014.

76. Valerie Wilson, "Women Are More Likely to Work Multiple Jobs than Men", Washington, DC: Economic Policy Institute, 9 July 2015.

77. Michael Madowitz and Danielle Corley, "The State of the U.S. Labor Market: pre-December 2015 Jobs release". Washington, DC: Center for American Progress, 3 December 2015.

78. Lonnie Golden, "Still Falling Short on Hours and Pay". Washington, DC: Economic Policy Institute, December 2016.

79. Jared Bernstein, "Jobs report: yes, the unemployment rate is 5.1%. No, we are not at full employment", *Huffington Post*, 4 September 2015.

80. Jeanna Smialek, "Workers in part-time limbo point to U.S. job-market slack", Bloomberg, 2 October 2014.

81. Lawrence Katz and Alan Krueger, "The Rise and Nature of Alternative Work Arrangements in the United States, 1995–2015". NBER Working Paper 22667, September 2016.

82. Executive Office of the President of the United States, "The Long-Term Decline in Prime-Age Male Labor Force Participation". Washington, DC, June 2016, p. 1.

83. Heidi Shierholz, "The Vast Majority of the 5.8 Million Workers Are Under Age 55". Washington, DC: Economic Policy Institute, 26 February 2014.

84. Binyamin Applebaum, "The vanishing male worker: how America fell behind", *New York Times*, 11 December 2014; and Martin Wolf, "America's labour market is not working", *Financial Times*, 3 November 2015.

85. Sarah O'Connor and Robin Harding, "US loses edge as employment powerhouse", *Financial Times*, 25 March 2014.

86. Shierholz, "The Vast Majority of the 5.8 Million Workers Are Under Age 55"; Josh Mitchell, "Some 2.3 Million Kids Live with Long-Term Unemployed Parent", *Wall Street Journal*, 14 January 2014.

87. Martha Ross and Natalie Holmes, "Report: Meet the out-of-work", Brookings Institution, 22 June 2017.

88. Pedro Nicolaci da Costa, "Unemployment trickles down to poorer workers, study finds", *Wall Street Journal*, 3 September 2014.

89. Edsall, "Why Trump now?".

90. Josh Bivens, "The Decline in Labor's Share of Corporate Income Since 2000 Means $535 Billion Less for Workers". Washington, DC: Economic Policy Institute, Economic Snapshot, 10 September 2015.

91. David Wessel, "The typical male U.S. worker earned less in 2014 than in 1973", *Wall Street Journal*, 18 September 2015.

92. Elise Gould, "More of the same: JOLTS is continued evidence of a slow moving economy". Washington, DC: Economic Policy Institute, 16 October 2015.

93. Filippo Occhino and Timothy Stehulak, "Behind the slow pace of wage growth". Cleveland, OH: Federal Reserve, 9 April 2015.

94. Lawrence Mishel, "Even Better Than a Tax Cut", *New York Times*, 23 February 2015.

95. *New York Times*, "You deserve a raise today. Interest rates don't", editorial, 7 September 2015.

96. Elise Gould and Julia Wolfe, "Income growth in 2016 is strong, but not as strong as 2015 and more uneven", posted on the Economic Policy Institute's Working Economics Blog, 12 September 2017.

97. Fatih Guvenen *et al.*, "Lifetime Incomes in the United States Over Six Decades". Cambridge, MA: NBER Working Paper 23371, April 2017.

98. Itrene Tung, Yannet Lathrop and Paul Sonn, "The Growing Movement for $15". New York: National Employment Law Project, 2015.

99. Michelle Chen "Almost Half of All American Workers Make Less Than $15 an Hour", *The Nation* 2015/6.

100. Michelle Park Lazette, "The Why of Weak Wages". Cleveland, OH: Federal Reserve Bank of Cleveland, 2015.

101. Brad Plumer, "How the recession turned middle-class jobs into low-wage jobs", *Washington Post Wonkblog*, 28 February 2013.

102. Peter Whoriskey, "After bailouts, new autoworkers make half as much as veterans in same plant", *Washington Post*, 25 July 2010; and Jim Tankersley, "Manufacturing jobs used to pay really well. Not anymore", *Washington Post*, 17 January 2013.

103. See "Only in America", *The American Prospect*, September/October 2013.

104. Gould, "2014 Continues a 35-Year Trend of Broad-Based Wage Stagnation".

105. Monique Morrissey, "Hotel housekeepers make the beds but can't afford to lie in them", Economic Snapshots, Economic Policy Institute, 21 May 2014.

106. Tung *et al.*, "The Growing Movement for $15".

107. Valerie Wilson *et al.*, "Black women have to work 7 months into 2017 to be paid the same as white men in 2016" Economic Policy Institute, Working Economics Blog, 28 July 2017.

108. Jake Rosenfeld, Patrick Denice and Jennifer Laird, "Union decline lowers wages of non-union workers", Washington, DC: Economic Policy Institute, 30 August 2016.

109. Elise Gould and Will Kimball, "'Right-to-Work' States Still Have Lower Wages". Washington, DC: Economic Policy Institute Briefing Paper #395, 2015.

110. On this, see Harold Meyerson, "How the American South drives the low-wage economy", *The American Prospect*, Summer 2015, pp. 32–6.

111. Gould & Kimball, "'Right-to-Work' States Still Have Lower Wages".

112. Lauren Leatherby, "Donald Trump's economic inheritance in 7 charts", *Financial Times*, 28 December 2016.

113. Mishel *et al.*, *The State of Working America 2008/2009*, pp. 365 & 377.

114. John Miller, "What's in a Name?", *Dollars and Sense*, July/August 2009.

115. Jim Morris, "Commentary: the unseen toll of workplace disease in America". Washington, DC: Center for Public Integrity, 23 December 2015.

116. Greenhouse, *The Big Squeeze: Tough Times for the American Worker*, p. 5.

117. Barack Obama, "The way ahead", *The Economist*, 8 October 2016.

3. CHASING HARD AND STANDING STILL: THE UK ECONOMY IN THE AMERICAN SHADOW

1. Martin Wolf, "The productivity challenge to the British economy", *Financial Times*, 27 January 2017.

2. Andrew Haldane, "Productivity Puzzles", speech at the London School of Economics, 20 March 2017.

3. Paul Kennedy, *The Rise and Fall of the Great Powers* (London: Unwin Hyman, 1988), p. 151.

4. *Ibid.*

5. Coates, *Capitalism*, pp. 11–14.

6. Coates, *Models of Capitalism*, pp. 135–41.

7. David Coates, *The Question of UK Decline* (London: Harvester-Wheatsheaf, 1994), pp. 249–84.

8. David Coates, *The Crisis of Labour: Industrial Relations and the State in Contemporary Britain* (Oxford: Phillip Allan, 1989), pp. 10–11.

9. David Coates, *The Labour Party and the Struggle for Socialism* (Cambridge: Cambridge University Press, 1975/2009), p. 44.

10. E. A. Brett, *The World Economy Since the War: The Politics of Uneven Development* (London: Macmillan, 1985), p. 140.

11. David Coates, "The New Political Economy of Post-War Britain" in Colin Hay (ed.), *British Politics Today* (Cambridge: Polity, 2002), p. 159.

12. David Coates, *Teachers' Unions and Interest Group Politics* (Cambridge: Cambridge University Press, 1972), pp. 94–100.

13. David Coates, *Labour in Power? A Study of the Labour Government 1974–79* (Harlow: Longman, 1980), pp. 86–146.

14. Coates, "The New Political Economy of Post-War Britain", p. 173.

15. Colin Hay, "Reflections on the Winter of Discontent after the Opening of the Archives". University of Sheffield: SPERI Paper No. 21, May 2015, p. 6.

16. Coates, *The Crisis of Labour*, pp. 38–40.

17. Coates, *Labour in Power?*, pp. 38–40.

18. Bob Jessop, "Conservative Regimes and the Transition to Post-Fordism: The Case of Britain and West Germany". University of Essex: Essex Papers in Politics and

Government, No. 47, 1988, p. 8; and David Coates, *Running the Country* (Milton Keynes: Open University Press, 1995), pp. 72–8.

19. Stuart Hall, "The Great Moving Right Show", *Marxism Today*, January 1979, pp. 14–20.

20. Coates, *The Crisis of Labour*, p. 165.

21. David Marsh, *The New Politics of British Trade Unionism* (London: Macmillan, 1992), p. 74.

22. Coates, *The Crisis of Labour*, pp. 121–7.

23. Coates, *Running the Country*, p. 6.

24. Coates, *Models of Capitalism*, p. 92.

25. Coates, *Running the Country*, p. 6.

26. Select Committee on Trade & Industry (1994), *The Competitiveness of UK Manufacturing Industry.* London: HMSO, 1994, p. 16.

27. Andrew Gamble, *Between Europe and America: The Future of British Politics* (London: Palgrave Macmillan, 2003), p. 45.

28. Porter, *The Competitive Advantage of Nations*, pp. 484–94.

29. Coates, *Models of Capitalism*, p. 93.

30. On the negative long-term economic legacy of Margaret Thatcher, see Christopher Kirkland, "Thatcherism and the Origins of the 2007 crisis", *British Politics* 10:4 (2015), pp. 514–35.

31. Coates, "The New Political Economy of Post-War Britain", p. 175.

32. David Coates, Matthew Bodah and Steve Ludlam, "The Development of the Anglo-American Model of Trade Union and Political Party Relations", *Labour Studies Journal* 28:2 (2003), pp. 1–22.

33. David Coates, *Prolonged Labour: The Slow Birth of New Labour Britain* (London: Palgrave Macmillan, 2005), pp. 26–30.

34. Philip Arestis and Malcom Sawyer, "The Economic Analysis Underlying the 'Third Way'", *New Political Economy* 6:2 (2001), p. 263.

35. Stephen Driver and Luke Martell, *New Labour* (Cambridge: Polity, 2002), p. 44.

36. David Coates and Joel Krieger (with Rhiannon Vickers), *Blair's War* (Cambridge: Polity, 2004).

37. David Coates, "Darling, it is Entirely My Fault! Gordon Brown's Legacy to Alistair and Himself", *British Politics* 3:1, 2008, p. 5.

38. Helen Thompson, "UK Debt in Comparative Perspective: The Pernicious Legacy of Financial Sector Debt", *British Journal of Politics and International Relations* 15 (2013), p. 480.

39. David Coates, "Labour after New Labour: Escaping the Debt", *British Journal of Politics and International Relations* 13 (2013), p. 39.

40. Craig Berry, "Are we there yet? Growth, rebalancing, and the pseudo-recovery". Sheffield: SPERI Paper No. 7, 2013, p. 7.

41. The term normally given to the years of unbroken economic growth that began with the Clinton presidency in the US and during the Major premiership in the UK.

42. BBC, "Budget: UK faces worst cuts since WWII, says IFS", 23 June 2010.

43. Larry Elliott, "George Osborne told by IMF chief: rethink your austerity plan", *The Guardian*, 13 April 2013.

44. Martin Wolf, "How Austerity has Failed", *New York Review of Books*, 11 July 2013.

45. Aditya Chakrabortty, "The graph that shows how far David Cameron wants to shrink the state", *The Guardian*, 15 October 2012.

46. Janan Ganesh, "The quiet success of Britain's anarchic economic model", *Financial Times*, 5 April 2016.

47. Chris Giles, "IMF to make U-turn over criticism of UK economic strategy", *Financial Times*, 6 June 2014; and Nicholas Watt, "IMF chief hails UK economic recovery", *The Guardian*, 16 January 2015.

48. David Blanchflower, "As good as it gets? The UK labour market in recession and recovery", *National Institute Economic Review* 231, February 2014, pp. F76–80.

49. Heidi Shierholz, "Six Years from its Beginning, the Great Recession's Shadow Looms over the Labor Market". Washington, DC: Economic Policy Institute, Issue Brief #374, 2014.

50. David Coates, "Building a Growth Strategy on a New Social Settlement: The UK Case". Sheffield: SPERI Paper No. 25, 2015, p. 8.

51. See Larry Elliott, "Why has the UK economy defied predictions of doom", *The Guardian*, 5 January 2017.

52. Amit Kara, "Prospects for the UK economy", *National Institute Economic Review* No. 241, August 2017, p. F9. The IMF projection was equally low – 1.7 per cent for 2017. On this, see the *Financial Times*, 25 July 2017.

53. Larry Elliott, "UK GDP: economy grows by just 0.3% amid 'notable slowdown'", *The Guardian*, 26 July 2017.

54. Jonathan Perraton, "The coming crisis: secular stagnation for the UK?", posted on speri. comment, 11 May 2016.

55. SPERI, "Has the UK economy been rebalanced?" Sheffield: SPERI Paper No 14. 2015.

56. Gemma Tetlow, "The UK economy in numbers in 2016", *Financial Times*, 29 December 2016.

57. BBC, "UK car manufacturing hits 10-year high in 2015", 20 January 2016.

58. Elliott, "March of the makers remains a figment of Osborne's imagination".

59. Anna Valero and Isabel Roland, "Productivity and Business Policies". London: Centre for Economic Performance, Election Analyses Series, 2015, p. 3.

60. Sarah O'Connor, "I quit! Job resignations and the UK labour puzzle", *Financial Times*, 25 March 2015.

61. Dan Milmo and Phillip Inman, "'True' UK unemployment is 6.3 million, says TUC", *The Guardian*, 14 February 2012.

62. Mark King, "UK employees work third longest hours in EU, says ONS", *The Guardian*, 8 December 2011.

63. Diane Abbott, "Young, black and unemployed: the tragedy of the 44%", *The Guardian*, 5 March 2012.

64. Sarah O'Connor and Robin Harding, "US loses edge as employment powerhouse", *Financial Times*, 24 March 2014.

65. Jason Heyes, "Job creation under the Coalition government", posted on speri.comment, 30 April 2015.

66. *Ibid.*

67. Sarah Butler, "Nearly 10 million Britons are in insecure work, says union", *The Guardian*, 5 June 2017.

68. Blanchflower, "As good as it gets?".

69. Samuel Brittan, "Britons want to work more – let's help them do so", *Financial Times*, 16 May 2013.

70. David Blanchflower, "The chancellor needs to get his facts straight", *New Statesman*, 17 August 2011.

71. TUC, "Job recovery and rising work pressures have led to record levels of unpaid hours". London: Trades Union Congress, 2014.

72. Matthew Taylor, "50% rise in long-term unemployment for young ethnic minority people in the UK", *The Guardian*, 10 March 2015.

73. Heather Stewart, "Temporary and part-time jobs surge promoted inequality, says OECD", *The Guardian*, 21 May 2015; and OECD, *In It Together*. Paris: OECD, 21 May 2015.

74. Scott Lavery, "Public and private sector employment across the UK since the financial crisis". Sheffield: SPERI British Political Economy Brief No. 10, 2015.

75. Jeevan Vasagar, "UK technology job creation outpaced other sectors", *Financial times*, 20 October 2013.

76. Tamsin Rutter, "O'Grady, Frances: 'Britain has been good at creating bad jobs'", *The Guardian*, 30 March 2015. For the latest data on this, see Hannah Wheatley, "The Rise of 'Bad Jobs'". London: New Economics Foundation, 15 August 2017.

77. Angela Monaghan, "Real wages likely to take six years to return to pre-crisis levels", *The Guardian*, 7 February 2014.

78. Rui Costa and Stephen Machin, "Real Wages and Living Standards in the UK". LSE: Centre for Economic Performance, Election Analyses Series, June 2017, p. 1.

79. Jamie Doward and Gaby Bissett, "British workers are suffering biggest slip in real wages since economic crises in the 1860s and 1870s, according to TUC", *The Guardian*, 11 October 2014.

80. Nick Broughton *et al.*, "Wealth in the Downturn: Winners and Losers". London: Social Market Foundation, March 2015.

81. David Finch and Matt Whittaker, "Under New Management". London: Resolution Foundation, November 2016, p. 3.

82. TUC, "Emergency workers earning far less this Christmas than five years ago, finds TUC". London: 23 December 2016.

83. Richard Blundell *et al.*, "What can wages and employment tell us about the UK's productivity puzzle?", *Economic Journal* 124 (2014), p. 381.

84. Sarah O'Connor, "Self-employed earn less than they did 20 years ago", *Financial Times*, 17 October 2016.

85. Costa & Machin, "Real Wages and Living Standards in the UK", p. 1.

86. Craig Berry, "The hyper-Anglicisation of active labour market policy". Sheffield: SPERI Paper No. 14, June 2014, p. 1.

87. Larry Elliott, "Why UK wages aren't growing in line with jobs", *The Guardian*, 17 February 2016.

88. Martin Wolf, "Economic ills of the UK extend far beyond Brexit", *Financial Times*, 29 September 2016.

89. Andrew Gamble and Scott Lavery, "Brexit Britain: Where does the UK growth model

go from here?". Sheffield: SPERI "Divergent Capitalisms?" Series, Brief No. 3, March 2017, p. 1.

90. Colin Hay, *The Failure of Anglo-Liberal Capitalism* (Basingstoke: Palgrave Macmillan, 2013), pp. 2–3.

91. Wolf, "Economic ills of the UK extend far beyond Brexit".

4. THE FADING OF THE AMERICAN DREAM?

1. https://www.linkedin.com/pulse/reason-call-american-dream-because-you-have-asleep-felix (accessed 15 December 2017).

2. Kali Holloway, "Nothing will really change until America reckons with race", posted on Alternet.org, 9 February 2017.

3. In Robert J. Shiller, "The Transformation of the 'American Dream'", *New York Times*, 4 August 2017.

4. For a fuller survey and evaluation, see David Coates, *Making the Progressive Case* (New York: Continuum, 2011), pp. 115–40.

5. For the continuing depth and relevance of America's urban-rural divide in the age of Donald J. Trump, see the fascinating reporting of Jose A. DelReal and Scott Clement in *Washington Post*, 17 June 2017.

6. See, for example, the argument that middle-class incomes stalled (NBER Working Papers No. 22211 and 23371) and that they did not (NBER Working Papers 17164 and 23292).

7. See Nicholas Kristof, "It's now the Canadian Dream", *New York Times*, 14 May 2014.

8. See Christian W. Weller and Jessica Lynch, "Household Wealth in Tatters", Washington, DC: Center for American Progress, April 2009; Federal Reserve, "Changes in U.S. Family Finances from 2007 to 2010: Evidence from the Survey of Consumer Finances", *Federal Reserve Bulletin* 98:2, June 2012, pp. 1–75; and also Economic Opportunity Institute, "How the Great Recession cratered America's middle class", EOI, 12 June 2012.

9. Anne Case and Angus Deaton, "Rising morbidity and mortality in midlife among white non-Hispanic Americans in the 21st century", *PNAS*, 17 September 2015.

10. Anne Case, "The media gets the opioid crisis wrong. Here is the truth", *Washington Post*, 12 September 2017.

11. Pew Research Center, "The American Middle Class is Losing Ground". Washington, DC: Pew Research Center, December 2015, p. 2.

12. Pew Research Center, "America's Shrinking Middle Class: A Close Look at Changes within Metropolitan Areas". Washington, DC: Pew Research Center, May 2016, p. 2.

13. Pew Research Center, "The American Middle Class is Losing Ground", p. 2.

14. Richard Reeves, "The dangerous separation of the American upper middle class". Washington, DC: Brookings Institution, 3 September 2015. For the full argument, see his *Dream Hoarders*. (Washington, DC: Brookings Institution Press, 2017).

15. Les Leopold, "Big Lie? America doesn't have #1 middle class in the world ... we're ranked 27th", posted on Alternet.org, 18 June 2013.

16. Robert J. Samuelson, "The roughed-up American", *Washington Post*, 14 September 2014.

17. Pew Research Center, "The Lost Decade of the Middle Class". Washington, DC: Pew Research Center, August 2012, p. 3.

18. Cliff Zukin, Carl Van Horn and Allison Kopicki, "Unhappy, Worried and Pessimistic: Americans in the Aftermath of the Great Recession". Rutgers: Edward J. Bloustein School of Public Policy, August 2014.

19. J. P. Morgan Chase & Co Institute, "Weathering Volatility: Big Data on the Financial Ups and Downs of U.S. Individuals". New York: May, 2015.

20. Neal Gabler, "My secret shame", *The Atlantic*, May 2016, pp. 52–61.

21. Robert Reich, "Why the sharing economy is harming workers – and what can be done", posted on socialeurope-eu, 30 November 2015.

22. Gabler, "My secret shame", p. 56.

23. Patricia Cohen, "Middle Class, but Feeling Economically Insecure", *New York Times*, 10 April 2015.

24. Jennifer Erickson (ed.), "The Middle-Class Squeeze". Washington, DC: Center for American Progress, September 2014, p. 9.

25. Jeffrey Sparshott, "Congratulations, Class of 2015. You're the Most Indebted Ever (For Now)", *Wall Street Journal*, 8 May 2015.

26. Arkadi Gerney, Anna Chu and Brendan V. Duke, "The Middle Class at Risk". Washington, DC: Center for American Progress, July 2015.

27. Larry Mishel and Heidi Shierholz, "A lost decade, not a burst bubble: the declining living standards of middle-class households in the US and Britain" in Sophia Parker (ed.), *The Squeezed Middle: The Pressure on Ordinary Workers in America and Britain* (Bristol: Policy Press, 2013), p. 17.

28. Ken Jacobs *et al.*, *Producing Poverty: The Public Cost of Low-Wage Production Jobs in Manufacturing*. UC Berkeley Center for Labor Research and Education, May 2016, p. 1.

29. Harry Holzer, "Job Market Polarization and U.S. Worker skills: A Tale of Two Middles". Washington, DC: Brookings Institution, April 2015.

30. Didem Tüzemen and Jonathan Willis, "The Vanishing Middle: Job Polarization and Workers' Response to the Decline in Middle-Skill Jobs", *Federal Reserve Bank of Kansas City*, Economic Review, First Quarter 2013. https://www.kansascityfed.org/publicat/econrev/pdf/13q1Tuzemen-Willis.pdf (accessed 15 December 2017)

31. Max Ehrenfreund, "Bernie Sanders is right: The top 0.1 per cent have as much as the bottom 90 per cent", *Washington Post*, 19 November 2015.

32. Paul Buchheit, "How 14 people made more money than the entire food stamp budget for 50,000,000 people", posted on NationofChange, 6 October 2014.

33. Sarah Anderson, "100 CEOs have as much retirement wealth as 41% of American families", posted on Alternet.org, 16 December 2016.

34. See Coates, *America in the Shadow of Empires*, p. 28.

35. Data from the EPI report by Lawrence Mishel and Jessica Schieder, posted 12 July 2016.

36. And even a bigger ratio in 2015. See Lawrence Mishel and Alyssa Davis, "Top CEO Makes 300 Times More Than Typical Worker". Washington DC: Economic Policy Institute, Issue Brief #390, 21 June 2015.

37. Pew Research Center, "The American Middle Class is Losing Ground", p. 2.

38. Zoe Carpenter, "A Staggeringly Lopsided Economic Recovery", *The Nation*, 26 January 2015.

39. Research findings by Emmanuel Saez, released by the Washington Center for Equitable Growth, 1 July 2016.

40. Paul Krugman (citing Alan Kreuger), "The great Gatsby Curve", *New York Times*, 15 January 2012.

41. Suzanne Mettler, "Reconstituting the Submerged State: The Challenge of Social Policy Reform in the Obama Era", APSA, *Perspectives on Politics* 8:3 (2010), pp. 803–24.

42. Raj Chetty *et al.*, "The Fading American Dream: Trends in Absolute Income Mobility Since 1940". NBER Working Paper 22910, December 2016.

43. Harold Meyerson, "Seeing What No one Else Could See", *The American Prospect*, July/August 2012, pp. 66–70.

44. John Cassidy, "Relatively Deprived", *The New Yorker*, March 2006.

45. Robert Rector and Rachel Sheffield, "Air Conditioning, Cable TV and an Xbox: What is Poverty in the United States Today?". Washington, DC: Heritage Foundation Backgrounder No. 2575, 18 July 2011.

46. Data from US Census, Income, Poverty, and Health Insurance Coverage in the United States 2014.

47. Emily Cuddy, Joanna Venator and Richard V Reeves, "In a Land of Dollars: Deep Poverty and its Consequences", Brookings Institution, 7 May 2015. See also Kathryn Edin, *$2.00 a Day: Living on Almost Nothing in America* (New York: Houghton Mifflin Harcourt, 2015) and Christopher Jencks, "Why the Very Poor Have Become Poorer", *New York Review of Books*, 9 June 2016, pp. 15–17.

48. Michael Snyder, "Extreme poverty is now at record levels", posted on Alternet.org, 14 November 2011.

49. Alisha Coleman-Jensen *et al.*, *Household Food Insecurity in the United States in 2015*. Washington, DC: US Department of Agriculture, Economic Research Report No. 215, September 2016.

50. Brad Plummer, "One in three Americans slipped below the poverty line between 2009 and 2011", *Washington Post*, 8 January 2014.

51. Center for American Progress, "From Poverty to Prosperity: a national strategy to cut poverty in half", Washington, DC, 25 April 2007.

52. James Lin and Jared Bernstein, "What We Need To Get By". Washington, DC: EPI Briefing Paper #224, 29 October 2008.

53. Barbara Kiviat, "Below the Line", *Time*, 28 November 2011.

54. On both, see Jeff Madrick, "America: The Forgotten Poor", *New York Review of Books*, 22 June 2017.

55. Peter Edelman, "Poverty in America: Why Can't We End It?", *New York Times*, 28 July 2012.

56. Peter Edelman, "The State of Poverty in America", *The American Prospect*, 22 June 2012.

57. Doug Hall, "Low-Wage Workers Have Experienced Wage Erosion in Nearly Every State", EPI: Economic Snapshot, 18 February 2014.

58. Deborah Povich, Brandon Roberts and Mark Mather, "Low-Income Working Families: The Racial/Ethnic Divide". The Working Poor Families Project, Policy Brief, Winter 2014–15.

59. Harold Meyerson, "For retailers, low wages aren't working out", *Washington Post*, 20 August 2013.

60. National Employment Law Project, "It's Time To Raise the Minimum Wage". Washington, DC: Economic Policy Institute, 23 April 2015.

61. Marianne Bitler and Hilary Hoynes, "The More Things Change, the More They Stay the Same: The Safety Net, Living Arrangements and Poverty in the Great Recession". Cambridge, MA: NBER Working Paper 19449, September 2013.

62. Alan B. Kreuger, Judd Cramer and David Cho, "Are the Long-Term Unemployed on the Margins of the Labor Market", paper to the spring 2014 Conference on the Brookings Papers on Economic Activity.

63. Josh Bivens, "Historically Small Share of Jobless People Are Receiving Unemployment Insurance". EPI Economic Snapshot, 25 September 2014.

64. Brad Plumer, "What happens when jobless benefits get cut? Let's ask North Carolina", *Washington Post*, 24 January 2016. See also Jesse Rothstein and Robert G. Valetta, "Scraping By: Income and Program Participation After the Loss of Extended Unemployment Benefits", NBER Working Paper 23528, June 2017.

65. Diane Whitmore Schanzenbach, Lauren Bauer and Ryan Nunn, "Who is Poor in the United States?". Washington, DC: Hamilton Project, 17 June 2016.

66. See Alana Semuels, "The Near Impossibility of Moving Up After Welfare", *The Atlantic*, 11 July 2016.

67. Bill Clinton, "How We Ended Welfare, Together", *New York Times*, 22 August 2006.

68. Elizabeth Kneebone and Natalie Holmes, "Fighting Poverty at Tax Time through the EITC". Brookings Institution, 16 December 2014.

69. Melissa Boteach *et al.*, "The War on Poverty: Then and Now". Washington, DC: Center for American Progress, January 2014.

70. "Overlooked but Not Forgotten: Social Security Lifts Millions More Children Out of Poverty". Washington, DC: Center for Global Policy Solutions, July 2016.

71. Peter Edelman, "The War on the Poor", *The American Prospect*, Winter 2016.

72. Ron Haskins, Vicky Albert and Kimberley Howard, "The Responsiveness of the Temporary Assistance for Needy Families Program During the Great Recession". Brookings Institution, August 2014.

73. Yonatan Ben-Shalom, Robert A. Moffitt and John Karl Scholz, "An Assessment of the Effectiveness of Anti-Poverty Programs in the United States". Cambridge, MA: NBER Working Paper 17042, May 2011.

74. Zachary Goldfarb, "The best case that the war on poverty has failed", *Washington Post*, 19 February 2014.

75. Liana Fox *et al.*, "Waging War on Poverty: Historical Trends in Poverty Using the Supplemental Poverty Measure". Cambridge, MA: NBER Working Paper 19789, January 2014.

76. See note 40.

77. *Wall Street Journal*, "Nearly Half of U.S. Lives in Household Receiving Government Benefits", Editorial, 18 January 2012; and Jonathan Cohn, "Blue states are from Scandinavia, Red states are from Guatemala", *The New Republic*, 5 October 2012.

78. See note 54.

79. Robert J. Samuelson, "The life-expectancy gap", *Washington Post*, 27 September 2015.

80. Diane Whitmore Schanzenbach, Lauren Bauer and Greg Natz, "Twelve facts about food insecurity and SNAP". Brookings Institution, 21 April 2016.

81. Elizabeth Roberto, "Commuting to Opportunity: The Working Poor and Commuting in the United States". Brookings Institution, February 2008.

82. On cycles of deprivation, see Coates, *America in the Shadow of Empires*, pp. 214–7.

83. David Cooper, Mary Gable and Algernon Austin, "The Public-Sector Jobs Crisis". Washington, DC: Economic Policy Institute, Briefing Paper #339, 2 May 2012.

84. Valerie Wilson, "State unemployment rates by race and ethnicity at the end of 2015 show a plodding recovery". Washington, DC: Economic Policy Institute, 11 February 2016.

85. Brad Plumer, "Charts: the economic gap between blacks and whites hasn't budged for 50 years", *Washington Post*, 19 August 2013.

86. Algernon Austin, "Reversal of Fortunes". Washington, DC: Economic Policy Institute, Briefing Paper #220, 18 September 2008.

87. Valerie Wilson, "Broad-based Wage Growth is Essential for Fighting Poverty and Narrowing Racial Wage Gaps". Washington, DC: Economic Policy Institute, 19 June 2014.

88. Pew Research Center, "Demographic Trends and Economic Well-being", posted 27 June 2016 (the data is for 2014).

89. Deborah Povich *et al.*, "Low-Income Working Families", p. 1.

90. Valerie Wilson and William Rogers III, "Black-white wage gaps expand with rising wage inequality". Washington, DC: Economic Policy Institute, 20 September 2016.

91. Pew Research Center, "The American Middle Class is Losing Ground", p. 22.

92. Rakesh Kochhar, Richard Fry and Paul Taylor, "Wealth Gaps Rise to Record High between Whites, Black and Hispanics". Washington, DC: Pew Research Center, 26 July 2011.

93. Joshua Holland, in *The Nation*, 9 August 2016.

94. Elise Gould and Tanyell Cooke, "Unemployment for young black grads is still worse than it for young white grads in the aftermath of the recession". Washington, DC: Economic Policy Institute, 11 May 2016.

95. Judith Scott-Clayton and Jing Li, "Black-white disparity in student loan debt more than triples after graduation". Washington, DC: Brookings Institution, 26 October 2016.

96. Plumer, "Charts".

97. Sean F. Reardon, "Growth in the Residential Segregation of Families by Income, 1970–2009". Stanford, CA: Center for Education Policy Analysis, November 2011.

98. Algernon Austin, "The Unfinished March". Washington, DC: Economic Policy Institute, 18 June 2013.

99. Elizabeth Kneebone, "The Growth and Spread of Concentrated Poverty, 2000–2012". Washington, DC: Brookings Institution, 31 July 2014.

100. Richard Reeves, Edward Rodrigue and Elizabeth Kneebone, "Five Evils: Multidimensional Poverty and Race in America". Washington, DC: Brookings Institution, April 2016.

101. "Top Nixon aide admits 'war on drugs' was excuse to target blacks and hippies", posted on Daily Kos, 23 March 2016.

102. Michelle Alexander, "The failed drug war has created a human rights nightmare", posted on Alternet.org, 3 May 2011.

103. The Pew Center on the States, "One in 100: Behind Bars in America 2008". Washington, DC: Pew Center, 29 February 2008.

104. Danielle Paquette, "One in nine black children has had a parent in jail", *Washington Post*, 27 October 2015.

105. Justin Wolfers, David Leonhardt and Kevin Quealy, "1.5 Million Missing Black Men", *New York Times*, 20 April 2015.

106. Michelle Alexander, *The New Jim Crow*. New York: New Press, 2012, p. 180.

107. Eyal Press, "Will This New Book Change the National Debate on Poverty?", *The Nation*, 29 March 2016.

108. Eileen Applebaum, Heather Boushey and John Schmitt, "The Economic Importance of Women's Rising Hours of Work", Washington, DC: Center for American Progress, 15 April 2014; see also Heather Boushey, "Home Economics", *Democracy Journal* 40 (2016) and her *Finding Time* (Cambridge, MA: Harvard University Press, 2016).

109. For details, see Pew Research Center, "Modern Parenthood: Roles of Moms and Dads Converge as They Balance Work and Family". Washington, DC, 14 March 2014.

110. Elise Gould, Jessica Schieder and Kathleen Geier, "What is the gender gap, and is it real?" Washington, DC: Economic Policy Institute, 20 October 2016.

111. Danielle Paquette, "The group that seriously out-earns white men", *Washington Post*, 1 July 2016.

112. Yian Q. Mui, "Young women from these college majors earn more than men", *Washington Post*, 6 August 2015.

113. Kaitlin Holmes and Danielle Corley, "The Top Ten Facts About the Gender Wage Gap". Washington, DC: Center for American Progress, 12 April 2016.

114. *Ibid.*

115. See, for example, Stephanie Coontz, *The Way We Never Were: American Families and the Nostalgia Trap* (New York: Basic Books, 2016); and Shelley Lundberg, Robert Pollak and Jenna Stearns, "Family Inequality: Diverging Patterns in Marriage, Cohabitation and Childbearing". Cambridge, MA: NBER Working Paper 22078, March 2016.

116. Holmes & Corley, "The Top Ten Facts About the Gender Wage Gap".

117. https://singlemotherguide.com/single-mother-statistics/ (accessed 15 December 2017).

118. Valerie Wilson, "African American women stand out as working moms play a larger economic role in families", Washington, DC: EPI Working Economics Blog, 11 May 2017.

119. Elise Gould, "Two in five female-headed families with children live in poverty". Washington, DC: EPI Economic Snapshot, 14 November 2012.

120. Diane Archer, "In retirement, income gap worsens for women", posted on Just care, 16 March 2016.

121. Sarah Jane Glynn *et al.*, "Facts on Who Has Access to Paid Time Off and Flexibility". Washington, DC: Center for American Progress, 26 April 2016.

122. Lonnie Golden, "Irregular Work Scheduling and Its Consequences". Washington, DC: Economic Policy Institute briefing paper #394, 9 April 2015.

123. The White House Task Force on the Middle Class, 2010, pp. 29–30.

124. The title of a report by Rasheed Malik and Jamal Hagler, published by the Center for American Progress, 5 August 2016. See also the Center's "The Missing Conversation About Work and Family: Unique Challenges Facing Women of Color", authored by Jocelyn Frye and published 3 October 2016.

125. Michael Modowitz *et al.*, "Calculating the Hidden Cost of Interrupting a Career for Child Care". Washington, DC: Center for American Progress, 21 June 2016.

126. *Ibid.*

127. Francine D. Blau and Lawrence M. Kahn, "Female Labor Supply: Why is the US Falling Behind?", NBER Working Paper 18702, January 2013.

128. Leila Schochet and Rasheed Malik, "2 Million Parents Forced to Make Career Sacrifices Due to Problems with Child Care". Washington, DC: Center for American Progress, 13 September 2017.

129. Pew Research Center, "Raising Kids and Running a Household: How Working Parents Share the Load", 4 November 2015.

130. Anne Johnson *et al.*, "The Student Debt Crisis", Washington, DC: Center for American Progress, 25 October 2012.

131. Chuck Collins, "Congrats, Graduates! Here's Your Diploma and Debt", posted on Alternet.org, 20 April 2017.

132. Ryan Foley, "New CDC data understate accidental shooting deaths of kids", *USA Today*, 9 December 2016.

133. Mark Follman, Julie Laurie and Jaeah Lee, "What does gun violence really cost?", *Mother Jones*, May/June 2015, pp. 24–5.

134. On this, see the latest NBC/*Wall Street Journal* poll, 4 May 2017.

135. Richard Fry, "For First Time in Modern Era, Living With Parents Edges Out Other Living Arrangements for 18- to 34-year-olds", Pew Research Centre, 11 June 2016.

136. Brendan Duke, "When I Was Your Age: Millennials and the Generation Wage Gap". Washington, DC: Center for American Progress, 3 March 2016.

137. Mandi Woodruff, "One in five millennial parents is impoverished, study finds", posted at Yahoo Finance, 30 April 2015.

138. But still very deep in the US. On this, see the National Low-Income Housing Coalition Report, "Out of Reach 2017: The High Cost of Housing", Washington, DC: 2017. In the introduction to the report, Congressman Keith Ellison notes that "rents are soaring in every state and community at the same time when most Americans haven't seen enough of an increase in their paychecks. The result: more than 7 million extremely low-income families do not have an affordable place to call home, and half a million people are living on the streets, in shelters, or in their cars on any given night". The other result: "the average full-time minimum wage worker can't afford rent in ANY state". (*Huffington Post*, 17 June 2017).

5. THE SLOW DISINTEGRATION OF THE UK'S POSTWAR SOCIAL SETTLEMENT

1. Jeremy Corbyn, 29 April 2017: quoted on BBC "General Election 2017" website.

2. Will Hutton, *How Good We Can Be: Ending the Mercenary Society and Building a Great Country* (London: Little Brown, 2015), p. 113.

3. There is now, in 2017 for the first time, a World Baseball Classic Championship, pitting national teams against each other. The US beat Puerto Rico 8–0 to win the first WBC title!

4. Jeremy Paxman, *The English* (London: Penguin, 1998), p. 3.

5. David Coates, *Prolonged Labour: The Slow Birth of New Labour Britain* (New York: Palgrave Macmillan, 2005), p. 178. The latest data suggests that car buying may now – at least temporarily – have peaked. On this, see Peter Campbell, "UK car market hits peak, says industry body chief", *Financial Times*, 5 January 2017.

6. David Coates, *Running the Country* (London: Hodder & Stoughton, 1991/5), p. 119.

7. Coates, *Prolonged Labour*, p. 21.

8. Patrick Butler, "Most Britons regard themselves as working class, survey finds", *The Guardian*, 29 June 2016.

9. For the BBC schema, see Mike Savage, Fiona Devine and Niall Cunningham, "A New Model of Social Class? Findings from the BBC's Great British Class Survey Experiment", *Sociology* 47:2 (2013), pp. 219–50.

10. James Plunkett, "Growth without Gain: the faltering living standards of people on low-to-middle incomes". London: Resolution Foundation, May 2011.

11. Matthew Whittaker, "Squeezed Britain". London: Resolution Foundation, January 2012, January 2013.

12. Quoted in Jessica Elgot, "Six million low-income families 'worse off' than ten years ago", *The Guardian*, 29 September 2016.

13. See notes 10 and 11 for these findings.

14. Gavin Kelly, "Why the 'squeezed middle' is here to stay", *The Guardian*, 22 May 2011.

15. Elgot, "Six million low-income families 'worse off' than ten years ago".

16. Sarah Lyall, "Watch: how to break our reliance on private debt". London: New Economics Foundation, 3 February 2016.

17. TUC, "Why we need action to help over-indebted households". London: Trades Union Congress, August 2016, p. 27.

18. Angela Monaghan and Sally Weale, "UK student loan debt soars to more than £100bn", *The Guardian*, 15 June 2017.

19. Gonzalo Vina, "UK graduates leave university with more debt than US peers", *Financial Times*, 28 April 2016.

20. Gemma Tetlow, "Two-thirds of UK students will never pay off debt", *Financial Times*, 4 July 2016.

21. *Ibid.*

22. Hutton, *How Good We Can Be*, p. 94.

23. George Eaton, "The strange non-rise of inequality", *New Statesman*, 11 August 2017, p. 17.

24. Gemma Tetlow, "Is income inequality increasing in the UK", *Financial Times*, 11 December 2016.

25. Alan Milburn, in his foreword to "Time for Change: An Assessment of Government Policies on Social Mobility 1997–2017". London: OGL, June 2017, p. 5.

26. High Pay Commission, "More for less: what has happened to pay at the top and does it matter". London: HPC, May 2011.

27. Larry Elliott, "Inequality in the UK: 5% of households have assets in excess of £1.2m, 9% have none", *The Guardian*, 19 November 2015.

28. Brian Bell & Stephen Machin, "Clinging on to a middle-class life?", Policy Network, 15 April 2014.

29. Richard Adams, "UK's social mobility problem holding back Thatcher generation, says report", *The Guardian*, 16 November 2016.

30. Social Mobility Commission, *2016*. London: OGL, 2016, pp. iv, 1.

31. Larry Elliott, "Middle-income families in UK resemble the poor of past years, says IFS", *The Guardian*, 19 July 2016.

32. See Office of the Deputy Prime Minister, "Breaking the Cycle: A Report by the Social Exclusion Unit". London: September 2004.

33. Coates, *Prolonged Labour*, pp. 76–9.

34. Will Paxton and Mike Dixon, "The State of the Nation: An Audit of Injustice in the UK". London: IPPR, 2004, p. 60.

35. David Freud, "Reducing dependency, increasing opportunity: options for the future of welfare to work". London: Department of Work and Pensions, 2007, p. 30.

36. Richard Dickens, "Child Poverty in Britain: Past Lessons and Future Prospects", *National Institute Economic Review*, October 2011, p. R11.

37. *Ibid*.

38. Larry Elliott, "Up. Up. Up. Child poverty, pensioner poverty, inequality", *The Guardian*, 11 June 2008.

39. Rachel Williams, "Child poverty grows as 2 million children have no parent at work", *The Guardian*, 3 November 2009.

40. Gemma Tetlow, "Wage stagnation driving up the number of working poor", *Financial Times*, 6 January 2017.

41. In Adam Tinson *et al.*, "Monitoring poverty and social inclusion, 2016". York: Joseph Rowntree Foundation, 2016.

42. For the daily reality of those ills, see Mary O'Hara, *Austerity Bites* (Bristol: Policy Press, 2014).

43. Rajeev Syal, "One in eight workers struggle to afford food, finds TUC survey", *The Guardian*, 7 September 2017.

44. Felicity Lawrence, "Fuel poverty affects a quarter of UK's households as bills soar and pay freezes", *The Guardian*, 1 December 2011.

45. Adam Tinson *et al.*, "Monitoring poverty and social inclusion, 2016".

46. Patrick Butler, "Number of rough sleepers in England rises for sixth successive year", *The Guardian*, 25 January 2017.

47. Patrick Butler, "More than a million people in UK living in destitution, study shows", *The Guardian*, 27 April 2016.

48. Press Association, "UK workers on zero-hours contracts rise above 800,000", *The Guardian*, 9 March 2016.

49. *The Economist*, 25 June 2016, p. 49.

50. Tetlow, "Wage stagnation driving up the number of working poor".

51. NPI, "Disability and Poverty". London: New Policy Institute, January 2017.

52. Federica Cocco, "Lowest-paid are the only group to get real-terms wage rise in a decade", *The Financial Times*, 31 March 2017.

53. Katie Allen, "A third of people in the UK have experienced poverty in recent years", *The Guardian*, 16 May 2016.

54. Frances Ryan, "From in-work poverty to out-of-work cuts: five horrors of 2017", *The Guardian*, 5 January 2017.

55. Glen Bramley *et al.*, "Counting the cost of UK poverty". York: Joseph Rowntree Foundation, 16 August 2016.

56. Stewart Lansley and Joanna Mack, *Breadline Britain* (London: Oneworld, 2015), p. 62.

57. This from David Coates and Sarah Ottinger, "Two steps forward, one step back: the gender dimensions of Treasury policy under New Labour" in Claire Annersley, Francesca Gains and Kirstein Rummery (eds), *Women and New Labour* (Bristol: Policy Press, 2007), pp. 117–32.

58. Gordon Brown, speech to the House of Commons, 12 July 1997.

59. Gordon Brown, speech to the House of Commons, 18 April 2002.

60. Clive Dobbs, "Patterns of Pay: Results of the Annual Survey of Hours and Earnings 1997–2005". London: Office of National Statistics, February 2006, p. 47.

61. Tinson *et al.*, "Monitoring poverty and social inclusion", p. 7.

62. Allegra Stratton, "Women main drivers of living standards", *The Guardian*, 6 December 2011.

63. Tinson *et al.*, "Monitoring poverty and social inclusion, 2016", *passim*.

64. *Financial Times*, "The UK's slow march to gender pay equality", *Financial Times*, 24 August 2016.

65. Katie Allen, "TUC analysis highlights 'pay penalty' for women having children early", *The Guardian*, 8 March 2016.

66. Jamie Doward, "For UK women in low-paid jobs, a second child is a mixed blessing", *The Guardian*, 6 August 2016.

67. Anushka Asthana, "Gender pay gap to remain for thousands, says Conservative MP", *The Guardian*, 7 March 2016.

68. Allen, "TUC analysis highlights 'pay penalty' for women having children early".

69. Anne Richardson, "Half the mothers I know have been driven from their jobs", *The Guardian*, 8 August 2013.

70. Claire Annesley, "The Impact of the Economic Crisis on the Situation of Women and Men and on Gender Equality Policies: the UK Report". Brussels: European Commission, 18 July 2011, p. 2.

71. *Ibid.*, p. 3.

72. Patrick Wintour, "Women are the losers in child benefit cuts, say Labour", *The Guardian*, 6 January 2013.

73. Patrick Butler, "Women and the coalition: mothers' and child benefits", *The Guardian*, 20 May 2011.

74. Esther Shaw, "How parents are working out a way of paying the £5,500-a-year childcare bill", *The Guardian*, 25 August 2013.

75. Jill Rutter, *Holiday Childcare Survey 2015*. London: Family and Childcare Trust, 2015.

76. Rachel Case and Daniel Wright, "Working parents hit living standards due to high childcare costs". York: Joseph Rowntree Foundation, July 2016.

77. Data in the *New Statesman*, 12 August 2014 (from CPAG).

78. Martin Sandbu, "Think of the children", *Financial Times*, 1 June 2015.

79. Zoe Williams, "The reasons mothers work – and Tories try to stop them", *The Guardian*, 12 May 2011.

80. Clive Cowdery, "Gaining from Growth: the final report of the Commission on Living Standards". London: Resolution Foudation, 2012, p. 10.

81. Alice Martin and Josh Ryan-Collins, "The financialization of UK homes". London: New Economics Foundation, 2016.

82. On this, see DETR, "Quality and Choice: A Decent Home For All". London: Department of Environment, Transport and the Regions, December 2000.

83. Coates, *Prolonged Labour*, p. 171.

84. *Ibid.*, p. 172.

85. Details in David Coates and Kara Dickstein, "A tale of two cities: financial meltdown and the Atlantic divide" in Terrence Casey (ed.) *The Legacy of the Crisis* (London: Palgrave Macmillan, 2011) pp. 60–78.

86. David Coates, "The Housing Crisis of the Young". http://www.davidcoates.net/2016/02/25/the-housing-crisis-of-the-young/ (accessed 15 December 2017).

87. *Ibid.*

88. James Pickford, "Bank of Mum and Dad is ninth-biggest lender with £6.5bn loans", *Financial Times*, 2 May 2017.

89. Phillip Inman, "Asking prices for homes rise to record average of £313,655", *The Guardian*, 24 April 2017.

90. Kate Allen, "UK housing: the £24bn property puzzle", *Financial Times*, 1 June 2015.

91. Helena Bengtsson and Kate Lyons, "Revealed: the widening gulf between salaries and house prices", *The Guardian*, 2 September 2015.

92. Lucy Daltroff, "Mortgage debt reaches £1 trillion in the UK", *Ham & High Property*, 16 February 2016.

93. Press Association, "1.1 million UK Households had mortgage debts worth 4.5 times their income in 2013", *The Guardian*, 7 October 2015.

94. Hilary Osborne, "Home ownership in England at lowest level in 30 years as housing crisis grows", *The Guardian*, 2 August 2016.

95. Gwyn Topham, "Home ownership £200,000 cheaper than a lifetime of renting", *The Guardian*, 18 June 2012.

96. Shelter, "House affordability for first time buyers: March 2015". London: Shelter, 2015.

97. Hilary Osborne, "Outright owners of homes outstrip mortgage holders for the first time since 80s", *The Guardian*, 25 February 2015.

98. Danny Dorling, *All That Is Solid* (London: Penguin, 2015), p. 165.

99. Hilary Osborne, "UK faces shortfall of 1.8 million rental homes, warns housing body", *The Guardian*, 4 October 2016.

100. Hilary Osborne, "Buy-to-let rents rise to all-time high as demand for homes outstrips supply", *The Guardian*, 8 September 2016.

101. Judith Evans, "Estate agents predict steep rent rises for the UK", *Financial Times*, 4 November 2016.

102. Coates, "The Housing Crisis of the Young".

103. On this, see Toby Helm, "Housing benefit cuts for young people may be scaled back", *The Guardian*, 25 February 2017.

104. Michael Edwards, "The housing crisis: too difficult or a great opportunity?", *Sounding Futures*, 2016, p. 27.

105. Toby Helm, "Housing policy is a mess – and the budget's 'mortgage guarantee' will not change that", *The Observer*, 30 March 2013.

106. Stephen Clarke *et al.*, "The housing headwind". London: Resolution Foundation, June 2016, p. 4.

107. Hilary Osborne, "Outright owners of homes outstrip mortgage holders for the first time since 80s".

108. Larry Elliott and Hilary Osborne, "Under-35s in the UK face becoming permanent renters, warns think-tank", *The Guardian*, 13 February 2016.

109. Dawn Foster, "If people in work struggle with rent, what hope for people out of work?", *The Guardian*, 12 May 2017.

110. Toby Helm, "Housing crisis threatens a million families with eviction by 2020", *The Guardian*, 24 June 2017.

111. Dawn Foster, "Today's housing crisis means strangers are now sleeping two to a bed", *The Guardian*, 29 October 2015.

112. Katie Evans and Nigel Keohone, "Locked Out". London: Social Market Foundation, February 2016, p. 4.

113. *Ibid.*

114. Angus Armstrong, "Commentary: UK Housing Market: Problems and Policies," *National Institute Economic Review*, No. 235, February 2016, p. F5.

115. Larry Elliott, "Prosperity and poverty in a country scared by the slump, with some parts doing fine while people at the bottom rely on food banks", *The Guardian*, 16 June 2014.

116. Social Mobility Commission, *2016*, p. 1.

117. On this, see Coates, *The Labour Party and the Struggle for Socialism*, pp. 5–6, 218–30.

118. On this, see Coates, *Prolonged Labour*, pp. 81–101; and Steve Ludlam, Matthew Bodah and David Coates, "Trajectories of solidarity: changing union-party linkages in the UK and USA", *British Journal of Politics and International Relations* 4:2, June 2002, pp. 222–44.

119. John Lanchester, "Brexit Blues", *London Review of Books*, 28 July 2016, p. 3.

120. The details are at Daniel Trilling, "Britain's last anti-Jewish riots", *New Statesman*, 23 May 2012.

121. See, for example, Owen Jones, "Brexitland: 'Too many foreigners – way, way too many'", *The Guardian*, 10 March 2017.

122. Hilary Osborne, "Almost a third of would-be buyers move back in with parents, report says", *The Guardian*, 8 June 2015.

123. Sally Weale, "Half of graduates who paid £9,000 tuition fees live with parents", *The Guardian*, 17 August 2015.

124. Sarah Marsh, "Which countries have the worst drinking cultures?", *The Guardian*, 15 April 2016.

125. Michael Orton, *Something's Not Right*. London: Compass, 2016, p. 4.

6. THE CONTINUING COST OF EMPIRE

1. Address "The Chance for Peace", delivered before the American Society of Newspaper Editors, 16 April 1953.

2. Quoted in Coates, "The Long-Term State of the Union – Counting the Cost of Empire?", *Huffington Post*, 18 April 2014. http://www.huffingtonpost.com/david-coates/the-long-term-state-of-th_b_4798647.html (accessed 15 December 2017).

3. Quoted in Coates, *America in the Shadow of Empires*, p. 33. Much of the content of Chapter 6 draws on this work, and on chapter 5 of the earlier *Making the Progressive Case*.

4. See Stockholm International Peace Research Institute, data on military expenditure by country as a percentage of GDP, 2006–15.

5. William Hartung, "The Trillion-Dollar National Security Budget", TomDispatch.com, 25 July 2017. www.tomdispatch.com/blog/176311 (accessed 15 December 2017).

6. War Resisters League, https://www.warresisters.org/resources/pie-chart-flyers-where-your-income-tax-money-really-goes (accessed 15 December 2017).

7. Coates, *America in the Shadow of Empires*, p. 10.

8. *Ibid.*, p. 49.

9. *Ibid.*, pp. 10–11.

10. *Ibid.*, pp. 13–14.

11. The details are at https://www.theguardian.com/uk-news/2016/jul/06/iraq-inquiry-key-points-from-the-chilcot-report (accessed 15 December 2017).

12. For this and other examples, see Coates, *America in the Shadow of Empires*, p. 13.

13. Coates, *America in the Shadow of Empires*, p. 177; and Robert Pollin and Heidi Garrett-Pelier, "The US Employment Effects of Military and Domestic Spending Priorities: 2011 Update", PERI: University of Massachusetts Amherst, December 2011.

14. For a recent overview, see Ron P. Smith, "The Economic Costs of Military Conflict", *Journal of Peace Research* 51:2 (2014), pp. 245–56.

15. A. Markusen and J. Yudken, *Dismantling the Cold War Economy* (New York: Basic Books, 1992), p. 63.

16. Coates, *Models of Capitalism*, pp. 203–10.

17. T. Sandler and K. Hartley, *The Economics of Defense* (Cambridge: Cambridge University Press, 1995), p. 220.

18. *Ibid.*, p. 220.

19. Colin Read, *The Rise and Fall of an Economic Empire* (London: Palgrave Macmillan, 2010), p. 200.

20. Coates, *America in the Shadow of Empires*, p. 27.

21. Colin Crouch, "Privatized Keynesianism", *British Journal of Politics and International Relations* 11:3 (2009), pp. 382–99.

22. Herman Schwartz, *Subprime Nation: American Power, Global Capital and the Housing Bubble* (Ithaca, NY: Cornell University Press, 2009), pp. 3–4.

23. Robert Cox, "Beyond Empire and Terror: Critical Reflections on the Political Economy of World Order", *New Political Economy* 9:3 (2004), p. 312.

24. Helen Thompson, "Debt and Power: The United States' Debt in Historical Perspective", *International Relations* 21:3 (2007), p. 316. See also Schwartz, *Subprime Nation*, 220–21.

25. United Nations, *World Happiness Report*, March 2017, p. 2.

26. Robert Boyer, "Capital-Labour Relations in OECD Countries: from Fordist Golden Age to Contrasted National Trajectories" in J. Schor (ed.), *Capital, the State and Labour* (Aldershot: Elgar, 1996); and Ian Clark, "Employment Resistance to the Fordist Production Process: 'Flawed Fordism' in post-War Britain", *Contemporary British History* 15:2 (2001), pp. 28–52.

27. For the distinction between positive and negative deindustrialization, see Coates, *The Question of UK Decline*, pp. 10–12; and for the original, Bob Rowthorn, "Deindustrialization in Britain" in R. Martin and B. Rowthorn (eds), *The Geography of Deindustrialization* (London: Macmillan, 1986), p. 23.

28. Bob Rowthorn and John Wells, *De-industrialization and Foreign Trade* (Cambridge: Cambridge University Press, 1987), p. 91.

29. Martin Wolf, "Why Britain has to curb finance", *Financial Times*, 22 May 2009.

30. Perry Anderson, "Figures of Descent", *New Left Review* 161 (Jan/Feb 1987), p. 34.

31. On this, see David Rubinstein, *Capitalism, Culture and Decline in Britain* (London: Routledge, 1993), p. 28.

32. P. J. Cain & A. G. Hopkins, *Innovation and Expansion 1688–1914* (Harlow: Longman, 1993), p. 44 (see also in their *Crisis and Deconstruction*, p. 298).

33. The next two paragraphs are from Coates, *America in the Shadow of Empires*, p. 122.

34. Bernard Porter, *Empire and Superempire* (New Haven, CT: Yale University Press, 2006), pp. 50–2.

35. David Currie and Ron Smith, "Economic Trends and Crisis in the UK Economy" in David Coates and John Hillard (eds), *The Economic Decline of Modern Britain: The Debate between Left and Right* (Brighton: Wheatsheaf, 1986), p. 226.

36. The term is David Edgerton's, in his *Warfare State: Britain 1920–70* (Cambridge: Cambridge University Press, 2005).

37. Ron Smith, *Military Economics: The Interaction of Power and Money* (London: Palgrave Macmillan, 2009), p. 103.

38. David Edgerton, "Liberal Militarism and the British State", *New Left Review* 185 (1991), p. 164.

39. Tim Radford, "Military dominates UK science, says report", *The Guardian*, 20 January 2005.

40. Edgerton, "Liberal Militarism and the British State", p. 164.

41. *Ibid.*, pp. 140–1.

42. Ben Fine and Lawrence Harris, *The Peculiarities of the British Economy* (London: Lawrence & Wishart, 1985), p. 243.

43. For a strident critique of what he termed "illusions of grandeur", see Sidney Pollard, *The Wasting of the British Economy* (London: Croom Helm, 1982) pp. 135–40, 185–6.

44. Corelli Barnett, "British economic decline, 1900–1980" in Patrick O'Brien and Armand Cleese (eds), *Two Hegemonies* (Aldershot: Ashgate, 2002), pp. 144–5.

45. *Ibid.*, pp. 143–4.

46. Andrew Gamble, "Hegemony and Decline" in O'Brien & Cleese, *Two Hegemonies*, p. 139.

47. For details, see "The $600bn question", *The Economist*, 17 June 2017.

7. THE FOLLY OF AUSTERITY POLITICS

1. https://me.me/i/our-congress-passes-laws-that-subsidize-corporations-farms-oil-companies-8388427 (accessed 15 December 2017).

2. Owen Jones, "Now we find out the real cost of austerity – our lives cut short", *The Guardian*, 18 July 2017.

3. For more on the return of Austerity politics, see Mark Blyth, *Austerity: The History of a Dangerous Idea* (New York: Oxford University Press, 2013); Paul Krugman, "How the Case for Austerity Has Crumbled", *New York Review of Books*, 6 June 2013; Suzanne J. Konzelmann, "The Political Economics of Austerity", *Cambridge Journal of Economics* 38:4 (2014), pp. 7–41; and Johnna Montgomerie, "Austerity and the Household: The Politics of Economic Storytelling", *British Politics* 11:4 (2016), pp. 418–37.

4. http://davidstockmanscontracorner.com/why-this-sucker-is-going-down-again/

5. This, and further details, in Coates, *Making the Progressive Case*, p. 20.

6. Coates, *Prolonged Labour*, p. 63.

7. The details are in David Coates and Kara Dickstein, "A Tale of Two Cities: Financial Meltdown and the Atlantic Divide" in Terrence Casey (ed.) *The Legacy of the Crisis* (London: Palgrave Macmillan, 2011), pp. 60–78.

8. Shawn Donovan, "US declares victory in G20 growth versus austerity debate", *Financial Times*, 31 August 2016.

9. Ruth Marcus, "The stimulus was a policy success but a political disaster", *Washington Post*, 19 February 2014.

10. Alan S. Blinder and Mark Zandi, "The Financial Crisis: Lessons for the Next One". Washington, DC: Center on Budget and Policy Priorities, 15 October 2015.

11. Michael Grunwald, "5 years after stimulus, Obama says it worked", posted 17 February 2014.

12. Edward Luce, "RIP Obama's stimulus: funeral for a policy process", *Financial Times*, 23 February 2014.

13. Details at "Stacking the Debt", *The Nation*, 11/18 March 2013.

14. Details at https://www.cato.org/blog/economists-against-stimulus (accessed 15 December 2017).

15. Andrea Louise Campbell, "Paying America's Way", prepared for the Working Group on Obama's Agenda and the Dynamics of US Politics, Russell Sage Foundation, New York, October 2010, p. 14.

16. The story is told in Noam Scheiber, "EXCLUSIVE: The Memo that Larry Summers Didn't Want Obama to See", *The Atlantic*, 22 February 2012.

17. See, for example, Paul Krugman and Robin Wells, "The Way Out of the Slump", *New York Review of Books*, 14 October 2010; and Robert Kuttner, "Recovery and Debt: Squaring the Circle", posted on *The Huffington Post*, 29 November 2009.

18. Christopher Ingraham and Kennedy Elliott, "Explore 60 years of budget deficits in one chart", *Washington Post*, 4 March 2014.

19. "Cutting the fiscal deficit: the workout begins", *The Economist*, 22 May 2010.

20. BBC News, "Spending Review 2010: George Osborne wields the axe". London: BBC, 29 October 2010.

21. https://www.theguardian.com/uk/2010/jun/22/emergency-budget-full-speech-text (accessed 15 December 2017).

22. For details of the "bedroom tax", see Dorling, *All That Is Solid*, pp. 147–54.
23. "Austerity's cruel pantomime", editorial, *New Statesman*, 7 July 2017, p. 3.
24. Martin Wolf, "Austerity is dead. Long live austerity", *Financial Times*, 16 June 2017.
25. Patrick Wintour and Larry Elliott, "Osborne moves to cut spending to 1930s level in dramatic autumn statement", *The Guardian*, 4 December 2014.
26. Patrick Wintour, "Britain can become the world's richest economy, says George Osborne", *The Guardian*, 14 January 2015.
27. BBC News, "Draw up 40% cuts plans, George Osborne tells Whitehall departments". London: BBC, 21 July 2017.
28. On this, see Polly Toynbee, "With a whiff of sulphur, George Osborne was gone – but for how long?", *The Guardian*, 20 April 2017.
29. See Ruth Cain, "The Gendered Impact of Universal Credit", posted on speri.comment, 17 June 2015.
30. Patrick Wintour, "Conservatives to withdraw key benefits from unemployed under-25s", *The Guardian*, 2 October 2013.
31. Yvonne Roberts, "Anger as lone parents face benefit cuts", *The Observer*, 20 May 2012.
32. Helene Mulholland, "IDS targets families of more than two children for benefit cuts", *The Guardian*, 25 October 2012.
33. Richard Adams, "Osborne's student loan overhaul betrays a generation", *The Guardian*, 25 November 2015.
34. Patrick Butler *et al.*, "Welfare cuts will cost disabled people £28bn over 5 years", *The Guardian*, 27 March 2013.
35. John Harris, "'End of austerity? A silent crisis in local services tells the true story", *The Guardian*, 26 November 2015. See also Sally Gainsbury and Sarah Neville, "Austerity's £18bn impact on local services", *Financial Times*, 19 July 2015.
36. John Harris, "The housing benefits cap means a wretched life for thousands in B&Bs", *The Guardian*, 16 September 2012.
37. Patrick Wintour, "Cuts to housing benefit could make claimants £570 a year worse off", *The Guardian*, 18 November 2015.
38. Heather Stewart, "George Osborne's hidden cuts will take away 30% of income for poorest families", *The Observer*, 25 November 2012.
39. Jamie Doward and Toby Helm, "Child poverty rise across Britain 'halts progress made since 1990s'", *The Guardian*, 20 June 2015.
40. Quoted in Daniela Tepe-Belfrage and Sara Wallin, "Austerity and the hidden costs of recovery: inequality and insecurity in the UK households", *Political Studies* 11:4 (2016), p. 390.
41. On this, see Simon Wren-Lewis, "The Austerity Con", *London Review of Books*, 19 February 2015, and his "The economic consequences of George Osborne: covering up the austerity mistake", *New Statesman*, 19 May 2015; Martin Wolf, "How Austerity Has Failed", *New York Review of Books*, 11 July 2013, and his "Britain can only walk tall if productivity is reignited", *Financial Times*, 19 March 2015.
42. Pamela Duncan, "UK growth not being converted to increased wellbeing, says report", *The Guardian*, 21 July 2016.
43. Martin Wolf, "Autumn Statement 2014: A political chancellor's delusional plan", *Financial Times*, 3 December 2014.

44. Larry Elliott, "Figures show Corbyn is right to say Labour did not cause financial crisis", *The Guardian*, 9 August 2015.

45. Laurie McFarlane, "More evidence that the cuts have failed", *The NEF Blog*, 27 May 2016.

46. John Van Reenan, *Austerity: Growth Costs and Post-Election Plans*. London: Centre for Economic Performance, 2015.

47. Michael Ellman, "The UK Coalition Government and Heterodox Economics", *Cambridge Journal of Economics* 39 (2015), pp. 1458–9.

48. Paul Krugman, "The austerity delusion", *The Guardian*, 29 April 2015.

49. Peter Dominiczak *et al.*, "BBC Question Time: Ed Miliband savaged over economic record during leaders' special", *The Telegraph*, 1 May 2015.

50. On this, see three pieces by David Coates: *Answering Back*, pp. 235–43; "Separating Sense from Nonsense in the US Debate on the Financial Meltdown", *Political Studies Review* 8, pp. 15–18; and *Making the Progressive Case*, pp. 161–4.

51. T. E. Woods, *Meltdown* (Washington, DC: Regnery Publishing, 2009), p. 47.

52. Johann Norberg, *Financial Fiasco* (Washington, DC: Cato Institute, 2009), p. 6.

53. *Ibid.*, pp. 134–5.

54. *Ibid.*, p. 134.

55. Letter in *Wall Street Journal*, 25 March 2013, from George P. Shulz, Gary S. Becker, Michael J. Boskin, John F. Cogan, Allan H. Meltzer and John B. Taylor.

56. Phil Gramm and Steve McMillin, "The Debt Problem Hasn't Vanished", *Wall Street Journal*, 22 May 2013, p. A15.

57. Chris Edwards, "10 Reasons to Oppose a Stimulus Package for the States", *Cato Institute Tax and Budget Bulletin* 51, December 2008.

58. By me in *Answering Back*, pp. 243–63; *Making the Progressive Case*, pp. 164–8; "Separating Sense ...", pp. 18–25; and *Observing Obama in Real Time* (Winston-Salem, NC: Library Partners Press, 2017), pp. 41–52.

59. The Financial Crisis Inquiry Report, *Final Report*. Washington, DC: US Government, January 2011, pp. xvii–xxv.

60. *Ibid.*, pp. xxvi–xxvii.

61. Sahil Kapur, *Who Really Caused the Deficit?* posted on TPMDC, 15 May 2012.

62. davej, "Three charts to email to your right-wing brother-in-law", posted on Daily Kos, 28 August 2014.

63. Michael Ettlinger and Michael Linden, "The Failure of Supply-Side Economics". Washington, DC: Center for American Progress, 1 August 2012.

64. On this, see Robert Reich, "The Three Biggest Lies about Why Corporate Taxes Should Be Lowered", posted on NationofChange, 6 August 2013.

65. See Thomas L. Hungerford, "Let's Face It – We're Far From Broke". Washington, DC: Economic Policy Institute, 28 April 2015.

66. On this, as a conscious ideological construction with serious negative consequences, see Daniela Tepe-Belfrage and Sara Wallin, "Austerity and the hidden costs of recovery", pp. 389–95.

67. Robert Skidelsky, "The Scarecrow of National Debt", posted on socialeurope-eu, 26 August 2016.

68. William Mitchell, "Beyond Austerity", *The Nation*, 4 April 2011.

69. On this, see Michael Hudson, "The Big Threat to the Economy is Private Debt and Interest Owed on It, Not Government Debt", posted on Alternet.org, 16 March 2013; and David Coates, "A Progressive Primer on the Issue of America's Debt Problem: Ten Things You Really Need to Know", posted on *The Huffington Post*, 3 September 2013, and reproduced in Coates, *Observing Obama in Real Time*, pp. 73–82.

70. For the relevant comparative data, see Christopher House *et al.*, "Austerity in the Aftermath of the Great Recession", NBER Working Paper 23147, February 2017.

71. See Mark Peters, "Many States' Tax Receipts Remain Depressed", *Wall Street Journal*, 10 March 2015.

72. See Anna Chu, "The Impact of the Sequester on Communities Across America". Washington, DC: Center for American Progress, 22 February 2013.

73. Elise Gould, "Austerity at all levels of government has created a teacher shortfall", Washington, DC: Economic Policy Institute, 7 October 2016.

74. Joseph Stiglitz, "Why Stupid Politics is the Cause of Our Economic Problems", posted on Alternet.org, 26 January 2015.

75. On this, see Jacob Hacker and Paul Pierson, "What Krugman and Stiglitz Can Tell Us", *New York Review of Books*, 27 September 2012.

76. Josh Bivens, "Why is recovery taking so long – and who's to blame?". Washington, DC: Economic Policy Institute, 11 August 2016.

77. John Weeks, "Brexit, the UK Economy and Public Policy: Discredit Where Discredit is Due", posted on Social Europe, 27 April 2017. On the "fiscal drag", see also Barry Z. Cynamon and Steven M. Fazzari, "Inequality, the Great recession and slow recovery", *Cambridge Journal of Economics* 40:2 (2016), pp. 373–400.

78. *National Institute Economic Review* 231, February 2015, p. R16.

79. On his ultimate resignation in frustration, and for a reflective overview of his strengths and weaknesses, see Amelia Gentleman, "The IDS way: Victorian morality, reforming zeal and gross incompetence", *The Guardian*, 20 March 2016; and Ben Margulies, "Weren't these neoliberals? Ian Duncan Smith, George Osborne and the limits of Thatcherism", posted on Political Insight, the PSA blog, 22 March 2016.

80. For more on this, see Coates, *Answering Back*, pp. 57–84.

81. Quoted in Alan Rappeport, "Federal Debt Projected to Grow by Nearly $10 Trillion Over Next Decade", *New York Times*, 24 January 2017.

82. Paul Volker and Peter Peterson, "Ignoring the Debt Problem", *New York Times*, 21 October 2016.

83. On the various faces of this, see Tom Coburn, "Subsidies of the Rich and Famous", Washington, DC: Congress, November 2011; Tad DeHaven, "Corporate Welfare in the Federal Budget", Washington, DC: Cato Institute, 25 July 2012; and Michael Cooper *et al.*, "Business in the United States: Who Owns It and How Much Tax Do They Pay?" NBER Working Paper 21651, October 2015.

84. See, for example, Nan Roman, "The Devastating Impact of Sequestration on the Poor and Vulnerable", posted on *The Huffington Post*, 5 March 2013.

85. See Larry Elliott and Katie Allen, "UK faces return to inequality of Thatcher years, says report", *The Guardian*, 31 January 2017.

86. See Phillip Inman, "UK tax burden will soar to highest level for 30 years, warns IFS", *The Guardian*, 7 February 2017.

87. Heather Stewart and Rowena Mason, "May signals break with Thatcherism in manifesto for 'community and country'", *The Guardian*, 18 May 2017.

88. Mike DeBonis, "House GOP unveils budget plan that attaches major spending cuts to coming tax overhaul bill", *Washington Post*, 18 July 2017.

89. Karl Marx, *The Eighteenth Brumaire of Louis Bonaparte*. London: 1852.

90. On the blatant immorality of the American Health Care Act that House Republicans voted to support as a replacement to the Affordable Care Act, see my "Wishing the Democratic Party a Healthy Easter Recess" at http://www.davidcoates.net/2017/04/16/wishing-the-democratic-party-a-healthy-easter-recess/ (accessed 15 December 2017).

8. TOWARDS A BETTER FUTURE

1. Barack Obama, "The Way Ahead", *The Economist*, 8 October 2016, p. 24.

2. Colin Hay and Tony Payne, "The Great Uncertainty". Sheffield: Sheffield Political Economy Research Institute, Research Paper No. 5, September 2013, pp. 2–3.

3. Obama, "The Way Ahead", p. 23.

4. Hay & Payne, "The Great Uncertainty", pp. 2–3.

5. This point is developed more fully in Coates, *Building a Growth Strategy on a New Social Settlement*.

6. For a recent and compelling overview of how general and deep these problems run, see Andrew Gamble, "The Coming Crisis: we do not have much time", posted on speri.comment, 13 July 2016. See also his *Crisis without End?* (London: Palgrave Macmillan, 2014).

7. Robert Gordon, "The Demise of US Economic Growth: Restatement, Rebuttal and Reflections", NBER Working Paper 19895, February 2014; see also Robert Gordon, "Is US Economic Growth Over? Faltering Innovation Meets the Six Headwinds", NBER Working Paper 18315, August 2012; and Robert Gordon, *The Rise and Fall of American Growth: The US Standard of Living Since the Civil War* (Princeton, NJ: Princeton University Press, 2016).

8. Martin Wolf, "Blame feeble productivity growth for stagnant living standards", *Financial Times*, 5 March 2015.

9. Stiglitz, "Why Stupid Politics Is the Cause of Our Economic Problems".

10. On this, see NBER working papers 20836 (Eichengreen), January 2015; 22172 (Summers *et al.*), April 2016; 23093 (Eggertsson *et al.*), January 2017; and 23160 (Blanchard *et al.*) February 2017; plus the IMF Working Paper 16/121 on *Income Polarization in the United States* and Thomas Palley's "Explaining Stagnation: Why It Matters", posted on social-europe.eu, 20 March 2013.

11. Daniel Alpert, "The Rut We Can't Get Out Of", *New York Times*, 30 September 2013.

12. Stiglitz, "Why Stupid Politics Is the Cause of Our Economic Problems".

13. David Weil, *The Frissured Workplace*. Cambridge, MA: Harvard University Press, 2014.

14. On this, see David Coates, "The UK economy: less a liberal market economy, more a post-imperial one", *Capital and Class* 38:1 (2014), pp. 171–82.

15. Loukas Karabarbounis & Brent Neiman, "The Global Decline of the Labor Share", NBER Working Paper 19136, June 2013. See also Matthew Rognlie, "Deciphering the fall and rise in the new capital share", *BPEA Conference Draft: Brookings Papers on Economic Activity*, 19–20 March.

16. Martin Sandbu, "A rising tide lifting all boats but one", *Financial Times*, 19 May 2016.

17. Robert Solow, "The future of work: why wages aren't keeping up", posted on *Pacific Standard*, 11 August 2015.

18. Robert Reich, "The Share-The-Scraps Economy", posted on socialeurope.eu, 3 February 2015.

19. Paul Pierson, *The New Politics of the Welfare State*. Oxford: Oxford University Press, 2001.

20. On this, see Mark Walker, *Free Money for All*. London: Palgrave Macmillan, 2016.

21. See also John Kay, "Miracles of productivity hidden in the modern home", *Financial Times*, 11 August 2015.

22. On this, see also Chad Syverson, "Challenges to Mismeasurement: Explanations for the US Productivity Slowdown", NBER Working Paper 21974, February 2016.

23. Kermal Dervis and Zia Qureshi, "How To Solve the Productivity Paradox", posted on social-europe.eu, 16 September 2016.

24. Anne Wren, "The rise of the service economy", posted on Policy Network, 8 May 2014.

25. This is a key theme in the OECD report, *The Future of Productivity* (Geneva, 2015). See also Martin Sandbu, "Great transformations", *Financial Times*, 4 March 2016; and his "Arithmetic and the golden age of growth", *Financial Times*, 17 May 2016.

26. Dervis & Qureshi, "How To Solve the Productivity Paradox".

27. The data is that of Robert Pollin and colleagues, reported in note 12 in Chapter 6.

28. See Coates, *America in the Shadow of Empires*, pp. 187–91.

29. On this, see the exchange between Martin Sandbu and Robert Wade in *Financial Times*, 17 February 2017.

30. The title of a much-discussed book by Stephen Cohen and John Zysman, published by Basic Books in 1987.

31. On this, see Josh Bivens, "Adding insult to injury: How bad policy decisions have amplified globalization's costs for American workers". Washington, DC: Economic Policy Institute Report, 11 July 2017.

32. See, for example, OECD, "Trends in Income inequality and its impact on economic growth". Paris: OECD, 7 January 2015; and "Why Less Inequality Benefits All". Paris: OECD, 21 May 2015.

33. The IMF has also shifted their position on this. See, for example, Jonathan D. Ostry *et al.*, "Redistrubution, Inequality and Growth", Washington, DC: IMF Staff Discussion Note, February 2014.

34. On this, see Margaret Heffernan, "Making a fetish of overwork bodes ill for productivity", *Financial Times*, 25 October 2016.

35. Paul Krugman, "Cheap Money Talks", *New York Times*, 11 July 2016. See also Free Lunch, "The problem is not too many robots, but too few – productivity is sluggish because of weak investment in capital", *Financial Times*, 5 April 2017.

36. See Jonathan Rothwell, "The Hidden STEM Economy". Washington, DC: Brookings Institution, June 2013.

37. On this, see for example, Josh Bivens, "A 'high-pressure' economy can help boost productivity and provide even more 'room to run' for the economy", posted on the website of the Washington-based Economic Policy Institute, 12 March 2017.

38. On the huge economic costs of continued gender-discrimination in workplaces and

professions, see recent reports by the McKinsey Global Institute, and by the International Monetary Fund, in reports in *Financial Times*, 24 September 2015.

39. See, for example, "The Power of Parity: How Advancing Women's Equality Can Add $12 Trillion to Global Growth". Washington, DC: McKinsey Global Institute, 2015.

40. See, for example, Sherrod Brown's "Working Too Hard for Too Little: A Plan for Restoring the Value of Work in America". Washington, DC: US Senate, March 2017.

41. See, for example, Joe Cox, "Sustainability and a Good Society". London: Compass, March 2015.

42. See, for example, "People, planet, power; towards a new social settlement". London: NEF, 17 February 2015.

43. See, for example, RSA's Inclusive Growth Commission, "Making our economy work for everyone". London: Royal Society of Arts, 7 March 2017.

44. See, for example, the Economic Policy Institute's "Raising America's Pay", http://www.epi.org/pay/ (accessed 15 December 2017).

45. See, for example, Lawrence Summers and Ed Balls, "Report on the Commission on Inclusive Prosperity", Washington, DC: Center for American Progress, January 2015; and Carmel Martin *et al.*, "Raising Wages and Rebuilding Wealth: A Roadmap for Middle-Class Economic Security", Washington, DC: Centre for American Progress, 8 September 2016.

46. See Hutton, *How Good We Can Be.*

47. Anthony Atkinson, *Inequality: What Can Be Done?* Cambridge, MA: Harvard University Press, 2015.

48. See, for example, Joseph Stiglitz, "Here's How to Fix Inequality", *The Atlantic*, 2 November 2015.

49. Heather Boushey, *Finding Time: The Economics of Work-Life Conflict.* Cambridge, MA: Harvard University Press, 2016.

50. Robert Gordon, *The Rise and Fall of American Growth.* Princeton, NJ: Princeton University Press, 2016, pp. 641–52.

51. E. J. Dionne *et al.*, "Faith in Equality: Economic Justice and the Future of Religious Progressives". Washington, DC: Brookings Institution, 2014.

52. See, for example, Joseph Stiglitz, "Principles and Guidelines for Deficit Reduction", New York: Roosevelt Institute, Working Paper No. 6, 2 December 2010.

53. See, for example, Lawrence Summers, "Strategies for sustainable growth", *Washington Post*, 6 January 2014.

54. See, for example, Michael Spence and David Brady, "Delivering on Promises to the Middle Class", posted on Facts & Arts, 8 April 2017.

55. See, for example, Rachel West, "EITC Expansion for Childless Workers Would Save Billions – and Take a Bite Out of Crime". Washington, DC: Center for American Progress, 4 August 2016.

56. See, for example, Nick Hanauer and David Rolf, "Shared Security, Shared growth", *Democracy Journal*, Summer 2015, p. 20.

57. John McDonnell, speech to the Labour Party conference, 28 September 2015.

58. See Mariana Mazzucato, *The Entrepreneurial State: Debunking Public vs. Private Sector Myths.* London: Anthem, 2014.

59. See NEF, "21 Hours". London: NEF, April 2016.

60. See, for example, the exchanges on basic income in "What will kill Neoliberalism?", *The Nation*, 4 May 2017.

61. Colin Hay and Tony Payne, *Civic Capitalism*. Cambridge Polity, 2015.

62. R. H. Tawney, "The Choice Before the Labour Party", first published in 1932, and reprinted in William. A. Robson (ed.), *The Political Quarterly in the 1930s*. London: Allen Lane, 1971.

63. John B. Judis, "The Millennials Are Moving Left", *The Atlantic*, 9 June 2017.

64. Tawney, "The Choice Before the Labour Party", reprinted in Robson, *The Political Quarterly in the 1930s*, pp. 101, 105, 107 & 109.

Index